Kimball Wiles
1913–1968

The High School of the Future: A Memorial to Kimball Wiles

Edited by

William M. Alexander
University of Florida

CHARLES E. MERRILL PUBLISHING COMPANY
A Bell & Howell Company
Columbus, Ohio

This volume is a collection of papers contributed by professional friends and associates of the late Kimball Wiles and edited by William M. Alexander for the Kimball Wiles Memorial Committee, College of Education, University of Florida.

Standard Book Number: 675-09439-9
Library of Congress Catalog Card Number: 70-80034

1 2 3 4 5 6 7 8 9 10—73 72 71 70 69

PRINTED IN THE UNITED STATES OF AMERICA

Each member of Kim's family felt a part of his professional life. We supplied him with a "built-in" laboratory and in return he shared his dreams for the future.

How fitting for this Memorial Volume to enlarge upon those dreams!

Kimball Wiles' family

Preface

The tragic death of Kimball Wiles in an automobile accident in February, 1968 robbed American education of one of its most dynamic leaders. Kim Wiles was truly a man for the times. With American education everywhere in ferment, searching for ways to meet the pressing new demands of modern society, it was natural that Dr. Wiles should rise to important positions of leadership. His love for education and teaching was matched only by his enjoyment of innovation and the high drama of bringing it about. Through his writing, speaking, administering, and teaching, he provided stimulation and direction for thousands of persons at every level of the educational structure. In addition, his ebullient spirit and boundless energy made him seem so indestructible that news of his death came as a very great shock to educators everywhere. To those of us who worked most closely with him at the University of Florida, the loss was especially poignant, for we missed his leadership as

Dean and the warmth and excitement of his personality around the College of Education.

When the immediate shock of Kim's passing had begun to recede, the College appointed a committee to plan an appropriate memorial to him. This committee was unanimous in its feeling that whatever was done should contribute to furthering the work to which Dean Wiles so unstintingly gave his life. As a consequence, it has planned three things:

1. The establishment of a Kimball Wiles Memorial Fund and the use of this fund in the furtherance of Dr. Wiles' goals.

2. The establishment of a Kimball Wiles Memorial Conference to be held at the University of Florida annually.

3. The publication of a memorial volume on "The High School of the Future," a topic dear to Dean Wiles' heart and one on which he had, himself, written most persuasively.

This volume, of course, is the expression of the last of these objectives. It seemed to the committee that there could hardly be a more fitting memorial than a volume devoted to a topic about which Kim cared so deeply and written by his contemporary leaders in American education who had, in one way or another, "labored in the vineyard" with him. It also seemed right that this book should be produced under the editorship of Bill Alexander, Kim's long-time colleague and friend. The committee is deeply grateful to Dr. Alexander for the superb volume he and his contributors have produced.

It is especially appropriate that this volume should be published by the Charles E. Merrill Publishing Company for whom Dean Wiles had served as Consulting Editor for the International Series in Education since November, 1963. Merrill's generous assistance has made it possible to produce this volume in considerably less time than is usually the case. We are appreciative, too, of the helpful suggestions, research, and enthusiastic support provided this project from Dean Wiles' family, his friends, and his former students.

We shall leave it to Dr. Alexander to introduce the authors of this volume in greater detail in the following pages, but the committee would like to express here its heartfelt thanks for the contributions these authors have made to this Memorial Volume.

To Mrs. Judy Johnson, Dean Wiles' former secretary, the committee owes a special debt for her gracious assistance and skillful aid.

Finally, it will please the readers of this book to know that the royalties it earns will go to the Kimball Wiles Memorial Fund and so continue the work for education Kimball Wiles so deeply loved and lived and inspired.

The Kimball Wiles Memorial Committee

Hilda Wiles

Maurice Ahrens
William Alexander
Derwood Baker
Bert Sharp

Arthur Combs, Chairman

Gainesville, Florida
November, 1968

The Contributors

Maurice R. Ahrens, Chairman, Division of Curriculum and Instruction, University of Florida, Gainesville

William M. Alexander (editor), Director, Institute for Curriculum Improvement, College of Education, University of Florida, Gainesville

Morton Alpren, Professor of Curriculum and Instruction, College of Education, Temple University, Philadelphia, Pennsylvania

Robert H. Anderson, Proffessor of Education, Graduate School of Education, Harvard University, Cambridge, Massachusetts

Vernon E. Anderson, Dean, College of Education, University of Maryland, College Park

Arthur W. Combs, Chairman, Foundations of Education Department, College of Education, University of Florida, Gainesville

Robert S. Fleming, Proffessor of Education, Virginia Commonwealth University, Richmond

Jack R. Frymier, Chairman, Curriculum Faculty, College of Education, The Ohio State University, Columbus

Robert S. Gilchrist, Director, Mid-continent Regional Educational Laboratory, Kansas City, Missouri

Glen Hass, Professor of Education, College of Education, University of Florida, Gainesville

Earl C. Kelley, Profressor Emeritus of Education, Wayne State University, Detroit, Michigan

John T. Lovell, Dean, College of Education, University of Bridgeport, Bridgeport, Connecticut

Trafford P. Maher, S. J., Chairman, Human Relations Center, Saint Louis University, St. Louis, Missouri

Alice Miel, Professor of Education, Teachers College, Columbia University, New York City

Hollis A. Moore, Jr., Vice President for Academic Affairs, George Peabody College for Teachers, Nashville, Tennessee

Franklin Patterson, President, Hampshire College, Amherst, Massachusetts

Chandos and Theodore Rice, T. Rice, Professor of Education, College of Education, Wayne State University, Detroit, Michigan

Galen Saylor, Professor of Education, Teachers College, University of Nebraska, Lincoln

William Van Til, Coffman Distinguished Professor in Education, Indiana State University, Terre Haute

Contents

part 5
Teachers and Teaching for the School of the Future

part 6
Leadership for Developing the School of the Future

part 1

Wiles' "High School of the Future"

chapter 1

Kimball Wiles

THE HIGH SCHOOL OF THE FUTURE*

All persons concerned with the improvement of the American secondary school are faced with the task of attempting to anticipate its emerging pattern. Each must use what he knows about learning, adolescents, the social trends, the new technology, to try to see what may be accomplished and the hazards that may be encountered. Unless professional people concerned about the welfare of the country, the world, and adolescents, try to invent the future, the nature of the secondary school will be shaped by the salesmen with the most convincing pitch or by political pressure fomented by irresponsible, sensational presentations via the mass media.

NEEDED RESEARCH

Many of the present answers to questions about the type of secondary curriculum needed must be based on inferences made by consulting research data from related disciplines. This approach is not satisfactory. Basic research studies designed to provide evidence concerning the

---

* Chapter 15 from Kimball Wiles, *The Changing Curriculum of the American High School* (Englewood Cliffs, N.J.: Prentice-Hall, Inc., 1963).

needs of youth and the most effective educational procedures should be undertaken.

Some areas that should be investigated immediately are:

1. How is mental health fostered?
2. How is the creative potential of an individual released?
3. How is commitment to values developed?
4. How are self-direction and the ability to deal effectively with change developed?
5. How is communication accomplished in person-to-person situations? in classrooms? by mass media?
6. How do the perceptions of teachers and pupils differ concerning the curriculum content? the transactions in the classroom?
7. What is the cultural heritage essential for all in our era of increasing specialization?
8. What skills are needed by all who are awarded high school diplomas?
9. What content and skills can be taught by teaching machines and mass media?
10. What type of pupil development can only be nurtured adequately through face-to-face, person-to-person communication?
11. What size and structure of groups most effectively promote the various types of growth sought in the secondary school?
12. How can the pupil growth that the secondary school seeks to promote be measured?

ANTICIPATED DEVELOPMENT

Evidence from research of the type outlined will enable concerned persons to modify the existing program realistically. Until it is available, attempts to anticipate and project the future program must be based on empirical evidence and inferences.

The remainder of this book is the effort of a person who has spent twenty-seven years working in and with secondary schools to predict the development of the next twenty-five years. It is hoped that these hypotheses will help each reader to formulate his own expectations, which may differ from those of the writer, and to plan his work for the type of change he deems desirable.

Values, Skills, Understandings Will Be Fostered

Although it is possible that schools in 1985 will be used as instruments of thought control and social classification, the writer is nevertheless optimistic enough to believe that there will continue to be a social commitment to freedom, creativity, and equality of opportunity. With this basic assumption, an attempt is made to project the changes that technological advances and social problems will produce in the next few decades.

In 1985, as at present, the planners of education for adolescents will hope that each pupil will develop a set of values to guide his behavior; acquire the skills necessary to participate effectively in the culture; gain an understanding of his social, economic, political, and scientific heritage; and become able to make a specialized contribution to the society.

The program of the school designed to promote these goals will be divided into four phases: analysis of experiences and values, acquisition of fundamental skills, exploration of the cultural heritage, and specialization and creativity.

Analysis of Experiences and Values

In the school, each pupil will spend six hours a week in an Analysis Group. With ten other pupils of his own age and a skilled teacher-counselor he will discuss any problem of ethics, social concern, out-of-school experience, or implication of knowledge encountered in other classes. No curriculum content will be established in advance for the Analysis Groups. The exploration of questions, ideas, or values advanced by group members will constitute the primary type of experience.

The purpose of the Analysis Group will be to help each pupil discover meaning, to develop increased commitment to a set of values, and to offer opportunity to examine the conflicts among the many sets of values and viewpoints held by members of the society.

The membership of the Analysis Group will be carefully selected to provide a group composed of persons of relatively equal intellectual ability, but varied social and economic values. The group will remain a unit throughout the high school program of its members. Changes will be made only when a deep emotional conflict develops between students or between a student and the teacher-counselor.

The teachers of Analysis Groups will be emotionally mature people. They will be selected early in their teacher education program because

they display a high degree of empathy and are warm, outgoing personalities whom other people like. They will be given special training in
counseling, communication, and value analysis. Each will be taught to
see his role as one of helping others to feel more secure, to clarify their
values, and to communicate more effectively with their colleagues. If a
teacher of an Analysis Group attempts to sell his viewpoint, he will be
considered unsuccessful and replaced.

Each Analysis Group teacher will meet three groups, or thirty-
three students, during the week. His time beyond the eighteen hours
in the discussion groups will be for individual counseling with the
thirty-three pupils and their parents.

The Analysis Group will be considered the basic element of the
educational program. In the late sixties, it will begin to be recognized
that unless citizens have values they accept, understand, and can apply,
the social structure will disintegrate until authoritarian controls are
applied. To counter the danger of collapse of the democratic way of
life, the school will be assigned the task of making as sure that each
child develops a set of values as it does that he is able to read. The
Analysis Group will evolve as the best means of performing the values
development function.

Acquisition of Fundamental Skills

Citizens in 1985 will need fundamental skills far superior to those
considered necessary in the early sixties.

In the home and in the elementary school, children will learn to
read, spell, and compute at their own rate of learning by the use of
teaching machines. In the school for adolescents, mathematics, foreign
languages, and many scientific processes and formulas will be taught
by machines supervised by librarians and a staff of technicians. Machines will teach basic skills as effectively and efficiently as a teacher.

The skills needed by all citizens will be stated, and each student
planning a high school program will be told the skills that he *must*
master. He will work through the needed programs as rapidly as he
can. When he wants to work on a skill, he will go to the librarian,
schedule a machine and a program, and go to work.

Some students will complete their basic skills work early in their
high school program. Others will work on them until they leave the
high school. Certain skills considered vocational in nature will be added
to a student's program if he indicates he has college entrance or a
specific vocation as a goal.

Two librarians, one to issue programs and the other to help on request, and a staff of mechanical technicians will supervise the work of two hundred students. Disorder will be at a minimum because each person will work on his own level and with his own goals. Moreover, each student will work in a private soundproofed cubicle.

The teaching machines laboratories for the various subject-matter areas—mathematics, languages, grammar—will be an integral part of the Materials Center of the school.

Exploration of the Cultural Heritage

The explosion of available knowledge in the last half of the twentieth century will confront educators with the need for selecting, synthesizing, interpreting, and seeking better methods of transmitting that knowledge. The things that an effective citizen will need to know in 1985 will be a multiple of the knowledge necessary in 1960. Textbooks taught by less than master teachers will not be enough, and ways of bringing each student into a working relationship with the best teachers available will be sought. Basic knowledge from the essential fields will be prepared in the most easily understood media and presented as dramatically and forcefully as possible. This knowledge, from the humanities, the social sciences, and the physical and biological sciences, will be considered the Cultural Heritage.

Roughly a third of the program of each high school student will be scheduled to help him acquire the basic knowledge of his culture. By exposure to the experiences, ideas, and discoveries of the past, the individual will be expected to become literate enough about the basic ideas of his culture to participate in discussions of them or to understand reference to them. For some, it will be expected that the experiences in the Cultural Heritage portion of the program will develop a desire to enhance further the values on which the society is based.

Classes in the Cultural Heritage program will be large. Sometimes as many as five hundred or one thousand will be in a single section. Teaching will be by television, films, or a highly skilled lecturer. No provision will be made for discussion, because ideas that produce a response can be discussed in the Analysis Groups. Only one teacher and an assistant will be needed in each subject-matter field in each school. The teacher will lecture or present the material through an appropriate medium. The assistant will prepare quizzes and examinations and record the marks made on the machine-scored tests. The high pupil-teacher ratio in the Cultural Heritage area, one teacher for each five hundred to fifteen hundred students, makes possible the low ratio, one to thirty-three, for Analysis Groups and highly individual instruction for the exceptional student.

Teachers for the Cultural Heritage program will be selected early in their teacher education program. They will speak well, like to be before an audience, have a sense for the dramatic, and be attractive persons. In addition to intensive work in their field, they will be given work in speech, dramatics, logic, and communication via the mass media.

Specialization and Creativity

The Analysis Groups, the Cultural Heritage courses, and the Fundamental Skills work will constitute the program required of all. But in addition each student will be encouraged to develop a specialization. It will not be required, but the opportunity will be presented.

Shops, studios, and work laboratories will be available for specialized activities. All students will be encouraged to engage in some creative activities, since the Cultural Heritage phase of the program will be essentially a passive one. Writing laboratories, for example, will be staffed to help students who want to develop creative writing ability. School newspapers, magazines, and telecasts will be written in the laboratories.

Other students will select work experience in various industries and businesses in the community. These students will have decided that they will not seek a higher education and will use their specialized program to insure a smooth transition to regular employment.

Special opportunities will be available for the persons who qualify for them in terms of ability and intensity of purpose. Seminars in the various content fields, and some of an interdisciplinary nature, will be available. Students must have displayed unusual ability and show evidence of a desire for individual investigation in a field before they will be permitted to enroll. Seminars will be limited to fifteen students. They will meet for two two-hour periods each week, and the remainder of the time the students will conduct independent research in the library or laboratories.

Small science laboratories will be kept open for full-time use by the individual researchers from the seminars. In fact, students who are not expected to become scientists or technicians in an area will not use laboratory facilities. Laboratory experience will have been abandoned as a general education procedure by the seventies.

In the specialized fields the pupil-teacher ratio will be low, one to forty or fifty pupils. Teachers will give individualized supervision and plan with the Analysis Group teachers the experiences individuals should have.

No longer will the colleges blame the secondary schools for inadequate preparation. Graduation days will have been eliminated. Students will continue to work in the secondary school until they pass their college entrance examinations or move to a job. Most students will enter the secondary school at thirteen, but some will leave at fifteen and others at twenty. A student's decision to leave the program will be conditioned by his completion of the Cultural Heritage experiences, his acquisition of fundamental skills, and his individual goals.

The School Plant

The school plant will have rooms of many different sizes. Buildings with uniform size classrooms will be obsolete. Analysis Groups, specialized education classrooms, studios, and laboratories will be small. Cultural Heritage courses will be held in large halls equipped for lectures and mass media programs. Libraries and shops will be large. Areas where individuals work with teaching machines to perfect basic skills will be divided into small work cubicles.

Basis of Support

The program will be paid for from federal funds. It will be recognized in the sixties that, with a truly mobile population, neither local communities nor the national government can afford to allow the great differences in educational opportunity to continue. No community is immune to poor education in another, and the national government cannot afford thus to neglect a large percentage of its human resources.

The Steps in the Evolution

Many voices arose in the early sixties clamoring for a copying of the European education system. Some wanted to use tests and allocate the pupil to a specialized curriculum as early as ten years of age and to give him the required courses the experts deemed suitable for him. They proposed restricting the curriculum of the secondary school to the intellectual pursuit of information in certain areas of knowledge. Values and social development were to be left to the home and church.

However, increasing juvenile delinquency, more homes with both parents working, increasing cases of mental and emotional disturbances could not be ignored. The secondary school program had to be made broad enough to deal with values, human relations, fundamental skills in communication, and the cultural heritage, and at the same time offer opportunities for work in a student's special field.

The program described for 1985 will not occur overnight. It will involve a step-by-step change produced by social pressures and technological advance. The steps that will lead to the 1985 program will be as follows:

1960-1965

Increased emphasis on guidance, science, mathematics, and foreign languages, with continuing federal support. The National Defense Education Act has produced desirable results. As more money has been fed into these portions of the secondary school program, better-trained guidance, science, mathematics, and foreign language teachers have been secured, and programs in these areas have been improved because of better facilities and equipment. Little chance exists that the present support for these phases of the program will be decreased.

Increased flexibility in the high school program, with courses becoming available to pupils on the basis of intensity of purpose and level of achievement instead of chronological age. In spite of the arguments by some critics of secondary education for a return to fundamental courses, this change will not occur. The demands of the American society for courses in art, music, family life, psychology, sociology, and even driver training will prevail. Various pressure groups that recognize the importance of each of these areas will stand back of the phase of the program in which they are interested if that portion of the secondary school comes into real jeopardy. They will become as vocal as the advocates of so-called basic education have been. As improved guidance personnel are secured, the fallacy of insisting that certain elective courses be assigned to a given grade level will be recognized. An increased concern for providing for the gifted will loosen some of the fetters that have made the school program unnecessarily rigid.

Increased number of seminars and opportunities for individual research for gifted students. Many high schools are experimenting with advanced seminars and individual research. Some are providing small laboratories where gifted individuals may work on their own outside of class. These efforts are proving so successful that the practice will spread.

Increased use of TV and other mass media and of teaching machines. All of the evidence available indicates that as far as facts alone are concerned, classes taught by a good teacher over TV and other mass media can get results equal to those of regular classes. This knowledge will bring increased use of TV instruction, particularly in the elective courses not available in all schools. Research in the use of teaching machines will lead many schools to use them for teaching skills.

Development of new structural forms for the high school plant. As mass media use increases, the need of some classrooms that are large and other work areas that are smaller will be more apparent. Architects will begin to design more buildings that have classrooms of varying size or more space with movable walls.

1965-1970

Federal support for citizenship education. By the late sixties it will be realized that federal support for vocational education, science, mathematics, and foreign languages is not enough. The nation will become increasingly aware of the need for developing greater commitment to democratic values. Out of the evident shortcoming in this area will come a cry for federal support for citizenship education, even though no one is sure as to how this can best be done. The NDEA will be expanded or some similar bill enacted to provide federal support for the social studies-humanities area of the curriculum.

Use of large classes for teaching the cultural heritage area of the curriculum (literature, social studies, and sciences). Classes will acquaint students with our cultural development by means of lectures, television, and demonstrations. Classes of one hundred to two hundred will not be unusual. Such classes will be developed in school programs that provide seminars. Large classes in these areas will make possible a low pupil-teacher ratio for seminars and creative work. The seminars will provide opportunity for the analysis of information gained in the large classes. Accrediting associations and administrators will move away from the assumption that all teachers should have the same pupil-teacher load and perform the same type of function.

Workshop laboratories provided for the development of individual skills. Reading laboratories and workshops in grammar and spelling will provide individualized instruction permitting students to progress at their own rate. Laboratories will be used extensively in foreign language instruction. Success with the use of teaching machines will lead many schools to do most of their instruction in basic mathematics skills in laboratories where students work individually with machines. Much more of the classroom experience in secondary schools will be in laboratories, whether the field be science, art, foreign language, English, or mathematics.

1970-1980

Guidance and the teaching function brought closer together. It will be recognized during the sixties that, in spite of the money being spent on guidance, satisfactory results are not being achieved. It will be seen that, no matter how well they are prepared, trained guidance personnel whom students see two or three times a year cannot do the job. Recognition will come that, for the typical student, guidance must be performed largely by a teacher with whom the student has long-term contact. A portion of the time provided for guidance will be allocated to classroom teachers. On the other hand, it will be recognized that all classroom teachers are not able to perform the guidance function, that teachers who provide guidance will need specialized training in counseling techniques, group discussion procedures, and value analysis.

The school program for an individual pupil will be organized in such a way that he spends some portion of each week, possibly as much as six hours, with one teacher who has a continuing relationship with him and with approximately ten other students. These eleven students will continue to work with this teacher during the period in which they are in the school. The six hours each week will be spent in discussing the kinds of experiences the group members have encountered in their other classes and in exploring the value conflicts that have arisen. It will be recognized by 1970 that the task of helping students develop values can no longer be assigned primarily to the home or the community. The continued increase in juvenile delinquency will provide the deciding evidence that the school must assume a major responsibility for the development of values to live by. So many value conflicts will be apparent to youngsters that they will need a situation in which they can explore them under trained leadership. Whether this person is called a counselor or a teacher will not be important. But this type of service will be provided by the staff of the secondary school. Specialized guidance personnel will be available as resource people to these counselors, and for referral of problems that the teacher is unable to solve.

Increased concern for mental health. It will be recognized that improvement of mental health is basic to citizenship education in a society in which one or more out of ten spend some time in an institution for the treatment of mental or emotional disturbance. Unless a person is emotionally capable of participating effectively in society he will be unable to use the skills and knowledge that he has acquired. He will be a dependent rather than a contributing citizen. Neither the public nor the profession will any longer be willing to say that the school's function is to develop the intellect alone. Both will recognize that the school must be equally concerned with mental health, and the administration, the teachers, and the program of the school will be evaluated in terms of their effect on mental health.

Revision in the pattern of teacher education. As the school program emerges it will be evident that one pattern of teacher education for secondary school teachers is not enough. The realization will come that some teachers spend their time primarily in the presentation of facts and ideas over the mass media to large groups, that another type of teacher spends the major portion of his time in working with individuals and small groups in value analysis and in counseling, and that still other teachers work with individuals as guides in the development of individual skills, in creative activities, and in vocational experiences. Different patterns of teacher education will be devised for each of these different types of teaching functions.

WHAT THE HIGH SCHOOL WILL BECOME

Change occurs a step at a time. It is stimulated by failure, social conflict, or disaster, which produce fear, frustration, anger, and cries for action. It occurs as a teacher, a school, a school system tries a new method, procedure, organization, or content. It is speeded by success, support, recognition, and approval.

What the high school will become depends upon the degree of dissatisfaction with the present, the range of lay and professional vision, the penetration of the decision-makers' insight, and the public's encouragement of experimentation. The quality of the program will be determined by the wisdom of the decisions made by the public, legislators, board members, administrators, teachers, pupils, and parents—by you and me.

chapter 2

William M. Alexander

The Editor's Introduction

To edit a book devoted to further review, development, and critique of the ideas of my friend and colleague, Kimball Wiles, has been both demanding and satisfying. Each contribution at many points touches on matters which Kim and I had discussed, even argued, always as friends, and on which we had been mutually engaged in expounding, implementing, and evaluating. The temptation to argue back with the contributor, and occasionally even with Kim, has been strong, but the editor in me has won out! As editor, I have felt it my job to get good contributions, group them in a sensible way, and let them speak out in their own ways.

The satisfying part of the job has been to work with such fine contributors, and to read the excellent development of Kim's and their ideas presented in these pages. I have had to stop and reminisce occasionally for Kim and I first got acquainted at ASCD in 1947, later came to Florida the same year (1950), and thereafter worked both separately and together with many of the contributors. But this book looks toward the future, not the past. High school education will be influenced for a long time by the ideas of Kimball Wiles, and the further treatment of these and related ideas found in this book.

14

WILES' "HIGH SCHOOL OF THE FUTURE"
(PART 1, CHAPTER 1)

I was attracted to Wiles' model of the "High School of the Future" upon its publication. As the reviewer of Kim's new book, *The Changing Curriculum of the American High School,* in May, 1963, I made the following comments on Kim's Chapter 15 for *Educational Leadership:*

> Wiles' "High School of the Future" is a far cry from today's schools. He sees all youth participating in "small analysis groups" (each group consisting of 11 pupils and a counselor for development of values; learning fundamental skills through machines; and exploring the cultural heritage through large classes (perhaps 500 to 1,000) taught by television, film, or a highly skilled lecturer. In addition each student would be encouraged to develop a specialization in creative activity, work experience, or independent study. Graduation would be eliminated, and students would leave the secondary school when they pass their college entrance examinations or move to a job.
>
> The reviewer is very much attracted both to this conception of what the high school might be like in 1985 and to Wiles' description of the steps needed to achieve such a school. There are questions, of course: Can fundamental skills be divorced from the other curriculum areas, and can they be taught with no more human direction than Wiles indicates? Should work experience be only for the students not planning to attend college? Is physical education not to be provided in 1985 and some type of organized student government or other student-directed activity? Such questions are intended as items for study in connection with, rather than basic objections to, Wiles' proposal. Indeed this final chapter is the most stimulating portion of a very stimulating book, and might well be read first and studied again and again by the reader looking for new solutions to the dilemmas of the secondary school curriculum.

These comments still reflect my appraisal of the Wiles model.

The strength of the Wiles model even encouraged me, as a professor, to work into my general and secondary curriculum courses an analysis of different models of the high school, including the then current ones proposed by Admiral Rickover, Dr. Conant, and Lloyd Trump, among others, and always ending with the Wiles model.

This approach seems sound, for students must indeed work through various, hopefully conflicting, ideas to firm up their own. The models change, of course, and already there are several new ones to be analyzed. But the process seems a good one.

Some five years later, I still have not found a more provocative model than the Wiles one. Hence, it is not only fitting to the purposes of this volume to place his first in the book, but it is in my judgment an exceedingly good model to provoke interest of students in the various analyses, modifications, and alternates presented in the chapters which follow.

THE SOCIETY OF THE FUTURE AND ITS SCHOOLS
(PART 2, CHAPTERS 3–8)

Kimball Wiles' own curriculum background was in the social sciences, and his views of schooling were profoundly affected by his concern with the interaction of school and society. In the introductory paragraph of his "High School of the Future" he stated that "unless professional people concerned with the welfare of the country, the world, and adolescents, try to invent the future, the nature of the secondary school will be shaped by the salesmen with the most convincing pitch or by political pressure fomented by irresponsible, sensational presentations via the mass media."

And so, this memorial volume includes as its first and largest group of essays, Part 2, six which seem to the editor to take their point of departure from the same vantage point as did Wiles. Indeed, Jack Frymier of The Ohio State University, a former student of Wiles, opens his speculations with the question, "What Is Tomorrow?" and goes on to the questions, "What Should the Schools Do?" "What Is Commitment?" and "What Is Essential?" Jack's posture toward these questions is as positive as it is inquisitive, for he observes in concluding his essay, "Truth is illusive. But it is an attainable goal."

Kim's friend from consulting activities in St. Louis, Father Trafford Maher of St. Louis University, seems with his chapter title, "Education for Survival," to be taking a somewhat grim view of the future—but not really so. True, he notes that more youngsters are committing suicide today that at any previous time in American history, but he explains "today" in the five explosions and revolutions (knowledge, space, population, religion, and personal freedom) with which he deals. He believes that schools can succeed in the new challenge of creating "models for constructive living," *if* there is "the courage, the depth of conviction, and the professional preparedness of school administrators, professional curriculum personnel, and the progressive independence of teacher educators who have the courage to break from the dull, unrealistic, irrelevant patterns into which teacher education programs are now pressured."

In Chapter 5, Alice Miel of Teachers College, Columbia University, associated with Kim as long ago as 1949 in the co-chairmanship of a very popular and influential ASCD yearbook, *Toward Better Teaching,* does a critique of Kim's rationale for a curriculum design in her usual analytical and forward-looking style. She leans heavily on the dilemmas of current American society, noting the impact to be made on education by the apparent lack of direction and commitment of many youth and suggesting that educators may "have to operate as if there were no commitment at all and help our young people distill anew the values essential to humane living in a crowded world." Although clearly seeking new ways out of the problems of our 1966 society, Alice concludes that "we have yet a long way to go before rising to the insights expressed in 1963 by one Kimball Wiles."

Franklin Patterson, of Hampshire College, co-author with Kimball Wiles of ASCD's 1959 *The High School We Need,* digs deep in Chapter 6 into the human issues in contemporary society. His introductory description of these issues invites the reading of his chapter:

> One of these (issues) revolves around the factor of drivenness and upward mobility that characterizes much of life in contemporary technological society as we know it. A second issue concerns the factor of meaninglessness which underlies and drains color and substance from individual lives when much of the foundation upon which our ethos was built over centuries is crumbling under the impact of massive mutations in man's cultural evolution. A third issue is based on the factor of disaffection, anger, and overt hostility, whose present and future dimensions are certainly not yet clearly or completely visible to us, but which are surely not limited in future potential to what we have already seen in the 1960's among black activists and rebellious white youth.

The editor can only agree with Patterson that "we cannot in any adequate way consider the *how* of the high school of the future—its appropriate mechanisms, arrangements, operations—without first trying to understand the questions of *what* and *why* that are imposed upon us all, in school and out, in an age of cultural revolution." This chapter will help the reader to understand these questions.

In Chapter 7, two long-time friends and former colleagues of Wiles, Theodore and Chandos Rice, address themselves chiefly to "the issue of youth identification in society and to the related role of the adult, especially the educational specialist, in helping youth determine (some might even say 'salvage') societal values and manifestations which may be useful in building the future." They give a very potent role to the school in describing how it can provide for the active involvement of the learner in all of his communities as well as in the international scene; how it can focus on the present and the future; and how it can aid in the development of esthetic and expressional valuing and production, the formulation of long-run personal-social goals, philosophy, and purposes, and the enhancement of the individual's own sense of personal worth. Their concluding "additions to the model school" add some very specific suggestions to the high school of the future.

As another past president of ASCD and professional peer of Kimball Wiles, William Van Til in Chapter 8 draws some parallels between the Wiles "High School of the Future" and a 1968 paper of his own. Since this book is focused on the Wiles model and its ramifications, Van Til, also a social philosopher, examines the high school of the future in terms of social projections for the years 1985 and 2000. He then makes his interesting predictions of "the most likely high school of the future," seen as a well-supported urban school, manned by coordinating teachers with supporting specialized staff, using versatile resource centers and computer technology, and having as its major concerns "value choices, especially as to leisure time use in an increasingly hedonistic society, and the crucial human problems in a society in which neither a Utopia nor an Inferno has arrived." The predictions are intriguing.

THE INDIVIDUAL AND HIS SCHOOL
(PART 3, CHAPTERS 9–11)

Although the individual is by no means neglected in the Wiles chapter (Part 1) or in the six chapters in Part 2 just introduced, the contributors grouped in Part 3 tend to focus more fully on the student.

Arthur Combs, associated with Kim at the University of Florida beginning in 1954, and Chairman of the Wiles Memorial Fund Committee responsible for this volume, brings to his analysis of the high school of the future his viewpoint as a humanist and perceptual psychologist. He notes that "the major problems of man have shifted from the physical to the cultural and psychological; from things to people" and that the Wiles high school "is a deeply human one." Combs, as one would expect and certainly hope, is concerned with student responsibility for learning, and feels that ways must be found to get students into the act. Combs in fact bewails the present situation, as do so many of us: "What a pity it is that Wiles had to forecast such schools for the future when we need them so badly right now." But Combs looks optimistically and far into the future, saying "I feel certain the high school of the future will be very much like what [Wiles] has described." "Our problem," he writes, is not "to find answers to be imposed on the future. Our problem is to apply the growth philosophy to the question—to get with it, participate in the process and see what we can make of it." In this process, Art concludes, "a good place to start is with the questions Kim Wiles posed for us."

Kim's long-time friend, Robert S. Fleming, now at Virginia Commonwealth University but known to us through associations such as New York University, the Southern Association of Colleges and Schools, the Association for Supervision and Curriculum Development, and elsewhere, deals in Chapter 10 very directly and forcibly with the need for greater student involvement. For his data, Bob went to the students themselves. His chapter includes the results of a series of recorded interviews with high school students held in several geographical areas. He found that the students were saying most frequently: "We want to be respected," "We want to be involved," and "We want to learn something that is important." Bob found these recurring themes "highly significant," as indeed we all should. And he goes on to tell the reader how the schools can respond by providing learning opportunities that very specifically meet the criteria suggested by the students and himself.

Demanding that we give more than lip service to "Humanizing the High School of the Future" is Earl Kelley, the veteran teacher and professional advisor of Wiles, Combs, and other contributors, recently retired from Wayne State University but still packing insightful and incisive comments in his Chapter 11. Either we get down to this business, he says, or else. ". . . no operation, business or public, can go on forever while losing thirty or forty per cent of its product without either changing or going out of business." He really questions the survival of the high school and doubts if it can survive unless the school substitutes something better for the pressure it has heretofore exerted "as an authoritarian device for bringing about our own adult purposes regardless of the ideas, feelings, or needs of our young." He is a bit pessimistic about change in our high schools but certain that there must be change if we are not to reject and alienate our youth. As he sees it, the fundamental change we need is a simple one, however hard we may have to work to effect it: "We need . . . to have more than just better facilities, lower class loads, and better pay. We need a change in the heart of teachers, so that they will become aware of the responsibility they have assumed and will try to do something about it." Teachers who read Earl's chapter might just be moved to make such a change!

THE PROGRAM OF THE SCHOOL OF THE FUTURE
(PART 4, CHAPTERS 12–15)

Kim's model of "The High School of the Future" focuses on its program, and Part 4 of this volume includes many fine contributions devoted to this topic. One contributor, Maurice Ahrens, associated with Wiles at the University of Florida since 1954 and even before that in ASCD and elsewhere, was not able to complete his paper because of added responsibilities as Chairman for planning and arranging the February, 1969, Kimball Wiles Memorial Conference. We especially wanted Maurice's contribution, not only because he was the first of the ASCD presidents now at the University of Florida, but because of his visions of schooling in the future.

Before we requested him to abandon his manuscript preparation to get conference planning under way, Ahrens had developed an outline of his chapter. This outline is sufficiently conceptual as well as provocative in content to merit inclusion here:

1. New developments and changes in young people, in education and in society which have occurred since Kim wrote his chapter seven years ago.
2. Keyed to these changes, the following possibilities for the high school of the 70's:
    a. A 210–day school year (but not an extension of academic work);
    b. A decentralization of the high school in which the total school enrollment is divided into unit groups of 200–300 students who become the responsibility of eight or more teachers. These teachers would work with the same group of students for four years assuming full responsibility for their high school education;
    c. A curriculum which provides three kinds of experiences for all students:
        (1) General education which would be focused on the personal, personal-social, social-civic, economic and political problems of youth and society;
        (2) Active participation in community (local, state, national, and international) affairs and in the solution of emerging problems;
        (3) Vocational preparation which would include vocational guidance, work experience preparation for college, and training in a technical skill for students who are terminal;
    d. Each unit would have adequate space for flexible space

arrangements in providing for one-half to two-thirds of the program. Available to the units would be resource labora-tories—science, art, music, media, vocational-technical, etc. —and in some cases resource teachers would be used;

e. The schedule would be completely flexible. For example, a full week at any appropriate time in the year might be used for students to conduct a house-to-house drive to encourage people to register for voting, or to work in a poverty area to help people clean up and improve their living conditions, or to make a survey of recreational facilities and opportunities for children and youth, etc. I expect to suggest many such activities.

Obviously, it is the reader's and the volume's loss that the final version of the chapter cannot be included.

The four chapters that are included, however, give an excellent review and extension of Wiles' own model. Morton Alpren of Temple University, a one-time doctoral student of Kim's, has written a chapter (12) which, as he says, "attempts to be both personal and deal with ideas." Mort also touches on Kim's concept of school and society and their interaction, but he dwells on Wiles' and his views of the curriculum. He calls special attention to two movements occurring after Kim had formed his model: the current curriculum movement with its emphasis on structure and other Brunerisms, and the "black, poverty, disadvantaged concern." Alpren's critique of the Wiles model in terms of these current and other concerns raises more questions than can be answered in his few pages, and provides a real stimulus to the reader's further study.

In Chapter 13, Robert H. Anderson of Harvard University, a more recent but nonetheless warm friend of Kim's, is also concerned with possible deficits of the Wiles model in terms of post-1963 developments. Bob takes a particularly interesting view of the high school from the elementary school point of view with which he works more actively, and finds "ideas and convictions in Kim's secondary school forecast that are relevant as well to the world of younger children." Long an advo-cate of the non-graded school, Bob also notes that "the high school of which Kimball Wiles dreamed would be essentially a non-graded school." Although questioning some aspects of Wiles' "Analysis Groups," he considers this proposal of Kim's "a major arrangement within the high school [that is] a creative idea worth developing." All in all, over and beyond his skillful questioning and additive explorations, Bob Anderson likes Wiles' "High School of the Future."

Hollis Moore of Peabody College, whose relatively recent friendship with Kim became more meaningful as their paths crossed more frequently, entitled his chapter (14) "In Search of Self." He finds the most meaningful section in the Wiles model to be "the analysis of experience and values," although he notes that the section was written "prior to the start of the current five-year period of violence." Moore develops the need for increased concern in the high school for "a planned effort to achieve maturity and emotional stability in spite of stress and tension" and sees "Kim Wiles' group" as "such an invention for the high school of the future." He adds to the Wiles model in this regard proposing an addition to the curriculum of "laboratory situations in which the contradictions of our own society and the essential elements of conflict and violence between the individual, his so-called neighbors, and his society came into clear focus."

In Chapter 15, "A Complete Education for Adolescents," Galen Saylor has done a scholarly and comprehensive job. Galen agrees wholeheartedly with two aspects of the Wiles proposal: the need for research in developing the high school of the future and the broad, complete scope of the high school program. He disagrees with Kim's vision of the high school of the future in regard to instruction in the cultural heritage phase of the program; specifically, he is "violently opposed to large group instruction as a regular, systematic aspect of the secondary school instructional program." Saylor's major additions to the Wiles model are in two areas that were treated only briefly by Kim: "the education of the disillusioned, the disenchanted, and the frustrated adolescent" and teacher education. His ideas here are both challenging and useful.

TEACHERS AND TEACHING FOR THE SCHOOL
OF THE FUTURE
(PART 5, CHAPTERS 16, 17)

Teachers and teaching for the high school of the future are described in many of the earlier chapters of the book (see, for example, the last section of Saylor's chapter just introduced), but these matters constitute the precise focus of Chapters 16 and 17.

Glen Hass, associated with Kim at the University of Florida for the past decade and his co-author of a readings book on the curriculum, has contributed a stimulating chapter on "Instruction Theory and the High School of the Future." Glen believes that "in planning for the high school of the future, we will have to think about changes required in teachers and teaching as well as changes in organization, content, and presentation of school subjects." In theorizing as to what these changes must be, he develops the position that the teacher of the future must "regularly test his assumptions about his teaching and seek a better diagnosis" and "value individual differences and vary his professional decisions accordingly." His chapter will help us develop such teachers.

In Chapter 17, Vernon Anderson of the University of Maryland, long associated with Kimball Wiles in ASCD and other professional organizations, goes far to describe the kind of teacher education needed to prepare the staffs of the high schools of the future. He dreams of teachers who will "teach young people to invent the future." But his chapter is much more than a dream, for he specifies the competencies needed by such teachers, describes the kind of "differentiation of pattern and time" required, and dwells, to this editor's delight, on the "independent study and self-direction" to dominate the high school and the education of teachers of the future. Further, he illustrates how such a program of teacher education is being carried on at his own institution, and describes how the public school can serve as "the best laboratory for teacher education." Both school and teacher education personnel will find his ideas inviting further exploration and implementation.

LEADERSHIP FOR DEVELOPING THE SCHOOL OF THE FUTURE (PART 6, CHAPTERS 18, 19)

Any memorial to Kimball Wiles must perforce acknowledge his contributions to the development of educational leadership, and build upon his ideas in this area for developing the leadership demanded for schools of the future. The final two chapters perform this role very well indeed.

Robert S. Gilchrist, currently with the Mid-Continent Regional Educational Laboratory but associated with Kim Wiles as long ago as the late 1930's at The Ohio State University and in many relationships thereafter, has made a unique contribution to the volume by involving some twenty-five other leading educators in its preparation. The chapter concerns the revolution in education and the question of whether there will be evolution or revolution in educational leadership. The consensus is clear that "the future must be planned in the present," although the ways and means of planning are uncertain. "Teacher power," "administrative power," and "citizen participation in power" are among the issues considered, but the need is emphasized for ever-more competent and vigorous leadership: "The educational leader today must set the stage for tomorrow's schools by becoming more sensitively aware of the dynamics of the present conflicts, and by becoming more vigorous in his determination to not weaken in pursuit of the quality of education needed in our nation's schools."

It is quite appropriate that the final chapter should have been written by one of Wiles' early doctoral students at the University of Florida, John Lovell, now at the University of Bridgeport, and that it should deal with the aspect of educational leadership to which Kim's first influential book was devoted—supervision. Lovell selects a number of ideas which he associates with Wiles and "which have had greatest meaning for [him] as a professional educator." The ideas include "proceeding from the known to the unknown," "sound evaluation," "change based on theoretical formulations and research findings from education," "change based on theoretical formulations and reseach findings from related disciplines," and a group of ideas about instructional supervision. John has done a unique job of sorting, selecting, and interpreting Wiles' ideas in this chapter and has made his own further contribution in his final statement on "Supervision in the Schools of Tomorrow."

TOWARD THE HIGH SCHOOL OF THE FUTURE

I could make many generalizations and predictions about the high school of the future, basing them on the fine proposals and judgments already presented by Wiles and by the contributors to this volume. But the present purpose is to help the reader interpret and use this book, not to review it further or to add to it more than a few words. These words, directly addressed to any interested reader, are:

1. Read as many of the chapters as possible, considering each from the standpoint both of its critique of the original model developed by Kimball Wiles and of the additional ideas it offers.

2. Then formulate your own model of what the high school of the future should be—making this *your* independent study, *your* beliefs, *your* model to put into practice as fully as *your* role in education makes possible.

This advice, I am positive, is exactly what Kim Wiles would have given you.

part 2

The Society of the Future and Its Schools

chapter 3

Jack R. Frymier

Some Answers Must Be Questioned

INTRODUCTION

With his head in the clouds and his feet on the ground, Kimball Wiles was forever dreaming but moving forward all the time. One basic posture which he often assumed included questioning conventional answers. Attempting to follow in that same path, this essay pursues some of the kinds of questions implicit in Wiles' concerns.

WHAT IS TOMORROW?

Life involves ordering reality. At any given moment of our being— laughing and loving, striving and struggling, thinking and talking—we are organizing and ordering reality.

The present reflects some order. The near past reflects more order. The near future reflects less order. The distant future is orderable, but we are uncertain how. As we thrust ourselves into the future, we seek to extend our past orderings on ahead of us to give us strength and assurance. We project the past and present forward and can sometimes confidently predict the future because we have prearranged the orderings which must then appear.

The future is sometimes awesome because it seems to hold that which death itself presumes—disorder, disintegration, and disorganization for us all. And when the pace of the times is so great that we are projected headlong into tomorrow before we have pressed our orderings on before us, then we are very naturally afraid. What we actually see—and have, in fact, confronted ourselves with—is our unordered perception of reality, scattered hither and yon. Little wonder that at moments like these our thoughts turn backward, to the safe and ordered past.

In the past, we have consolidated our knowledge and organized our experience—categorizing, canalizing, and compartmentalizing everything we know. We have made neat little bundles of experience and labeled them and stored them conveniently within the disciplines for use whenever we call.

But the order of the universe is rooted in change, and our task in life becomes one of finding a way to fit ourselves close against this changing order and eternal flow. Though we can try to shape the course of history, alter events or intervene, the man who lives life fullest steps boldly forward into the breach of tomorrow, feels for the order there, and then creates his own. If his benchmarks are only in the past, his course and effort will always fail, because tomorrow is not a repeat of yesteryear or yesterday or even today. Tomorrow represents a new order. New patterns, new relationships, new problems, new dimensions, and new motivations change the woof if not the warp of the fabric of time in every way. Can we learn to lean upon our conceptions of order but still create a new, evolving scheme? Can we profit from what we know, but elude the shackles of an overorganized, overordered world and mind?

The disarray of the ghetto, the disorganization of the riot, the plaintive wail of an orphan in Vietnam is tomorrow, but it has come today. There is no order. There is no plan. There is no logical way. The ghetto, the riot, and the orphaned child from a far away war tell us what we do not want to hear: tomorrow is here. Because it is not neat and tidy and because it lacks conventional labels and compartmentalized norms, we are afraid. We fear because we see in all the chaos and lack of order disintegration, instability, irrationality, and nonorderable matter—we see death. And we feel alone. Our rational, logical, categorical, rubrical efforts are to no avail.

The realities are hard and time goes on. We need more of the poet and the politician, but we call erroneously for the expert, the scholar, and the organizer to come up from the rear. They are reluctant to leave their organizing chores, for putting the past together is easier and inevitably safer than sensing the order of tomorrow which is inherent "out there." The expert and the scholar impose their organizational constructs from yesterday on tomorrow and we applaud their efforts, even though we know they are certain to fail. We applaud because they have absolved us of responsibility for building a new and better tomorrow out of a hazy and tangled today. That their efforts will fail will not become conspicuous for some while, and, in the meantime, we will say to ourselves that we have employed the talents of our most respected men to bring order to our tenuous ways. Such an effort seems both reasonable and good. Men will talk about the undertaking in rational and meaningful phrases. We are not really fooled, but we play the game, anyway—this is the way the game of life has always been played. We trust that somewhere, somehow, one naïve or simple or recalcitrant or creative soul will generate a new ordering scheme and create a new day.

In the back of our minds, though, are the gnawing questions: What is tomorrow? What if the creative man with the answer does not step forward? Can we depend upon one individual or even a few to create new directions or solutions for the complex tomorrows which are already here? Wells' often quoted statement that "history becomes more and more a race between education and catastrophe"[1] is infinitely more true today than when he wrote it half a century ago. Thus, the need for more effective schools is underscored again. But what should the schools do? Which paths should they follow? In which direction should they go?

WHAT SHOULD THE SCHOOL DO?

The basic purpose of schools is to help children learn. But helping children learn means *helping children learn*

1. to value learning
2. to want to learn
3. how to learn
4. to value knowledge
5. to acquire knowledge
6. to understand knowledge
7. to behave according to knowledge

The ultimate objective of the educational effort is to help youngsters learn to behave according to the best knowledge available; that is, to make intelligent decisions which are based upon the facts. To presume that people will naturally "do as well as they know," however, is utterly naïve. The world is replete with people who "know better" than they "do." Prisons are full of men who "knew" they should not do what they did, but who went ahead and did it anyway. Every smoker "knows" that smoking is detrimental to health, but he still smokes. Such behavior could hardly be described as "rational" or "intelligent" or the kind of behavior which characterizes truly "educated" men. Thus, the assumption that the ultimate objective of education is to help young people learn to *behave* according to the best information and the best ideas available at any given point in time is underscored.

Helping people behave according to factual knowledge is not possible, however, unless people *understand* that knowledge, unless they give meaning to that knowledge, based upon their own past experience. Meaning always comes from the individual and what he has already learned; understanding represents the union of past experience and new stimuli in the learner's mind. To behave according to the best knowledge available, children first need help to understand, comprehend, appreciate, and give meaning to those facts.

Even before schools can begin working to help young people understand, however, they must help them *acquire knowledge* and facts and concepts. This educational objective must be realized before moving on to objectives which include understanding and ultimately behaving.

In the very same way, helping children acquire knowledge is hardly meaningful unless those children *value knowledge* first. Unless they believe in and are committed to the importance and worthwhileness of information, facts, and knowledge, mere acquisition is pointless. Perhaps the problem of the prisoners or smokers previously mentioned is that they have not "acquired" or "understood" the knowledge available. In all probability, the more significant reason for their behavior is that they have not "valued" knowledge—they have not believed in the worth and importance of valid data as an operating basis for their personal lives. Persons who acquire or even understand certain factual data or knowledge without being committed to and valuing knowledge are less apt to use that knowledge regularly or even occasionally. Valuing knowledge enables a person to retain it longer, have it more readily accessible when needed, and integrate it more meaningfully into past experiences.

The logic extends further, though. Valuing knowledge is not possible unless people have *learned how to learn;* therefore, helping children learn how to inquire, how to relate, how to communicate, and how to interact, for example, are all prerequisites to valuing knowledge, acquiring knowledge, giving meaning to knowledge, and behaving according to that knowledge. The skills of learning are, in other words, means to more noble ends, but they are purposes in their own right if seen in this way.

If students have not *learned to want to learn,* though, learning how to learn is pointless. Teachers who are concerned that students will not "try to learn" should probably rephrase this and ask themselves what they can do to help those students "learn to try." Helping students learn to want to learn is an educational objective, in other words. It is a necessary, though not sufficient, condition to ensure attainment of the ultimate objective of helping youngsters use knowledge and information so that it is reflected in and consistent with what they do behaviorally.

Helping children learn to want to learn presumes the most basic educational objective of all, that of *valuing learning.* Unless children have learned to believe in the worthwhileness of learning as a human activity, nothing else will count much anyway. Unless they are committed to learning as a way of bettering their own lives and the lives of all mankind, and unless they believe in learning as a powerful, creative, and superbly human way of resolving problems and coping with reality and the myriad of other facets of daily living, they most certainly will not want to learn, nor will they learn how to learn. Further, it is hard to believe that such persons would ever value knowledge, or acquire it, or understand it; therefore, it could hardly affect their lives. It is in this sense that "helping children learn" must begin with helping children learn to value learning as an exquisite, exciting, practical, and lifelong human enterprise, which will carry over in countless practical, esthetic, intellectual, social, and personal ways.

Because these purposes are functionally related to one another, there is an inexorable logic to the direction which has been defined. This logic leads toward the idea of "rational man" (man who uses the power of intelligence so that his choices, actions, and thoughts are consistent with factual knowledge), then, presumably, to "the good life," and is thus consistent with the heritage of Western man struggling to realize that which is both "good" and "true."

The educator's task, therefore, is to sequence subject matter and generate experience which will lead the student along that learning highway—each educational objective is a "process" objective and, as such, serves as a means to a higher, more noble, and more worthy end.

The educator has to be both "pipeline" and "sparkplug"; he must provide the information, and he must help people feel that this information is so important that they cannot behave except according to the data that are available. He has to generate emotion about the facts, and that means helping people learn to value learning, learn to want to learn, and learn to value knowledge. Valuing is the basis for educational effort and the cornerstone of personal commitment.

WHAT IS COMMITMENT?

Commitments are important, but they must be based on fact. The demagogue is committed, and so is the authoritarian and the true believer. But the commitments of these men are based on prejudicial fancy, frustration, or fear. Schools must foster a kind of commitment which goes to the core of the best that men presently know.

Commitment and conviction require the individual to take a stand or demonstrate a belief. Such actions presume that the individual has, for the moment at least, closed himself off to further variations or modifications in his belief system or his value system. If closure precedes acquisition of knowledge and interpretation of truth, demagoguery will inevitably occur. If closure follows extensive experiencing and interaction with factual information from every source, commitment *based on fact* can most readily occur.

Working with students in ways which enable them to "stay open" to new experiences and new stimuli is not only desirable but absolutely essential in the development of educated, committed men. At the same time, helping young people learn to pause in the experiencing process, "close down" on what they know, and act on the basis of intelligence and conviction is the teacher's task, too. Such a task requires patience and sensitivity as well as understanding and skill.

The ultimate in desirable behavior would probably involve an uneven rhythm of "openings" and "closings" to the individual learner's learning style. He would learn to hold himself maximally open to new information and additional truths until the time for action came, then he would "close down" his perceptual apparatus and act on the basis of the best that he knew. Action would be followed by subsequent perceptual effort, and the never-ending curiosity and the desire to know would appear in a kind of pulsating cycle involving being "open" and being "closed."

Unless schools help the learner develop skill in timing his shifts from being "open" to being "closed," serious problems for both the learner and the teacher will inevitably arise. For example, if closure comes too soon, the individual may be firmly committed, but to an inadequate data base. On the other hand, if closure is delayed, the individual may be unable to act with assurance or effectiveness given the conditions which prevail. Precise timing is imperative, or the learner behaves in uncomprehending or inappropriate ways.

Any value system and commitment to action has an assumptive base; assumptions serve as postulating filters which give direction and energy to perceptual activities and personal life style.

Life is worthwhile. Life has value. Commitments which are life-supporting and life-enhancing should be encouraged. Commitments which are life-negating or life-destroying must be discouraged and denied the possibility of maturing and manifesting themselves in thought or deed in any form.

Facts are important. Man must know what the reality is. In the final analysis, however, men behave according to their feelings about the facts. Making information available to students so that they can develop strong feelings about the best that men know, therefore, is the most effective way for educators to function.

The teacher's task is to help students convert the "cold hard facts" into "hot feelings about hard facts." This demands both passion and compassion along with insight and foresight in order to sequence the logic of ideas to fit the logic of a growing learner's mind. Teaching is creating poetry in life. Concept, rhythm, and meter must blend into an enduring fire which consumes the truth.

In looking for models, the educator has to create his own blend. Journalists who present a maximum of information with a minimum of feelings are considered effective. Performing actors and comedians who communicate a maximum of feeling with a minimum of information, however, are generally considered most successful. The educator's endeavor must embrace the maximum effort of both of these: tremendous amounts of information in a dramatic, emotional way.

WHAT IS ESSENTIAL?

The conventional wisdom of education suggests that some skills and some knowledge are essential for all students if they are to participate responsibly and meaningfully in the complex, dynamic society of today and tomorrow. The only problem has been what these certain things should be: the traditional "liberal arts"; the "essentials" of Bagley;[2] or the "fundamental skills and cultural heritage" of Wiles, for example.

Other persons have argued in the opposite direction. Kelly and Rasey for instance, presume that some skills are undoubtedly essential but that no specific set or cut of knowledge can be singled out as absolutely essential in our complex day and age. "Who can say," they maintain, "that from the vast wealth of knowledge in the fields of literature and science and history and art, for example, just which facts and which concepts are so important that they absolutely must be taught and must be learned?"[3]

Thus, both the controversy and the dilemma are born. In the past, we have resorted to tradition, to empirical countings of present offerings, or to experts' estimates of the future needs for our answer. None of these approaches has proven adequate.

We dare not face the past and back into the future. Nor can we tally what schools now do and presume that to be good. And no man knows what the future will hold, because it is not here. Some guesses may be right, but most will always be wrong; the dynamics of an evolving situation will guarantee that. What can we do?

Suppose we postulate that learning is a part of life; and, just as man needs food and water and air in order to maintain physical life, perhaps we can also presume that man needs stimulation and experience in order to maintain intellectual and emotional life. The question then becomes, What educational nutrients are essential to life?

Those who work in the fields of nutrition and biology and related fields have worked to answer these questions:

a. What substances or conditions are essential to the maintenance of physical life?

b. How much of any given substance or condition is essential to the maintenance of physical life?

c. How much of these substances or conditions is present in foods or other matter which the individual might consume or otherwise utilize in order to maintain physical life?

That is, Which elements or forces or combination of elements and forces present in the world are essential to physical life? Yes or no answers to questions such as the following, would typify specific illustrations of Question "a" described above:

1. Is iron essential?
2. Is calcium essential?
3. Is oxygen essential?
4. Is chlorine essential?
5. Is lead essential?
6. Is hydrogen sulfate essential?
7. Is vitamin A essential?
8. Is beefsteak essential?
9. Are carbohydrates essential?
10. Is electricity essential?

11. Is gravity essential?
12. Is atmospheric pressure essential?
13. Are calories essential?

Such a list of questions reflects various levels of awareness of the problem. "Is oxygen essential?" and "Is beefsteak essential?" are questions of a very different order. We all know that beefsteak is not essential to life, but we also know that protein, which beefsteak has in abundant amount, is essential to life. Although the question sounds superficial, it may very well be that such questions were actually posed in the early years of research on problems of this kind. The point of the whole series of questions is simply to illustrate the fact that researchers in nutrition and allied fields have had to answer questions such as these in order to ascertain precisely which elements or combinations of elements or conditions are essential for the maintenance of life. And, interestingly, certain questions (such as, "Is gravity essential?") have only been posed in recent years. As man moves into outer space, the list of essentials for life may be extended, but the process for determining those essentials will proceed by asking questions such as those described above.

The second general question, "How much of any given substance or condition is essential to physical life?" can be asked only after the first question has been answered. It would be pointless to attempt to determine if thirty or seventeen or three milligrams of niacin per day are essential to life if it is not known whether niacin itself is essential. But once the essentialness of niacin, iron, iodine, calcium, or any other factor is known, then it is perfectly appropriate to attempt to determine precisely how much is necessary for the maintenance of life.

Finally, a whole series of questions relative to the nutritional content of particular foods emerges:

1. How much protein is there in a pound of beefsteak?
2. How much calcium is contained in a quart of milk?
3. How much carbohydrate is there is a boiled potato?
4. How much carbohydrate is there in a fried potato?
5. How many units of Vitamin C are there in an orange?
6. How many units of vitamin C does the body gain from an hour in the sun?
7. How much iron is there in a half-pound of liver?

Questions such as these are only answered by research aimed at *describing* the content of food in terms of the essentials identified.

Knowing *what* substances are essential, *how much* of each substance is essential, and *which foods* contain these essentials in *what amounts* enables the physician to *prescribe* a nutritional diet based on more than tradition or logic or whim. Furthermore, wide distribution of such information has put more and more people into a position to make intelligent personal decisions about which foods and how much they should eat.

Suppose we employ this kind of logic in education and curriculum building. The three kinds of questions which would emerge are set forth below:

a. What areas of knowledge are essential to intellectual and emotional life?

b. How much of these areas of knowledge are essential to intellectual and emotional life?

c. How much of these areas of knowledge are present in any given stimulus which the individual might experience or otherwise utilize in order to maintain intellectual and emotional life?

Regarding the first question above, we might ask, "Which concepts, which facts, which patterns of information, which generalizations, and the like are essential to intellectual and emotional life?" If we research how essential each factor is, it might be that we would actually discover that no particular area of knowledge, no particular facts or concepts or generalizations are actually essential to intellectual and emotional life. In all probability, we would find that some are essential, but which ones may not be important. Or, we may actually discover that certain facts, certain concepts, and certain relationships are, in fact, essential.

Assuming that the answer to Question "a" is that some knowledge is essential, then it would be appropriate to ask "How much?"

Discovering the content of content, so to speak, would be the next step. How many facts, how many relationships, how many concepts, or how many generalizations, for example, are contained within a given textbook, film strip, group activity, counseling session, field trip, or individual study experience that might be contrived by the curriculum-maker? If teachers and others are to be effective in planning and sequencing experiences with the intention of facilitating learning, they must know the content of any particular subject matter or process experience which might be prescribed for students in order to help them learn.

The answers to questions such as these are simply not known. Nobody knows for a certainty which facts, which concepts, or which anything are absolutely essential to the maintenance of intellectual and emotional life. Furthermore, even if we did know which ones were essential, we do not know how many. Finally, even if we knew which ones and how many were essential, we do not yet know where those might be found and in what degree, as far as educationally planned experiences go. The total field of curriculum, in fact, is characterized by the fact that we have dealt with problems of sequence, organization, and scope *before* we knew the essentialness that was involved. Such problems are legitimate and appropriate to tackle *after* we find out what is essential for intellectual and emotional life, but not before.

This discussion raises many problems—some practical, some theoretical, and some empirical. I do not know the answers to these problems at all. I do feel that they need the best thought and the most creative researching that curriculum planners can bring to bear.

In determining what knowledge is essential, asking experts in the field or surveying opinion is not the place to begin. Even when all of the men in the world thought the earth was flat, that did not negate that it is spherical. And, when all of the learned physicians of the day laughed at Semmelweis for his hunch that physicians themselves spread disease because they did not wash their hands clean, that did not negate the fact that he was absolutely correct. Pooled judgment and expert opinion may be right, but it may be wrong.

We need empirical studies for the deficiencies which arise when particular substantitive experiences are denied. We know from the work of men like Hebb[4] and Hunt[5] and from some of the work of researchers studying language and ego development patterns among young children from culturally disadvantaged backgrounds[6] that certain kinds of deprivation experiences obviously result in incomplete, inadequate, or inappropriate development in the areas of intellectual and emotional life. But, we still do not know precisely what *is* essential.

In the realm of curriculum materials and experiences, furthermore, we do not know what substitutions might occur or what equivalencies exist. In physical life, for example, we know that protein is essential, but protein can be obtained in hamburger, pork chops, milk, or lima beans. The "content" of such foods is equivalent in that respect, even though there are also unique ingredients in each.

In the physical realm, certain foods and materials may be ingested but not absorbed into the bloodstream and, therefore, not utilized in the life process. Or, they may be absorbed and processed through the organism but not utilized, eventually eliminated as waste. The same phenomena are apparent in learning. Books may be read but not under-

stood, films seen but not perceived, lectures heard but not compre-
hended, and so forth. Likewise, information may be "absorbed" but
later forgotten—learned but later lost to either recall or use in any way.

The most difficult but promising problem, however, appears to revolve around the quantity question, once the "essentialness" problems
have been resolved. Although the body's physiological needs manifest
themselves and function in a homeostatic way, intellectual and emotional needs appear and function in another form. The body needs protein, carbohydrates, oxygen, and water, for example, but it only needs
and in fact can only handle certain amounts of these various things at
any particular point in time. Water is essential, but only so much water
can be consumed and used. Oxygen and vitamin A and other nutrients
are essential, but the body can only accept and utilize limited amounts
of these essentials in any life-supporting way. Too much water and the
individual drowns. Too much protein and he becomes ill.

Is the same thing true for intellectual and emotional life? Can the
individual only take so much "cognitive stuffing," or are his learning
needs insatiable? I would hypothesize that educational nutrients are
essential for intellectual and emotional life indefinitely, or at least as
long as the individual physically lives. Like those ingredients necessary
for physical life, however, it may be that only limited quantities and
types can be psychologically consumed during any given learning time.
The question of maximums and minimums, therefore, would probably
need to be resolved in optimal terms. Just as there is tolerance or leeway in terms of physical needs, so too there is probably tolerance or
leeway in terms of intellectual and emotional needs. What those limits
are we do not know. Nor do we know whether the limits vary with the
interactions which might occur. For example, drinking alcohol and
eating fatty foods produces a very different physiological response than
drinking alcohol on an empty stomach with no fatty supplements. Thus,
it may very well be that the experiencing of a particular concept, in
relationship to a set of facts, along with a particular set of skills will
result in an entirely different learning experience from that of simply
experiencing the concept alone.

Finally, what is the difference between *maintenance* and *enhancement* of intellectual and emotional life. Certain foods, certain minerals,
and certain other phenomena are essential for existence—for elementary maintenance of physical life. Beyond this, additional things contribute to enhancing or improving physical life. Is this also true for
intellectual and emotional life? Are certain knowledges, certain skills,
certain facts and concepts essential just for the basic maintenance of

intellectual and emotional life, while other knowledge contributes to the improvement and enhancement of that aspect of human existence? The questions are poorly stated here, but they are real.

SUMMARY

Some answers must be questioned. That was Kimball Wiles' way. This paper has explored four different kinds of problem areas which were reflected in his concerns. The attempt here has not been to restate what Kimball Wiles felt and knew. This is already known. The attempt, rather, has been to press the areas of concern in different and hopefully productive directions for persons who are thoughtful about and interested in curriculum work in American schools. They have served me here as springboards into the unknown. The only real effort has been to follow the ideas wherever they might go. Truth is illusive. But it is an attainable goal.

References

1. H. G. Wells, *Outline of History* (New York: Garden City Publishing Company, 1920 and 1931), p. 1169.
2. William C. Bagley, "An Essentialist's Platform for the Advancement of American Education," *Educational Administration and Supervision,* XXIV (April, 1938), 241-256.
3. Earl C. Kelley and Marie J. Rasey, *Education and the Nature of Man* (New York: Harper and Brothers, 1952).
4. D. O. Hebb, *The Organization of Behavior* (New York: John Wiley & Sons, Inc., 1949).
5. J. M. V. Hunt, *Intelligence and Experience* (New York: The Ronald Press Company, 1961).
6. For example, see Martin P. Deutsch, "The Disadvantaged Child and the Learning Process" and David P. Ausubel and Pearl Ausubel, "Ego Development Among Segregated Negro Children," in A. H. Passow, ed., *Education in Depressed Areas* (New York: Teachers College Press, 1963).

chapter 4

Trafford P. Maher S.J.

Education for Survival

In central east Africa, Tanzania is the site of Olduvai Gorge. This is the ancient home of Zinjanthropus, early man of 1,400,000 years ago whose remains were found by Dr. Leakey and his wife.

When one views the skull of Zinjanthropus alongside that of modern man and reflects upon the years between the eras of these two representatives of Homo sapiens, some tall questions do indeed rush quickly to mind. For example, What essential progress has man made? Zinjanthropus and colleagues loudly barked at one another. Power made right! Magnitude of bark plus naked muscle designated leadership. A roving, aimless search constituted days and nights. A comprehensive, supportive love appears not to have been present.

Twentieth-century man, although the proud achiever of incredible technological feats, has not improved too much on Zinjanthropus's earlier condition.

YOUTH SUICIDES

There are many indices one could use to document the above. To use only one index, there is the staggering fact that more youngsters are committing suicide today than at any previous time in American history.[1] Some experts believe that as many as 36,000 school-age boys and girls commit suicide or attempt suicide every year.

Fact gatherers for the *Enquirer* show the following:

1. Suicide ranks third in the cause of deaths of youngsters, 15 to 19 years old. Only accidents and cancer claim more lives. In many accident cases, a suicide drive probably has been operative.
2. Among college students, suicide is the number two cause of death, with only accidents taking a greater toll.
3. Suicides among college students run fifty per cent higher than for non-students in the 18–22 age groups.
4. Suicide rates are highest among the brightest students in the best schools.
5. Boys commit twice as many suicides as girls.
6. For every successful youthful suicide there are between five and six unsuccessful attempts.

The United States Department of Health, Education, and Welfare lists suicide as the third cause of death among teenagers. Dr. Edwin S. Schneidman, Chief of the Center for Studies of Suicide Prevention in Washington, D.C., indicates that youthful suicides represents a growing crisis in our society. His estimate is that in America today there are 500,000 young people with borderline mental problems and another million who have serious mental disorders. Many of these will attempt suicide and far too many will succeed.

Dr. Stanley F. Yolles of the Washington, D.C., National Institute of Mental Health says that there are key factors of suicide characteristics which do seem to exist. For example, he notes that a New Jersey study of 41 children who killed themselves between 1960 and 1963 revealed that none of them had close friends. Another study in Southern California of 50 adolescents who had attempted suicide showed that 46 per cent had seen a doctor within a year of their suicide attempt; 64 per cent had become defiant and rebellious in the past five years; 73 per cent had withdrawn themselves; 44 per cent had run away from home; 76 per cent said they couldn't talk with their parents.

The late Dr. Kimball Wiles, this author believes, would have been among the first to agree that the high school of the future must seriously grapple with the awesome realities outlined above.

To attempt to assign causative factors of the drive toward suicide among youth, in the absence of hard, objective research evidence would be foolhardy indeed. One can, however, generally describe the cultural milieu which forms the context in which youth must confront itself and its problems. This milieu is characterized by five mighty explosions, each with its own revolution, which do undoubtedly smash against young lives.

EXPLOSIONS AND REVOLUTIONS

These explosions and revolutions are in a) knowledge; b) space; c) population; d) the released cultural forces of religion; and e) a new-found awareness and functioning of personal freedom. These explosions and revolutions have rocked many lives, particularly youthful lives, throughout the 1960's. Without question, these explosions and revolutions will be intensified throughout the 70's and 80's.[2]

The above forms a basis, this author believes, that makes it imperative for the curriculum of the high school of the future to focus on *Education for Survival*.

Suicide is not the only killer of our youth. There is another kind of death. It is the "death" which results from reacting to prolonged pressures from home, school, and community; the "death" which sets in when youth calls a psychological moratorium on life. Some young persons simply drop out of current life, a state that becomes symbolic of their rejection of cultural continuity and progress. Too often, these youths completely resist a view of man which expects rationality, work, duty, vocation, maturity, and material and intellectual success.

We need to explore curriculum possibilities, through experimentation, which will give us higher probability of producing a society of mature, free individuals, finding their personality in the common life of the community around them through free initiative. If and when we find that curriculum direction, we will have a society which will be very much better and ultimately very much stronger than what we have had until now.

A CURRICULUM FOR SURVIVAL

This chapter suggests that this new curriculum will probably be found under the formality of "Education for Survival."

What is this survival? It is something much more viable than the precarious state sustained by the recipient of a heart transplant who must live hour by hour. Survival is an habitual state in which a person is motivated by an abiding conviction that *he is equal* to whatever reality may be placed upon him. It is a conviction which is generated by definite knowledges and skills to keep one aware that he is adequate to the demands which confront him.

This survival is multiple: emotional, mental, spiritual, vocational, economic, social, political—and ultimately it is *personal.* Each of these "survival areas" has clear-cut implications for the curriculum.

While the specifics here are as yet unknown and still await the searchlight of a new kind of research and painstaking study, it can be realistically stated that the new curriculum will have to be implemented in a human school environment that is characterized by non-judgmental acceptance, non-selfconsciousness, sincerity, integrity, relevance, and participatory democracy. Each of these words has great significance and, if you will, implications for teacher education itself.

The term "non-judgmental acceptance" indicates here that the high school student must be confronted at every stage of his development in terms of who and what he is, and not in terms of some predetermined mold into which we attempt to fit him. "Non-selfconsciousness" means that the teaching communication skill has to function with overtones of a warm, working relationship, devoid of all affectation and stereotypes.

If the generation gap is not to widen even more disastrously, sincerity, integrity, and relevance must play a vital part in the schools of today and tomorrow. "Sincerity" demands of the teacher and the total school an approach generated by convictions rooted in evidence and free of all myth, legend, and folklore born of almost "deified" middle-class values. "Integrity" insists that the teacher and school never break faith with their youth no matter how insistent various societal and professional groups may become. "Relevance" means that the teacher and curriculum must make "here and now" sense to the student. The dishing out of cold packages from the accumulated stockpile of the past is not relevant to the developing human being. Work-study programs tend to keep schooling more relevant.

The high school of the future, "to foster life and to foster it more abundantly," must possess a curriculum that pursues and provides opportunities to acquire in deeply internalized ways the aforementioned factors of emotional, mental, spiritual, economic, social, political, and personal survival.

ADEQUACY

Here, the concept of *adequacy* needs emphasis. The drift of young lives today and current events make it reasonable to suspect that in the decades ahead conditions will be so intensified that persons must be helped to be as adequate as possible in as many foreseeable circumstances as possible. The Establishment's tyranny has been to educate individuals to be completely conforming, normal individuals. Yet life is too big and too varied to contain *normalcy,* which, at best, is a statistical term meaning mediocre. Today's youth have rejected this fate en masse. Young people seek, they need to claim and develop distinct individuality—the flowering of their own unique temperaments and personalities.

These are the relevant, inescapable stark realities which far too many comfortable, change-fearing, rut-entrenched, traditional educators are unwilling and often unable to face. School systems with their inherited power centers must, to save youth and ultimately the country itself, face up to the need to blast rigidities out of the present curriculum—dependent as they are on the equally rigid college demands for prerequisites called college preparatory programs.

One of the first ways to start is by designing a curriculum now and for the future that fosters adequacy as an insurance for productive survival.[3]

However the new curriculum is shaped and whatever it contains, it must achieve its goals through the process of forming the necessary and relevant values, loyalties, commitments, and their products: attitudes toward persons, places, issues, and things.[4]

A value is the meaning or rating a person attaches to his experience; a loyalty is the degree to which one is willing to adhere to his values; a commitment is the reason why, conscious or unconscious, one hangs on to the value he has placed on his experience. An attitude is the product of the value-loyalty-commitment chain. The attitude is one's readiness and posture for action.

Obviously, if the curriculum for today and for the 70's and 80's is to communicate, if it is to convey a deep sense of personal purpose, adequacy, and sound, convincing reasons which tellingly motivate youth to want to survive psychologically and physically, it must relate to youth in such a way that they can taste its short-range worth and trust its long-range promises.

The task proposed is enormous, complicated, and demanding. Two of the most frustrating aspects of the challenge are these: 1) No one really knows just where or how to start; 2) those in the professional positions charged with the responsibility of curriculum designing are actually too far removed from a personal feeling and awareness of how young people perceive the realities bombarding them. This prompts the suggestion that on every high school curriculum team there should be a substantial representation of persons not beyond sophomore year in college, whether they are from the field of education or not. The role of the professional here is to listen through many and long discussion sessions to what young people have to say.

SOME QUESTIONS THAT WILL NOT DISAPPEAR

On paper, the task does not appear too formidable or horrendous. When one operationally faces the assignment, however, questions that will not disappear keep nagging: How does one make relevant to young people of today and tomorrow in terms of their perceptions of adequacy and survival

1. values, loyalties, commitments in the emotional area?
2. in the mental area?
3. in the spiritual area?
4. in the vocational area?
5. in the economic area?
6. in the social area?
7. in the political area?
8. in the comprehensive personal area?

Let all educational professional organizations, school systems, appointed or elected lay and hired professionals, assigned committees and task forces know that the old system with its inherited approaches and procedures is outmoded, irrelevant, and dead. Effective processes and content must be researched and found, or unending friction, non-communication, human loss, and ultimate, perduring chaos will result.

In the absence of tested evidence, we can take no sure stand; however, we can speculate. It is more than likely that nothing is or will be more important than giving high school students training and education in personal communication skills to achieve psychological and physical survival.

PERSONAL COMMUNICATION SKILLS
NEEDED

The communication here referred to is that process embracing every action, reaction, and interpersonal reaction posited for the purpose of sending and receiving *meanings* and *feelings*. This is the communication that is needed for mental and emotional support in one's world of people. This is the process which builds "bridges among persons"; which forms "links in the human chain."[5]

Lest all of this remain just "paper talk" for curriculum specialists and committees, let it be remembered that the teaching process and knowledge can have a major formative impact on developing adolescents. Constructive, productive, supportive values, loyalties, commitments, and attitudes—the heart of the communication process—can be acquired by students in and through the secondary schools.

Learning skills to implement any process involves three stages: a) the opportunity to become aware of the lack in one's self and of the precise motivation and behavior that will fill the lack or gap; b) the chance to experience the use of the newly acquired skill in a wide range of concrete, human, living situations; c) the opportunity to solidify the skill by having frequent occasions (e.g., small group discussions) in which to verbalize the meaning and applicability of the skill. The latter exercise tends to deepen insights. Deepened insights strengthen motivation.

Traditionally, school curricula have tended to give emphasis to what "has been" in the humanities, social, and physical sciences. To youth, this gives learning an aura of irrelevancy and impersonality. While in no sense ignoring the past, the curriculum should give constant strong emphasis to what is to come. It is in this context that the highly sensitive communication skills are learned. The curriculum, teachers, and the total school environment need to be emphatically future-oriented. In this orientation, the search should be to penetrate to the essence of human living and understanding. Growth here means the acquisition of an abiding, vital sense of personal purpose.

Over and above the communication skill which is of central importance, school and school programs need to furnish learning opportunities to acquire the skills to *organize* knowledge, new and old, into coherent patterns designed according to rational priorities. As the student matures in the use of the organizing skill, gradually he comes to have a plan into which he can fit all new learnings. This yields a satisfying basis upon which to make constructive choices and judgments.

This consideration opens up a whole new area which has to do with personal values and personal goals, short- and long-range. Here, attention is drawn to the skill of assigning priorities to knowledge as well as to action plans. This skill can and indeed must become a habit of mind and emotions if one is to perform with any degree of adequacy as he moves from one life plateau to another. A life of purpose, the only kind which maximally insures survival, needs unity and cohesion. These can be achieved only when one has a set of value norms, freely formed and freely accepted, which make possible priorities and purpose.

Because of increased new learning materials and new aids for the rapid transmission of information, much more thought and effort can now be applied to the more subtle task of forming values, loyalties, commitments, attitudes, and communication and organizing skills.

SPECIAL SKILLS MAN NEEDS

This chapter would in no sense be complete without reflecting upon those special skills which man needs for looking at himself and at the vast universe of reality which is non-self. The human function of perceiving needs a special mode of observing the world and of giving meaning to these observations. This will most profoundly influence the choices man makes, the decisions he implements, the persons he prizes, the life-style values he formulates, the ideas and feelings he elects to communicate, and the knowledge and behaviors he considers of most worth.

The special mode of observing self and non-self needs a basic framework. The curriculum itself must yield this framework so that the student can form his own weltanschauung. Survival demands that one have a comprehensive conception or image of the universe and of man's relationship to it. If the high school student is to be equipped to cope with life, he cannot and should not be protected from the problems of pain, evil, failure, and even death.

At every stage of development, students need to be helped to differentiate reality from wishful thinking. This is no mean task but it can be effectively accomplished if teachers will work with the perceptual process. With lightning-like rapidity, human perception tends to interweave the past and the future with the present moment of perception. In learning to communicate accurately with self and others, the individual needs to become aware of this "interweaving process" within himself.

Help in differentiating can be given in a variety of ways: 1) by sensitizing the student to his own communications content in small group discussions; 2) by having the student report on an event; 3) by recording some of the matters the teacher hears a student saying. Later, student and teacher can explore these remarks; 4) by having the student express his meanings and feelings in some art form, no matter how primitive; 5) by having the student "free wheel" in his expression. The follow-up is to have the student label what is real and what is wishful thinking.

Direction and meaning come into a life through the individual's ongoing perceptions. Long ago, Lindworsky indicated that after the first four years of a child's life there is no such thing as a "pure perception." Memory of the past and expectation of the future rush to the present perception like unsummoned blood rushes to a cut in the skin. Lives that are to be constructive and productive—lives that are going to foster and maintain at least minimal stability and adequacy must have the skill to differentiate the elements in perception, or distortion will enter meanings. Distorted meanings yield mental and emotional as well as spiritual disorganization.

The curriculum and the teaching art itself can aid the student here. Needless to say, this presupposes that the curriculum has been designed to be proportioned to its moment of time and that teachers themselves possess the necessary skills regarding themselves and others.

The future looms large and uncertain as has been the case since man developed to the stage where the force of reason made the future a concern. All the facets of the science and technology of the present tantalize man concerning their wonders in the future. Realistically, however, we cannot be tantalized by man's relationship to man in the future if we are to use the ugly facts of the present as a basis for our prognostication. Much, much more time must be given in the secondary school to the factors of *love* and *loneliness* in human experience if the future is to be any improvement over the present.

Man's relationship to man cannot be left to happenstance as was the case with Zinjanthropous and company. We know that man turns to others with varying degrees of feeling and interest. We observe that man can be aloof, kind, angry, loving, or hateful. The question arises: Since man can love, how can we activate more of his potential for loving? The school must develop persons who are able to give and receive love.

Exclusive self-getting and self-protection are enemies of love. Since our culture tends to be predominantly thing-centered, the curriculum and teaching must exert an unusual counterforce by cultivating in manner and matter a people-centered focus. Students need to develop an habitual motivation which leads them to perceive the good, the dignity, and the worth in others and then to follow these perceptions by action plans which seek to further this good, dignity, and worth. Once this has happened, the developing student can begin to place in perspective his attachments and commitments.

Love has the potential for strength, positive feelings, and productivity. Paradoxically, love also possesses the potential for dissatisfaction, improductivity, and unhappiness. It is in the latter state that loneliness is experienced. There is, of course, a difference between loneliness and aloneness.

Loneliness is characterized by an abrasive feeling of being cut off from others; aloneness is merely solitude in which one has "quiet time" in which to keep vital, appropriate perspective. Students need much time and help to understand love, loneliness, and aloneness. Further, they need wise aid in acquiring the necessary skills to handle these human realities.

This chapter has moved from Zinjanthropus of 1,400,000 years ago to a consideration of love and loneliness. While this leap may seem ludicrous, it may be that actually there is no leap at all. Destructiveness was rampant in our earliest ancestoral beginnings. It is still with us! Witness the suicide figures plus the phenomena which indicate that many young people have dropped out of life psychologically.

OUR OPPORTUNITY

Fortunately, the secondary school of the future can turn over to the miracle of electronics the rapid transmission of information. This released time makes available to the curriculum and to teachers much creative time in which to cope with the subtle task of forming persons— communicating persons; persons who care about their world of man.

When this new type of school has had a chance to prove that it can introduce students to a sense of personal purpose and that it is capable of producing people who are unafraid of love (whether to give or to receive), who know that aloneness is necessary and that loneliness starves and leads to death, then models for constructive living will begin to mount in our statistical tables. Whether we continue to fail or to choose our own new destiny will depend on the courage, the depth of conviction, and the professional preparedness of school administrators, professional curriculum personnel, and the progressive independence of teacher-educators who have the courage to break from the dull, unrealistic, irrelevant patterns into which teacher education programs are now pressured.

References

1. *National Enquirer,* Vol. 43, No. 1 (Sept. 8, 1968), 22.
2. For a further development of this theme, see "The Peculiar Dimensions of Today's Cultural Transitions," in Trafford P. Maher, *Self, A Measureless Sea; Counseling Theory and Practice* (St. Louis: Catholic Hospital Association, 1966), Chap. 1, p. 3.
3. For a further development of this theme, see Maher, *op. cit.,* pp. 25-29; 110-112.
4. *Ibid.,* p. 35 ff.; 47 ff.; 51 ff.
5. *Ibid.,* p. 110 ff., "The Maher Hypotheses—Personalism and Communication."

chapter **5**

Alice Miel

Rationale for a Curriculum Design: A Critique

Every responsible author in a professional field has a common dread as he releases his written words to the relentless exposure of print. Will those words rise to haunt him in future years, or perhaps even as they come off the press only a few months after he places the final period on his manuscript? Will future readers, and those who quote and quibble, tend to view the words as something *said* at one point in time and within its own context? Or will they consider them as something the author *says* for all time?

Kimball Wiles would be the last to want any of his writing to be taken as a final pronouncement of his views. His hope in the chapter on "The High School of the Future" that "these hypotheses will help each reader to formulate his own expectations" shows clearly that he desired this particular writing at least to be considered tentative and suggestive to others.

To make points in the nature of "yes, but," "yes, if," and "no, unless" in continuing the discussion Wiles started in the early sixties is to do what any author should welcome. It is to pay him the honor of keeping ideas alive and growing. This is not to be confused with putting words in the mouth of another, either in the form of what he intended to say at the time or what he would say if writing today.

51

The forecast published first in 1963 contained predictions that the high school would take on certain forms within specified dates. Intriguing as these predictions still are, it is useful to read them not only as the only forms that could possibly be invented for the purpose stated or as forms that will inevitably become established, but rather as illustrative solutions that a man, writing in a particular year, considered promising enough to offer hypothetically.

When an author allows predictions to go into print, he is especially vulnerable and depends on his critics to make allowances for the limitations of human oracles. A good five years after a set of predictions has been published, it may be more productive to examine the ideas marshalled to rationalize the forecast than to probe into the details of the predictions themselves. That is the task undertaken in the present chapter.

Those ideas selected for discussion in the pages that follow are: 1) the need of each individual for "a set of values to guide his behavior"; 2) the need of each individual for "skills necessary to participate effectively in the culture"; 3) the need of each individual for "an understanding of his social, economic, political, and scientific heritage"; and 4) the need of each individual to "become able to make a specific contribution to the society." These ideas are examined for their relevance to education in general in the world that is shaping up.

VALUES TO GUIDE BEHAVIOR

In 1963, Wiles was "optimistic enough to believe that there will continue to be a social commitment to freedom, creativity, and equality of opportunity." His particular selection of words happened to lay stress on one segment of the values our society has stood for; namely, the rights accruing to the individual. Unmentioned was the other side of the coin, the responsibility of the individual to cooperate with others in achieving a kind of order within which the person can count on opportunities to exercise his rights. Yet, Wiles was an excellent prognosticator when he wrote: "In the late sixties, it will begin to be recognized that unless citizens have values they accept, understand, and can apply, the social structure will disintegrate until authoritarian controls are applied."

Already it begins to appear that commitment to both aspects of our basic value system is lagging. A few extremists in the youth group, both white and black, seem so intent upon destroying the power of an establishment they consider totally evil that they justify any means they choose to employ, demand freedoms they grant to no one else, and take a nihilistic approach to the problem of governance. More than a few of the older members of our society have reacted in fright and some in seeming hatred of youth in general. One politician, for example, has publicly equated beards with lack of brains. Some have excused the clubbing of demonstrators after they were under arrest. Tolerance of measures designed to secure any kind of order at any cost to individual freedom is on the increase.

It is frightening to contemplate the fact that the confrontation and reaction we are experiencing could lead to systems of thought control of the kind developed in Nazi Germany, but it would not be wise to expect the situation to right itself unaided. Professor George Counts, while lecturing to classes at Teachers College, Columbia University, used to point out the danger of the belief that "it can't happen here." He would give a long list of things that "just couldn't happen" in Europe in the thirties, but that nevertheless did happen. To see to it that "it doesn't happen here" may be the most significant charge to our educational system in the years ahead.

No doubt, we can still assume on the part of a large segment of the society a verbal commitment to the values of both freedom *and* self-imposed restraint, order *with* justice, caring deeply about people *and* using reason in solving problems of the society. But never before have both our institutional forms and our basic values been so sharply challenged in and of themselves.

It has always been true that each new generation has to be taught that democracy is a hard-earned achievement of man—an achievement that must be rewon time and again as conditions on this globe change and as new vistas of the potentialities of democracy for man open up. Political rights, civil rights, economic rights, social rights, and finally human rights—each expression suggests new worlds to conquer in the search for ways of improving the lot of mankind. Unfortunately, we have never carried on such teaching as if it really were a prime responsibility of our schools; thus, we have learned all too little about how to conduct education for value development. In the past dozen years, when there has been widespread pressure on young people to achieve academically above all else, we have probably done less than ever to help them with lessons so crucial for the survival and advancement of what we have called the free world.

Wiles was quite right in providing for direct attention to value development in his scheme for the future secondary school and quite right in affording "opportunity to examine the conflicts among the many sets of values and viewpoints held by members of the society," even though not all readers might agree that his "Analysis Group" or any one device would be "the best" means for the purpose.

If only the voices of the young people attending the 1960 White House Conference on Children and Youth had been listened to as they pleaded for help from their parents and teachers on value problems! They were aware, as their elders did not seem to be, of the importance of values in guiding behavior.

Now, rather than to assume an overall commitment to basic values we have too long taken for granted, we may, as educators, have to operate as if there were no commitment at all and help our young people distill anew the values essential to humane living in a crowded world. We may have to help them discover for themselves what decisions and what forms of behavior are fair and decent and what are unfair and indecent. If democratic values are as sound as many of us have believed, they will once again be found indispensable.

SKILLS FOR EFFECTIVE PARTICIPATION

Skills necessary to participate effectively in the culture include many which Wiles suggested could be taught by machines supervised by librarians and technicians. For example, reading, spelling, computing, handling a foreign language, and manipulating scientific formulas and processes were named. Effective participation in a complicated modern society also calls for skills of a quite different order. If values are to be applied in ongoing human situations, skills of social problem solving and skills of relating with fellow human beings are essential. More than teaching machines and technicians are required if such skills are to be learned. They can be acquired only through group experiences under wise leadership, through examined interpersonal and intergroup transactions. This aspect of a school program is not made explicit in the Wiles chapter although it has been the subject of much other writing by that author.

It is becoming more and more clear that not only have we failed to help the young activists of today to clarify their values and goals; we have also failed to help them with skills required for carrying out the obligation of each generation to make its society a better one. Where have our more radical youth turned for models and procedures for their crusade? To Che Guevara, Karl Marx, and other "heroes of the New Left." And what preparation have their more moderate peers had for tempering the tactics of the revolutionaries while continuing to be active in promoting useful change? Many have expressed bewilderment on finding themselves being manipulated by fellow students who have undergone a more realistic political education.

It is already very late to try to turn outrageous confrontation and enraged reaction to conversation characterized by mutual responding. But we must learn better than we have up to now how to teach the skills of constructive protest and useful conformity, the skills of claiming rights and exercising responsibility, the skills of questioning and listening to both the idea content and the emotional content of messages being communicated.

Given the temper of today's often militantly committed youth, we must not be so naïve or shortsighted as to urge them to forget their feelings and follow a cool, rational course. Many have highly legitimate complaints against the society that reared them and they care strongly about rectifying conditions. We must somehow help them to learn the difficult art of acting on the basis of both caring and thinking. This means, in part, enlarging the area of concern, going beyond the cause of the moment, and having regard for the impact of action on other human lives. This dual dimension of action highlights the role of understanding to which we now turn.

UNDERSTANDING THE CULTURAL HERITAGE

As Wiles used the term cultural heritage, it included basic knowledge from the humanities, the social sciences, and the physical and biological sciences. The expectation was that the individual would become literate enough to participate in discussions of, and understand references to, the experiences, ideas, and discoveries of the past. Only for some was it expected "that the experiences in the Cultural Heritage portion of the program will develop a desire to enhance further the values on which the society is based."

Development of understanding is a commonly expressed goal in education, yet it is such a broad and loose term that it is difficult to know what it includes. Since Wiles' treatment of understanding the cultural heritage is necessarily brief, it seems useful to expand upon it at this point.

There is a kind of understanding which allows a person to show that he is "educated," for he can exhibit a familiarity with a great range of information. There is another kind of understanding which illuminates something—a current problem, one's own behavior, or an aspect of the human condition. For example, one can study the French Revolution and even recite glibly a list of its causes but still have no understanding of the basic phenomenon of revolution and no insight into the revolution in progress in our own society. A generation maturing in an age of violent upheaval will need help in acquiring a longer perspective and becoming aware that a non-violent period of hard work must follow if institutions are to be redesigned and a new order is to be achieved.

As Fred Hechinger wrote in the *New York Times* for September 8, 1968, in commenting on the critical unrest in the nation's schools:

> Will the students who observe the power struggles of their parents, teachers, and older brothers and sisters be able to regard the clash of a society in crisis as a temporary phenomenon?
>
> Will force be more appealing to them than law? If the present power struggle in an education system in crisis is to be understood as an extraordinary rather than a permanent phenomenon, the pain of renewal rather than the prelude to dissolution, some very sophisticated, persuasive teaching will be called for.[1]

Education for understanding what the problems of our society are made of and how and why people work on these problems, understanding that helps the individual feel oriented and able to examine critically what goes on around him—that is the level of understanding toward which curriculum plans should be geared and teaching should be aimed.

Young people will need help similarly in understanding their own motivations and actions, their own fears and hopes. Knowledge for understanding the culture is mentioned in the Wiles chapter; knowledge for understanding the self is not. The humanities and the social sciences may contribute to that end, but courses in those fields cannot be depended upon to function that way automatically. It takes concern and expertness to help young people reach deeper levels of understanding.

The particular stance taken in the cultural heritage section of the chapter being discussed raises additional questions. The most basic one has to do with making the cultural heritage synonymous with knowledge, leaving out the values and skills which have been developed in the culture. To some, these values and skills also are parts of a heritage belonging to all those born into a culture. Viewing the cultural heritage as knowledge alone perhaps justifies the essentially passive experience projected in this section of the forecast. This view, however, leads to other questions next discussed.

It is indicated that the goal is for the many merely to "understand" while a few may develop a desire to enhance values. If attention is given to knowledge acquisition at the expense of building connections between knowledge and values, it may be anticipated that few young people will be moved to work toward an improved value orientation in the society. Is it wise to create a situation encouraging such a result? Should we not plan and work deliberately for the opposite effect?

References only to knowledge accumulated in the past raise questions about the importance of the processes of creating knowledge going on ceaselessly in the present. The Wiles chapter was being developed in the period when the profession was shaking down its ideas about teaching the basic nature of the various disciplines. Today it is more clear that an essential economy in learning comes from grasping the way in which knowledge is produced in specialized fields and the organizing principles of different disciplines. Man's varied ways of knowing and his developed processes of inquiry and expression, in the opinion of many today, are in themselves part of the cultural heritage.

A final question arises from the implied gap between knowing and acting. However it is to be accomplished, the whole person needs to know how to engage in a complete process of seeing the need for information, gathering and processing pertinent information, making value judgments and decisions about the use of the information collected, and taking action on the decisions made.

As the co-chairman of the 1949 yearbook of the Association for Supervision and Curriculum Development, Wiles took the position that fostering problem solving and social action on the part of youth were important aspects of better teaching. For some reason, in his later description of the school of the future, he did not make explicit an action orientation. On the contrary, there is provision for machine-scored tests and the recording of marks, reinforcing the impression that for students to acquire a store of information is the chief purpose of the cultural heritage courses outlined. This is not to say that other purposes of education were not to be cared for elsewhere in the school, but it does mean that certain unfortunate separations were made in the analysis. The most basic of these separations was the provision that knowledge was to be transmitted to huge groups of students by live or canned performers, while examination of knowledge for meaning and application was reserved for another time and situation. By this very arrangement, students are silently being taught a lesson about compartmentalization of knowledge we would not wish them to learn.

ABILITY TO MAKE A SPECIALIZED CONTRIBUTION

In the Wiles chapter, the hope is expressed that *each* pupil would "become able to make a specialized contribution to the society." The part of the program designed to present the opportunities for such specialization was, however, left optional. This difference between the language of the goal statement and that used to describe the school program proposed for promoting the goal may have resulted from the linking of specialization and creativity in the fourth phase of the program. The author may have wished to avoid making creativity a required acivity! A further feature is that only certain students would be allowed to enroll in seminars and thus find their way to special science laboratories. Since there appears to be no provision for an inquiry or discovery type of experience in the projected program other than in this optional segment, this discriminatory feature is open to question.

On the other hand, the college-bound student from the middle class is not seen as a likely candidate for work experiences. Such experiences might well increase empathy for fellow men who will follow careers different from one's own. Recent studies of the attitudes of suburban youth suggest the need to develop just such empathy for those of a different social class.

In the late sixties, we have become much more conscious of the subtle ways in which children from certain parts of the society are kept from having chances to find or improve themselves. It is in managing access to opportunities for specialization and creativity that we have made many of our mistakes, putting ceilings on young people or setting entrance requirements to various opportunities but taking no steps to help individuals meet them. This section of the rationale has inviting possibilities for expansion and rethinking in the light of realities we are facing much more squarely today than ever before.

One more aspect of contribution to the society remains to be mentioned. Whether a young person is college-bound or not, he and his society will profit if he has opportunities to see himself as an individual who feels rewarded when he gives service to the community. The time is long since past when community service may be thought of as restricted to the middle class or to the established adult. Young people in every type of community and socio-economic group need to know how to give of themselves in concert with others to make their community better. Service occupations will absorb an increasing proportion of the population in the years to come. Therefore, participation in community service projects may well lead to a satisfying career for some.

CONCLUSION

The kind of rationale on which Wiles built his forecast is a valuable contribution in itself. The fact that certain questions have been raised is not to deny the worth of an analysis which permits planning a school program in manageable parts. The difficulty of providing for unity and integration in a large enterprise with so many interlocking facets underlines the importance of continuing to explore various comprehensive and harmonious curriculum designs wherein every student as a whole person is served.

Efforts must be continued also to find the best staffing patterns to implement such designs. It is clear that this society cannot afford to have highly trained specialists doing work that a less well-trained person can handle while the function the specialist could perform so well is neglected.

There are no easy answers to the problem of staff differentiation. A technician may supervise the use of a teaching machine, but who is to help the student know when and for what purpose to turn to the program on the machine? Who or what is to make this a relevant experience for the student? Is it enough to have a list of skills each student must master? Is this a promising way to develop thinking people? Who is to help each student gain fair access to opportunities challenging and right for him, especially the student who for some reason does not seek chances to adventure in his school life? What kind of staffing patterns will give students teachers of whom they can say, "They really care about *us*"?

The list of areas to be investigated with which Wiles opened his chapter shows that he shared many of the concerns voiced in this present piece. We have yet a long way to go before rising to the insights expressed in 1963 by one Kimball Wiles.

References

1. © September 8, 1968 by The New York Times Company. Reprinted with permission.

chapter 6

Franklin Patterson

Human Issues in Post-Industrial Society: The Context of Education Tomorrow

Some years ago I had the privilege of working with Kimball Wiles on a report entitled *The High School We Need.*[1] In that task, and in all of my other associations with Kimball Wiles, I was profoundly impressed by his remarkable capacity for combining intuitive insight, courageous vision, and operational practicality. This capacity was demonstrated in very nearly everything that Kimball Wiles did and wrote, including certainly his chapter on "The High School of the Future" which the present memorial volume takes as its point of departure. In his writing as in his teaching, Kimball Wiles deepened our insights, raised our angle of vision, and never let us forget the practical questions of operation and organization that education must face. He moved us to feel, and think, and act. The discourse in this volume is proof of that.

Reading his 1963 chapter, I find myself again in conversation with Kimball Wiles about human issues that are involved in the education of adolescents now and tomorrow—issues that he was concerned about along with us, and that we must go on to wrestle with as best we can. All of these issues arise out of the context, texture, and dynamics of a post-industrial technological society. All of them affect our children and youth, and all of them affect the high school as it is today and as it may be tomorrow. The effects of these human issues will occur whether we know it or not; as educators and citizens concerned for the welfare of young persons who are entering selfhood and society, it is crucial for us to understand these issues as best we can. Unless we try to do so, our efforts at building schools, colleges, and other educational enterprises that will be appropriate to the future will be even more vulnerable than they are likely to be anyway.

There is space here to touch only on three of the human issues of education for the future that one can descry in the present. One of these revolves around the factor of drivenness and upward mobility that characterizes much of life in contemporary technological society as we know it. A second issue concerns the factor of meaninglessness which underlies and drains color and substance from individual lives when much of the foundation upon which our ethos was built over centuries is crumbling under the impact of massive mutations in man's cultural evolution. A third issue is based on the factor of disaffection, anger, and overt hostility, whose present and future dimensions are certainly not yet clearly or completely visible to us, but which are surely not limited in future potential to what we have already seen in the 1960's among black activists and rebellious white youth.

These three issues indeed provide a sober stage on which to consider the high school of the future. That is, they do so if we consider them only negatively, or only as threats. For myself, I am trying to see the issues of human education that revolve around these factors as accurately and realistically as my limitations will allow, and at the same time explore ways in which the school and college can respond constructively, with some hope of reconstructing education so that significant help will be given to transforming the energies that are more and more absorbed by these factors into the energies it will take to build a new era in which man can be more human, rather than less so. The essential point is that we cannot in any adequate way consider the *how* of the high school of the future—its appropriate mechanisms, arrangements, operations—without first trying to understand the questions of *what* and *why* that are imposed upon us all, in school and out, in an age of cultural revolution. The discussion of the three issue areas that this paper attempts could provide at best only a limited, partial view of the major considerations that must enter into our thinking about the *what* and *why* of the high school of the future. We need much more development of these and other considerations if we are to understand with any adequacy what education must try to become and do.

THE NATURE OF POST-INDUSTRIAL SOCIETY

It has become virtually habitual to refer to the present as a time of trouble and crisis and to the society we live in as, in one way or another, sick. This hysterical or semi-hysterical cliché has become rather badly shopworn. In the long run, some artist may look back, as Dickens did on an earlier era of revolution, and say with balance, "They were the best of times; they were the worst of times." But as Lord Keynes remarked, "in the long run we are all dead." For us, day by day, the troubled present is all that we have, and we must be forgiven if we feel this trouble and fall into the analogy of sickness to describe it. But we ought to be aware of the danger that diagnoses may be wrong, and that it is certainly precarious to prescribe treatment for a disease without taking a hard look at its etiology. Often, we do not do the latter because it is hard work and almost always turns out to be full of complexity, loaded with troubling questions. Looking back for the causes of the disease seems academic and time-wasting when we are already preoccupied with the pangs of the affliction and want nothing more than for the doctor to give us a simple prescription which will make the whole thing go away.

As a society of pill-takers, we are conditioned, of course, to such an attitude. We put trust in our medicine men surely no less than allegedly primitive people have done, and we are reinforced in this by a long social history of experience with itinerant snake-oil salesmen, and a modern period in which television, our incessant teacher, persuades us that life has no headaches which some magic pill cannot quell in one magic moment.

We like our social remedies in simple packages. Sufficient unto the day is the headache thereof. It is enough to agree that the pain is there. The sensible course of action often seems to be to run, not walk, to the nearest medicine cabinet for the prompt relief our cultural dream has promised us.

Unhappily, social reality seldom turns out to be this simple. We can find quackery in the social medicine cabinet almost as easily as in the one at home. If we are lucky, the social medication we take may turn out to help. The act of taking it, or even the substance of the remedy, may provide us with a certain euphoria. On the other hand, there is a fair chance that, if the remedy is not a product of an understanding of the etiology of the condition for which it is intended, our social ills may in the long run be compounded by the medicine itself.

Slogans and short-term programs can make us feel warm inside and can reach and help a certain number of children and youth or people of other ages. Occasionally, a short-term program can be conceived with such perception of the need for fundamental change that it transcends the domain of gimmickry and is incorporated into our social system as a modification of long-lasting value. But the things that are wrong, or rather the things that need to be done in our society, run much deeper than slogans and short-range programs for the most part will reach. They require an amount of insight and adaptation which it would be innocent to suppose could be found at the end of any brief sawdust trail, no matter how enthusiastic the hallelujahs.

The central consideration essential to any useful understanding of what is going on in American life lies in the emergence of what Daniel Bell and others refer to as "the post-industrial society," characterized by a deep-set, tremendous, and continuing change in our economy and technology as its principal impulse, from which waves sweep out to alter all our lives and institutions. The second industrial revolution has overtaken us long before we have learned how to accommodate to the first. Technically speaking, the principal feature of the present revolution is the immense and accelerating growth of the technical-scientific nature of industry. The nature of production and distribution in our society is increasingly complex, increasingly rationalized, increasingly automated, increasingly impersonal, and increasingly capable of relentless output. In one way, as we will see, the post-industrial society is almost incredibly demanding of the manpower required to operate its economy and technology.

In another way, the post-industrial society, with its breakthrough into unlimited output and abundance, simultaneously presents us with enormous demands to be consumers dominated by a consumer mentality and operates to destroy the work ethic on which man's life was founded in all of the eons of scarcity prior to the present. A profound and terrible truth is contained in the remark Robert Hutchins once made, that the only *inherent* function of the technological revolution *is to make man superfluous, except as a consumer.* We possess, or are possessed by, the most brilliant technology in the world. Through it, even allowing for great inequities and for sectors of poverty, we are surrounded by affluence, abundance, and plenty beyond the dreams of men in ages past. Both the technology and its ceaseless material output are rapidly reshaping the conditions of our lives, and even more so, the lives of our children.

Thus far, most of the reshaping has been blind. Brilliant as it is, the technology is neutral, in the last analysis presenting in its performance only a mirror of what man himself is and wants. To the degree that man wants a full belly and material satiety, the technology gives these things to him with ease. To the degree that men want power—whether through abstract wealth or deadly weapons—the technology gives these easily and massively to the men who control it. Materially, whatever we want or are able to imagine wanting is to be gotten via this vast extension of man's capability to make and do, whether it be a hundred million private automobiles, sprawling and unplanned urbanism, men on the moon, nuclear power to destroy the earth, or what. The neutrality of technology, plus its fantastic growth and capability, plus man's nearly total lack of preparation for the revolutionary access to the unlimited scientific-technical power that he now finds on his hands, is a combination that has made this indeed what Michael Harrington called "the accidental century."

We have blundered into wars, radical social change, vastly altered individual lives, materialism, and a time in which the idea of work is very nearly obsolete, at least as a commanding imperative. We have gained great and good things, but we have gained many others that are dubious in quality, and we have clearly not begun to imagine what we can do with our technology that may really make it possible for man to become more fully human.

It is the essence of the post-industrial society that it gives us the chance, as Norbert Wiener said, to discover and enlarge the human uses of human beings, or to fail at this. More human or more inhuman, post-industrial society opens both doors for us. It is this, and the fact that man's state of wit and grace before these alternatives is so fragile, that helps define the responsibility that now falls upon all of education.

Drivenness: Sanity, Mobility, Opportunity

The post-industrial society has created, because of its need for a social order and economy geared to its performance and consumption demands, a vast, new, and predominant middle class. At the same time, the qualifications for participation in the technocratic order (as technicians, managers, etc.) and its abundance have been such as to lock out a significant sector of the population. Revolutionary changes in the conditions of economic production and consumption in American society during this century have created a huge, new, frenetic, and variously prosperous class, and at the same time have isolated a sector of the population whose members live in poverty because they are not equipped to cope with the conditions of production and, in the case of the Negro, for example, have been denied participation by prejudice and discrimination.

The new middle class of our time is new in its numbers, in the variety and significance of its occupations, and in being a direct outcome of large-scale economic activity. The growth of this new middle class has been phenomenal, and there are no indications that its central position in our social order is likely to decrease. The expansion of industry and technology is accelerating rather than slowing down in our society, and it continually increases the demand for technicians, managerial workers, professionals, sub-professionals, and clerical workers, except as automation operates to strike down categories of lower skill. This development is not simply a matter of numbers; it is a matter of the strategic importance that attaches to the new middle class in the society as a whole. Industry becomes more and more dependent on the possessors of technical knowledge and skills, both as producers and consumers, while the unskilled population languishes. The technicians are masters of the mysterious processes of a system of production which is infinitely more complex than production in the early stages of the first industrial revolution. And the strategic importance of the technologically based middle class grows socially as well as economically, as it becomes clear that the essential and predominant character of the civilization is technological in the modern sense.

Perhaps the most exciting and at the same time most troubling social feature of the modern economy and its technology has been its great impact on social mobility. A whole new dimension of "opportunity to rise in the world" has been opened up by the astonishing expansion of technical-managerial and professional employment and of great varieties of sub-technical and sub-professional occupations.

Millions of working-class parents struggled to make it possible for their children to take advantage of the opportunity to rise into the new, growing middle class and to share in its presumed benefits. Once in the new middle class, occupying the role of parents themselves in their turn, millions upon millions have fought to expand a foothold into a stepping stone, to reach up to the next rung of the golden ladder, and most of all to push their children ahead of them, not so much looking down to the abyss below as across to their neighbors and the neighbors' children, engaged with equal anxiety in the upward climb.

In all of this, the social order that we have created serves and reflects the performance and consumption demands of a modern, highly structured, technologically oriented economy. It is geared to exactness, uniform standards, time scheduling, high competence, and prodigious consumption. It is a materially productive, highly organized, machine-tooled society—whose prime ingredients for personal success include exact performance, precise time-sequencing, and unrelenting effort. The conditions of life in this kind of technological society are exquisitely calculated to produce tension and heighten anxiety. The pace is fast, and it is almost always someone else's pace or schedule. For the individual, there is constant competitive pressure, yet there is little chance to use one's best judgment in the fractionated processes of production and distribution. Proof of success or failure is not within the task usually, but rather in some superior's judgment, often far away, or from abstract, impersonal agencies of judgment. On the positive side, those who fit into the productive sector of the social order find access to abundance, the reward given them for conforming to the drive and performance-orientation that the system requires. They are the affluent consumers.

In terms of social mobility, opportunity, and access to material abundance, present circumstances and processes of the social order tend to deny movement, self-realization, and material fulfillment to those who live in poverty. But it would be empty and inaccurate to underestimate the individual and social damage done by our present mechanisms for motivation, selection, and advancement to *those who are not poor*. The performance-oriented social order of the technological society surely turns a harsh face toward the poor and their children. But besides being concerned about this fact, we must also be concerned about the psychic and moral consequences of the high-compression chamber within which children of relatively affluent families live today. Schools have made contributions of important, positive kinds to affluent and poor children alike. But we can ill-afford to ignore the fact that, in different ways, today's schools are failing *both* the affluent and the poor as institutions for coping in human terms with a revolutionary technological and economic order.

On the one hand, with the affluent, education in the schools is being heavily used to force middle-class children toward success within the terms of the technocratic system. In the middle class, we find it easy to be hysterical about achievement and competition. All children are judged to be underachievers until they can prove otherwise. The pressures on children to achieve, to do better and better, are universal, intense, unremitting. There is a desperate hurry to move children along, to find weaknesses and close gaps, to pressure them into conforming to ever-accelerating production deadlines. Donald McNassor has commented:

> . . . children are pretty sturdy people. What they cannot take without ill effect is the kind of unremitting pressure and competition that implies constant criticism and weakness. They cannot

remain physically and mentally healthy by going through school with the nagging feeling that, in some way, they are not the kind of persons that they are supposed to be; that no matter what they do, it is never enough. And they will not become truly imaginative, affectionate, and creative if they feel under pressure to be in a desperate hurry to compete for the best jobs, the top honors, the best grades, the good colleges, the better sections of classes at school, the classes most likely to yield high point averages. . . . A rich imagination and creative impulses are not produced in humans the way we create space vehicles and cars. Children need periods of incubation, a time to turn to an inner world of long thoughts, opportunities to become deeply involved in an idea or interest. They need to hear themselves sometimes, over the din of the noises in the competition market.[2]

For the middle-class child who "succeeds," life takes on some of the features it had for children who were workers in the mills and mines of a century ago. Even without conscious parental prodding, a reasonably able boy who is a junior in an eastern suburban high school today may well spend seventeen hours a day five days a week in school and in doing homework, with nearly as much time given to homework on the weekends. And ahead of him, after the SAT tests, the achievement tests, the college interviews, and all the rest, there is likely to be only more of the same. When he approaches college, it may seem to him as though he had been working as a slave in a galley-ship for twelve years of a long voyage, promised that at last he would land on a golden island called the "college of his choice." But when he lands on the island, he finds, alas, that it is not golden, and that it will take him four more years to cut his way through the jungle to the other side, where he will be expected to board another galley for another long voyage euphemistically called graduate school—duration unknown.

The fact is that the middle class, at all its levels, is constantly adapting to the rapidly evolving needs of a collective economic activity and changing technology. It has seized upon education, through patterned and formal institutions, as the principal vehicle for adapting itself and its young to these conditions. In the past ten years, college enrollments have risen from three million to seven million, and this is only one sign of the times. Social mobility should be natural to an open society, and education should be a natural and good vehicle for mobility and the release of individual talents. What is wrong within the middle class and the schools is a psychological surrender to the drivenness that is implicit in a society whose chief ends are material, and perforce ultimately both elusive and illusory. For the middle class and its children not to be ridden by this drivenness, and yet to maintain the best that the technological society produces, requires a reconsideration of both ends and means, both the meaning of being human and the meaning of education.

On the side of the poor, those who are excluded from the economic mainstream and caught in the sub-basement below those who enjoy the best jobs and the affluence of the technological society, there are two matters often overlooked. One is the need to see the problem of the poor as an integral part of our total social response to radical changes in technology and the economy, and the other is the need for measures not only to enlarge participation in the economic mainstream for the poor, but to transform the nature of that participation for all.

On the first matter, it is mistaken to think that only the poor are caught by what S. M. Miller has called the "credentials trap." Poor and affluent alike are affected by the pressure of the society for credentials amenable to the requirements of a technical social order—the poor because they do not have the credentials, the affluent because they identify the only desirable reality with the possession of them. In a technological world that demands qualifications, it is a terrible thing not to have them, or reasonable access to getting them. At the same time, it can be terrible in other ways to be caught up in the race for credentials. Of alcohol, the Japanese have an ancient proverb that after the third cup, the wine drinks the man. With grades and diplomas and credentials and climbing, it can be the same: these can become ends in themselves, consuming us. Yet qualifications, developed abilities, are essential—both for individuals to gain self-respecting entry into the mainstream of economic life, and for a productive system to be maintained. In our schools and colleges we need to ask ourselves how these gains can be made both for children of poverty and children of affluence without destroying more valuable human qualities in the process. Much more importantly, we need to ask ourselves how we can conduct education so that, without being prisoners of the requirements of a technological social order, youth can learn how to go on into adulthood able to use technology for increasingly human ends rather than being used by it.

We should, if we have imagination enough, be able to find alternative educational routes to qualification for full, vigorous membership in a social order which is both human and technological—routes to offset the rigid and elaborate credentialing system within which our schools and colleges are increasingly enmeshed. Also, we should have enough wit to be able to multiply the ways and times in which a person can acquire the "proper" credentials for various occupations during the course of his life. And we should be able to restructure jobs in the economy in order to enlarge opportunity, and reflect enlarged opportunity by our approach to boys and girls in school.

I am convinced it would be a wasteful mistake to conceive long-range solutions to the problem of opportunity and qualification development as lying largely outside the formal apparatus of education, either for the poor or the affluent. Our apparatus of education needs a great broadening and extension, and it is indeed useful to experiment outside of it. But what really is needed—and most feasible economically—is to use our schools and colleges for new and better purposes, transforming them to serve a new age, as they have been transformed from time to time in the past.

Much as I have applauded the spirit and intention of the so-called Poverty Programs, I cringe at their name. Our ultimate need is education for all our people that is diverse, flexible, and sane enough to meet all the needs of a diverse society—not one big system for the middle class and a number of disparate programs for the dispossessed. We have the capability of being the first truly educative society in history with a coherent educational effort that belongs at the center of all our lives, lasts for all our lives, and is not principally committed to what is, in effect, competitive manpower training. We need to undertake a great re-examination of what happens to exclude some and overdemand from others in school and society. Schools and colleges should indeed serve the manpower preparation needs of a society. And they should do this job well and fairly, with no potential ignored and no talent blighted.

But education must be far more than a manpower training ground if it is to mean anything worthy at all. Certainly, it cannot be justified simply as forced feeding for the sacrificial lambs of upward mobility. We owe our children more than jobs and a ride on the Big Escalator. And we can have more from education if we want it. This is what the most articulate and best of our young rebels are saying to us about their families, their schools, their colleges, and the general society.

Meaninglessness: Identity, Values, Anxiety

The freeing of children and youth from grinding labor, one of the first victories of industrial civilization, is a case example of the point that Robert Hutchins made about the only inherent function of the technological revolution. Today we have gone the whole distance and have freed most of our young from virtually all economic responsibilities except those of consumers. At present, we are far along in doing the same for our older citizens as well.

The extension of this process is in the offing for many of the rest of us. It is true, as mentioned in the preceding section, that automation will demand new levels of technically qualified manpower, and that production will continue to be an interesting venture—for those who actually participate. The fundamental course of things, however, makes really responsible involvement in production and service less and less necessary or possible for more and more of us. Technology may well lead us across a threshold to the truly human use of human beings. But there is the real possibility that technological advances will bring a civilization in which work is meaningful for relatively few, and non-work time (whether so-called "leisure" or "free" time, or whether disguised unemployment in the form of military service or compulsory school or college attendance) is abundant and meaningless for very many.

Meanwhile, the adolescent affords us a possible prototype of tomorrow's man. Here are—both in slums and suburbs—girls and boys whose new culture, born of a general if maldistributed affluence, indicates what tomorrow's culture may be like for the whole society. Here are meaningless free time, a consumer orientation, a standardization of taste and values by mass means, and a notable emptiness not wholly disguised by the "made work" of the school.

Many of us, like Rousseau, have romanticized children and youth, expecting from them a wisdom and discipline which we all too seldom exhibit ourselves as adults, and being surprised and dismayed when they instead behave with spoiled and ignorant arrogance. Avoiding both romanticism and rejection, we must try to understand that American youth today are exiled in certain damaging ways, and that a good many of them know it. In building the technological society, we have been remarkably successful in excluding youth from roles that are significant and necessary in their immediate context. In the nineteenth century and earlier, or even earlier in this century, this was not true for large numbers of young people who clearly were needed for work and family survival. Increasingly, as we have become a people of plenty, we have placed youth in a social vacuum with little to measure themselves against except standardized academic achievement scores, and peer standards that are evoked by advertising, consumer persuasion, and the disc jockey. Until the 1960's, the chief remaining roles for youth appeared to be those of passive students, consumers, dependents, and bored observers of the adult rat-race.

Identity is familiar as an essential quest of adolescence. But the quest for identity now is increasingly stalled for many adolescents, and carried over unfulfilled into adulthood. Great material abundance has been achieved through the great changes in the way we live and work. In the process, elements of crucial importance to self-definition and social definition have been seriously unsettled and diminished. Such elements as the family, the roles of father and mother, the community, religion, and the structure of general society are in flux under the shock of revolutionary technological change and a materialistically oriented economic culture. The questions of adolescence—"Who am I?" "Where am I going?" "What is the meaning of life?"—become harder and harder to answer in ways that are stable, satisfying, and socially constructive. In an economy of scarcity in earlier times, where constraints were painfully clear and the hard-work ethic prevailed, answers may have been fewer, but they were available and sanctioned by a tradition which made up in stability what it may have lacked in freedom. A sense of purpose, identity, and meaning was to be had in the imperatives of family organization, work, religion, and other institutions.

In contrast, individuals in the post-industrial society face the bigness and complexity of the present era with little armor except what they can contrive themselves. Family organization is less and less disciplined by the demands of economic scarcity and more and more disrupted by mobility and the seductions of consumer competition. Work, less commandingly necessary and often less available until one has gone through a long sequence of credentialing, and largely devoted to making the product-oriented machinery of society operate at accelerating speed, seems to many to be a poor source of self-definition. Even clergymen appear to find religion in deep trouble as a source of fundamental meaning, and relativism pervades most other traditional sources of value. The Western world in general, and America in particular, finds itself in a value crisis that reaches deep into individual lives and is the price for being first in the technological revolution that is sweeping the world.

Viewed in the broad scene, in the reflection of ourselves that we see in high culture and now in pop culture, the spectre of meaninglessness looms above all of us—not simply above the young. It is only that in the young and their anguish we see the spectre of meaninglessness most vividly.

The trouble is that the conquests made by our technology have finally brought us to a place where we are forced to ask, "What are human beings for?" and to have to find the answers ourselves. Always before, when men were less free from the constraints laid upon them by scarcity and by the institutions that operated to insure man's survival in spite of scarcity, the answer to that question was given to children and men and women by the circumstances of their lives. Now we are faced with the privilege and awesome responsibility of trying to cope with that question with intelligence and wisdom under conditions of nearly complete freedom from stable institutional constraints.

In terms of the school and college, this question becomes the *sine qua non* of education itself. Unless the education of adolescents and young adults in high schools and colleges of the future deals with this question as a concern of the highest priority, nothing else that education does will be fully or adequately relevant to human needs.

Disaffection: Hostility, Anger, Violence

It should not surprise us that the factors of drivenness and meaninglessness that make up part of the cultural context in which our schools and colleges share are accompanied by substantial disaffection in various forms. These factors certainly are not unrelated to each other, nor are they unrelated to the demands and character of an advanced technological society that still has not learned how to make the technological-product economy more than an end in itself. It is just beginning to dawn on us that in deep ways the present system distorts certain kinds of human behavior and seriously frustrates the fulfillment of some important human needs.

A technological society, which displays its material largess to the children of poverty via the vivid mass medium of television and simultaneously denies them access to education and careers which would make that largess available to them, should expect to elicit frustration and rage from the dispossessed. Almost at the same time that James Conant was calling attention to the fact that we were accumulating social dynamite in the slums of our cities, S. I. Hayakawa was pointing out the serious impact of television on Negro youth. Hayakawa's point was a simple one: that modern telecommunications and unremitting advertising put before every child of poverty a seductive vision of the riches that our society not only provides but demands that we consume, and that such children cannot avoid comparing this vision with the lack of riches and opportunity around them. Resentment, anger, protests, and violence are understandable outcomes of frustration bred by this comparison.

This is not to say that disaffection and activism can be explained or understood solely in terms of the impact of television and advertising on those who are denied full access to the affluence of our society. But Hayakawa's insight is valuable in helping us understand how these phenomena are closely related to the present nature of our product-oriented, technological society. Black disaffection in our time and in the probable future has innumerable roots and forms. It is essential in considering the future of schools and colleges, to try to understand this disaffection, to diagnose ways in which education and other agencies of the culture have helped generate such disaffection, and attempt to use education effectively in a more general effort to overcome its causes. It is easy to state this challenge, but it is extraordinarily difficult to respond to it with adequacy. Certainly, the schools cannot do the job alone. Hayakawa's point emphasizes how vastly powerful in their social consequences certain outside forces, such as commercial television, actually are.

In colleges these days, and increasingly in the schools, we are aware of the disaffection of many of our other youth, most of whom come from what could be regarded as well-advantaged backgrounds. Space here does not permit an adequate exploration of the nature, causes, and possible future meaning of the disaffection of affluent youth. Explanations and analyses abound, as we all know.

Kenneth Keniston of Yale has done more than anyone I know to provide us with intelligent, sympathetic insights into the ways in which many of our middle-class youth are responding to the technological society in which they find themselves. In his book, *The Uncommitted,* Keniston describes young men and women who, while conforming competently to the training and performance demands of our society, do so only superficially and not with genuine commitment of self. "The uncommitted" do nearly everything the system asks of them and do it well, but Keniston argues that their alienation and disaffection are shown in the fact that they turn to privatism for what they regard as real living. In a more recent book, *The Young Radicals,* Keniston tells us perceptively about other young people who are indeed *committed,* but not to the technological society I have been describing in this paper. Instead, their commitment lies in the direction of radical reform —or destruction and reconstruction—of our technological society as they perceive it. Disaffection is openly and actively expressed in their style of life, in their politics, and in nearly every way.

In a discussion of "Youth, Change and Violence,"[3] Keniston emphasizes our need to understand what he calls "the style of post-modern youth." Among these features of style are:

a. *Fluidity, Flux, Movement.* Keniston comments that post-modern youth display a special personal and psychological openness, a flexibility and unfinishedness. He suggests that our earlier fear of the ominous psychiatric implications of prolonged adolescence must now be qualified by an understanding that many adolescent concerns and qualities persist long past the time when (in earlier eras) they should have ended. "The vision of the personal and collective future is blurred and vague: later adulthood is left deliberately open."[4]

b. *Generational Identification.* Keniston comments that today's youth view themselves primarily as part of a generation rather than an organization, that "generational" distinctions are coming to involve five years and less, and that generational consciousness entails a feeling of psychological disconnection from everything about prior generations.

c. *Personalism.* Keniston finds youth, whether hippie or radical, rejecting what they regard as the depersonalization of the modern world and seeking their rewards in intimate, loving, open, and trusting relationships between individuals or among small groups of people. He finds personalism exemplified as well in the ardent desire of radical youth for personal confrontation with their opponents.

d. *Nonasceticism.* Keniston describes the style of post-modern youth as nonascetic, expressive, and sexually free. "It is of continuing importance to these young men and women to overcome and move beyond inhibition and puritanism to a greater physical expressiveness, sexual freedom, capacity for intimacy, and ability to enjoy life."[5]

e. *Inclusiveness.* Keniston underlies post-modern youth's search for personal and organizational inclusiveness as another basic element of style. Personally, nothing is to be considered alien; interpersonally, no other person of whatever race, nationality, or place is to be considered alien. "In post-modern youth, then, identity and ideology are no longer parochial or national; increasingly, the reference group is the world, and the artificial subspeciation of the human species is broken down."[6]

f. *Anti-technologism.* Keniston sees in contemporary youth a style which has grave reservations about many of the technological aspects in the contemporary world. His views on this aspect of style relate closely to the general position I have outlined in this paper:

> The depersonalization of life, commercialism, careerism and familism, the bureaucratization and complex organization of advanced nations—all seem intolerable to these young men and women, who seek to create new forms of association and action to oppose the technologism of our day. Bigness, impersonality, stratification and hierarchy are rejected, as is any involvement with the furtherance of technological values. In reaction to these values, post-modern youth seeks simplicity, naturalness, person-hood, and even voluntary poverty.

But a revolt against technologism is only possible, of course, in a technological society; and to be effective, it must inevitably exploit technology to overcome technologism. Thus in post-modern youth, the fruits of technology—synthetic hallucinogens in the hippie subculture, modern technology of communication among young radicals—and the affluence made possible by technological society are a precondition for a post-modern style. The demonstrative poverty of the hippie would be meaningless in a society where poverty is routine; for the radical to work for subsistence wages as a matter of choice is to *have* a choice not available in most parts of the world. Furthermore, to "organize" against the pernicious aspects of the technological era requires high skill in the use of modern technologies of organization: the long distance telephone, the use of the mass media, high-speed travel, a mimeograph machine, and so on. In the end, then, it is not the material but the spiritual consequences of technology that post-modern youth opposes. . . . What is adamantly rejected is the contamination of life with the values of technological organization and production. It seems probable that a comparable rejection of the psychological consequences of current technology, coupled with the simultaneous ability to exploit that technology, characterizes all dissenting groups and all epochs.[7]

g. *Participation.* The post-modern youth that Keniston talks about are committed to searching for new forms of groups, of organizations, and of action where decision making is collective, where arguments are resolved by "talking them out," where self-examination, interpersonal criticism, and group decision making are fused. The search emphasizes disaffection with present styles of life and present forms of organization and present forms of decision making—at least as these are perceived by the young.

h. *Anti-academicism.* Keniston comments that among post-modern youth, one finds a virtually unanimous rejection of the "merely academic." Keniston feels it would be wrong to label this trend "anti-intellectual," because many of the young are highly intellectual themselves and appear to him to be demanding that intelligence be engaged with the world, that action should be informed by knowledge.

To post-modern youth, then, most of what is taught in schools, colleges, and universities is largely irrelevant to living life in the last third of the twentieth century. Many academics are seen as direct or accidental apologists for the

Organized System in the United States. Much of what they teach is considered simply unconnected to the experience of post-modern youth. New ways of learning are sought: ways that combine action with reflection upon action, ways that fuse engagements in the world with understanding of it.[8]

i. *Nonviolence.* A final element of the style, as Keniston sees it, involves nonviolence:

> The basic style of both radicals and hippies is profoundly opposed to warfare, destruction, and exploitation of man by man, and violence whether on an interpersonal or international scale.

It is clear that Keniston's view of the style of youth is as sympathetic as it is perceptive, and that it relates principally to the affluent young. It is less clear to me that his description is adequately helpful to us in understanding the full realities and possible consequences of the disaffection shown by the youth he describes. On the other hand, he closes this discussion with some very sobering comments about problems that may be ahead:

> . . . the position of psychologically non-violent youth in a violent world is difficult and paradoxical. On the one hand, he seeks to minimize violence, but on the other, his efforts often elicit violence from others. At the same time that he attempts to work to actualize his vision of a peaceful world, he must confront more directly and continually than do his peers the fact that the world is neither peaceful nor just. The frustration and discouragement of his work repetitively awaken his anger, which must forever be rechanneled into peaceful paths . . . what they continue to find difficult to live with, what they still repress, avoid, and counteract is their own potential for violence. It remains to be seen whether, in the movement toward "resistance" and disruption of today's young radicals, their psychological non-violence will continue to be reflected in their actions. . . . Witnessing the acting out of violence on a scale more gigantic than ever before, or imaginatively participating in the possibility of world-wide holocaust activates the fear of one's own violence; heightened awareness of one's inner potential for rage, anger, or destructiveness increases sensitivity to the possibility of violence in the world.
>
> This same process of historical potentiation of inner violence has occurred, I believe, throughout the modern world, and brings with it not only the intensified efforts to curb violence we see in this small segment of post-modern youth, but other more frightening possibilities. Post-modern youth, to an unusual degree, remain open

to and aware of their own angers and aggressions, and this awareness creates in them a sufficient understanding of inner violence to enable them to control it in themselves and oppose it in others. Most men and women, young or old, possess less insight: their inner sadism is projected on to others whom they thereafter loath or abjectly serve; or, more disastrously, historically heightened inner violence is translated into outer aggression and murderousness, sanctioned by self-righteousness.[9]

I will return in a moment to the point touched upon by Keniston at the end of the statement above. But first I feel obliged by what looks to me to be historical reality to add a dimension which Keniston scarcely touches upon, and which seriously complicates the relationship between the articulate, activist youth he is describing and the rest of our society. This dimension does not apply to those youth who have taken the hippie route, but it certainly does apply to those who view themselves as activists or radicals—who are not only disaffected in terms of what they call "The Establishment," but publicly proclaim their intention to destroy it. This is the dimension of *power,* and its emergence as a factor has accelerated in the most recent past. Clark Kerr, in a conference in Puerto Rico in March, 1967, presented an analysis of the shift of modesetting students from apathy to confrontation that is somewhat different from Kenneth Keniston's analysis, although no less sympathetic. The difference is that Kerr singles out the dimension of power as one of the principal elements of confrontation politics as practiced within the radical activist style described by Keniston. Mr. Kerr comments:

There is an obsession with power. The refrain again and again is the acquisition of power. It seems to be assumed that, with power, evil can be eradicated; that, without it, nothing can be done. Participants want power versus the faculty, the college administration, industry, the unions, and government. There is a determination to combine the new morality of the students with the old power now held by other people.

The role of persuasion in getting results from those who have power is considered quite small. There is little realization of the extent to which power is actually fractionalized, subject to checks and balances, and often held in gentle hands.

The recurrent theme is how students, who really have no formal power, can obtain and exercise power. "Student power" can bring pressure on a university certainly, on a society possibly. It requires no reliance on a reluctant faculty, a quiescent labor movement, a non-existent peasant class. It also requires no fixed ideology. Ideologies divide as well as unite. They divided students

in the 1930's. But, after (Joseph) McCarthy in the United States
and polycentricism in the communist world, the line between the
moderates and the liberals versus the radicals is no longer so
sharply drawn or drawn at all. "Student power" allows a united
front. The old ideological barriers are largely gone.[10]

What Kerr refers to as an obsession with power, and the increasing
tendency of the radical activist fringe of youth to verge into the use of
force in its pursuit—or of provocation designed to precipitate a violent
repressive response that will "lay bare the true nature of the police-state
in which we live"—are facts that for me raise serious questions about
Keniston's analysis and the future course of events. Keniston's closing
statement seems to me dangerously romantic in its assumption that the
post-modern youth he describes have somehow arrived at a state of
grace not achieved by any prior generation: ". . . this awareness [of
their own angers and aggressions] creates in them *a sufficient understanding of inner violence to enable them to control it in themselves and
oppose it in others*" (italics added). Good as youth are, very few of
them can be the saints that such an assertion suggests. And there is considerable evidence, unhappily, that the youth Keniston describes can,
like other mortals, become swept up in their own expression of inner
anger through aggressive and sometimes violent behavior.

There is also considerable evidence that the disaffection, power-
orientation, rhetoric, and revolutionary activism of youth who take
Fanon and Guevara as their models is beginning to trigger the frightening kind of response Keniston touches on in his final sentence. This
response is capable of becoming a mass movement because it could give
millions of the relatively inarticulate a self-righteous way of release
from accumulated anxiety and anger.

If disaffection on the part of the black population and on the part of
affluent youth in schools and colleges were the whole story, the agenda
now before the society would be complicated enough. What is not yet
adequately realized is that there are great reservoirs of latent disaffection, hostility, anger, and violence in the rest of our society. These other
reservoirs, in their way, are fed by the factors of drivenness and meaninglessness and other features of the technological order and its
inequities fully as much as is disaffection among blacks and educationally advantaged youth. That they have not yet become as visible or
vocal should not lead us into a misapprehension that they do not exist.

The disaffection that I refer to here is, by comparison, diffuse, un-
focused, and widespread among the great sectors of our population that
are white, less-educated, and lower-income, whether in the working

class or the lower middle class. It is a disaffection encouraged into inchoate existence by the pressures of inflation, of a sense of being expected to buy too much with too little, of having to moonlight to stay afloat in the society, of having had to struggle hard to move out of scarcity into some share of affluence, of anxiety about preserving such gains of status and material well-being as have been gotten, and of finding a world that more and more seems confusing and uncertain.

Now a supremely dangerous focus for the disaffection of such people is beginning to emerge. This focus lies in the parallel phenomena of black activism and student activism. It is hard, if not impossible, for many in the white working class and the lower middle class to understand why it should be considered just for American Negroes now to lay claim to material benefits and opportunities which they regard themselves as having had to struggle hard for and win on their own initiative. It is equally hard for this large proportion of our people to understand the dress, the behavior, the language, and the political demands of student activists who come from affluent backgrounds, who seem arrogantly to reject both the standards of the general society and the opportunity for education.

The bewilderment, resentment, and antagonism that disaffection among black militants and some white students is evoking in this large middle group of our population should be of serious concern to anyone who has studied mass political and social movements in this century.

Symptoms of this reaction were to be found in the national election campaign of 1968. These symptoms go far beyond and cannot be explained solely by racial prejudice. They are evidenced in all parts of the country—north, east, south, and west. They reflect many anxieties and frustrations. It is urgent to understand that some millions of Americans, already pressed and disquieted by inherent change in the society, are reacting negatively with increasing articulateness to what appear to them to be dangerous attempts to alter, or even destroy, the social fabric within which they find and prize a certain stability. This developing reaction has begun to find the two elements that are essential for the mobilization of diffuse political discontent into political action: highly visible scapegoats, and highly effective political leaders. It is also important to understand that, in addition, a further essential ingredient of mass political action to serve the needs of this kind of disaffection is becoming available: money. The success of George Wallace of Alabama in securing enough funds to conduct an active national campaign in 1968 is a vivid case in point.[11]

What present symptoms reveal is a potentiality of the usually submerged two-thirds of the American body politic to become mobilized and active in sponsoring political and social repression. What is not understood by enough of us is the possibility that the dimensions of this repression could be, if sanity altogether fails us, as grand in scale as anything we have witnessed in European totalitarianism in this century. Many of us who are comfortable in our lives are also comfortable in a naïve faith that "it can't happen here." We are abstractly aware that genocide and totalitarian regimes have occurred in other presumably civilized nations in our time, and it is part of our provincialism to suppose that such potentialities could not exist within ourselves or our own nation. Some black militants appear aware of these potentialities much more clearly than the rest of us; it is testimony of their own desperate disaffection that they are willing to fight their battle even in the face of such absolute risks. Student radicals, on the other hand, including those who talk in the most extreme terms of a necessary total destruction of American society, appear profoundly naïve on this score, either wholly ignoring or underestimating the gigantic potential for violent repression that exists in the society, or conceiving it as something their tactics will suffice either to neutralize or transform.

Schools and colleges have three possible alternatives in the future vis-à-vis the forces of disaffection that I have touched upon here. One of these is to muddle along in a fantasy of business-as-usual. This, it seems to me, is clearly a dangerous alternative for central institutions of the society charged with the responsibility of attempting to link the past, present, and emerging future. A second alternative for schools and colleges, also easy to fall into or to be manipulated into, is to become politicized by one or the other of the sectors of disaffection, becoming captured by it and committed to its ends. I feel strongly that this would be a disastrous alternative for schools and colleges to take. It would mean the end of the educational institution as a source of mediation, freedom, and stability in a society that badly needs all three and has all too few such resources outside of education. It would mean the commitment of educational institutions in various ways to political conflict and possible civil war.

The third alternative, by far more difficult to take, is also the only intelligent one, as I see it. This is for the high school and college of the future to commit themselves to the fullest possible understanding of what is right and wrong about post-industrial civilization, to the fullest possible understanding of the potentials and limitations of formal education in helping individuals realize themselves, and to the fullest possible understanding of how education may be reconstructed in ways that will contribute to a sane human society. It is only from the foundation of such a commitment that any very useful discourse about the high school of the future can proceed. We cannot afford to reject this alternative on the grounds that it is impossible for us to handle. To do that would be to default without honor before the real challenge of the work we have accepted as ours.

BECOMING HUMAN

I have suggested three aspects of post-industrial society by which all of us are in one way or another affected, and with which schools and colleges need to be creatively concerned if they are to make intelligent commitment of human energy and resources in the future. The factors of drivenness, meaninglessness, and disaffection provide a somber backdrop against which to build education for tomorrow. There are other far happier factors in the modern human situation, and these of course should be recognized, honored, and worked with. But all will come to nought, or to far less than we need, if we do not try to cope with these less happy factors.

In thinking about educational requirements for the future we will be trapped if we think of people as things, as though our task were simply to continue to serve the manpower needs of the technological social order. We will be trapped, also, if we see our task solely as that of filling more and more people with more and more knowledge.

It seems clear to me that we must conceive the nature of our task in education at a far higher level than this. Certainly, education needs to make its contribution to the development of better technical, scientific, and informational training for our whole population than we have ever before thought about. But our view of the task of the high school and college for the future needs to be qualitatively different from this limited conception.

Our problems are always really in the *present*. The future is always being born in every passing moment, and its question, as Kathleen Nott has said, is "How can men become human?"[12]

There are certain imperative educational needs of the present which are encompassed by this question, and which should inform our best estimates about tomorrow. These needs relate directly to the three factors that I have discussed here and to other aspects of life. There is not space to spell out these needs in detail, but a brief mention of them may indicate the direction in which I think we must move. The following list is in the form of propositions and questions, which rightly suggests that I do not know how the needs can be met. I only know that we must try to meet them.

- *First proposition:* The concepts people hold about themselves are powerful directives of their behavior. *Question:* How can education help concepts of self be such that individual life and the life of society will be healthy and free? How can it do so when vast centrifical forces in the society have eroded the effectiveness of older institutions, when the most impressive characteristic of general social reality is its kaleidoscopic quality?[13]

- *Second proposition:* Social groups have a significant relation to individual human behavior. How can education help individuals gain a realization of themselves through the whole range of group relationships in which they are—or will become—involved? Especially, how can schools find ways to cross over the compartmentalization of urban life, the gulf between the inner city and the suburb, the black-white relationship, the generational gap?

- *Third proposition:* Since much of what one "sees" in anything is the stereotype to memory of an earlier perception, one's reactions to situations are often preconditioned and unrealistic. *Question:* How can we encourage the continual re-education of perception so that human behavior will be more effective in terms of a swiftly changing environmental reality?

- *Fourth proposition:* Human communication is constantly subject to distortion. We are most apt to note and recall messages we already know, or those which harmonize with our beliefs, or those which meet our needs. *Question:* How can education help individuals and groups learn to communicate with a minimum of damaging distortion?

- *Fifth proposition:* Effective problem solving in our changing environment is one of the most crucial types of human behavior and requires us to conceive problem solving as a flexible process for working out solutions to problems for which no man has a ready answer. *Question:* How can a flexible approach to problem solving be built by education for people of all backgrounds?

- *Sixth proposition:* Human behavior is goal-oriented, and men in defining and striving for their goals choose among alternative modes of thought or behavior. *Question:* How can education help people to make these choices not as sheep or as children, but as men and women?

These shorthand propositions and questions deserve consideration and discussion as we think about the high school of the future and about the college. They are put too briefly here, but I trust that they suggest my concern that we must identify as educational needs those things which have to do with the areas in which our feeling, thinking, and action must rapidly change in order for us to close the gap between our capabilities and our environment. The real needs are in the areas of developing a sense of meaningfulness in the midst of change, of overcoming a sense of powerlessness, of developing taste and the uses of leisure in a civilized form, of achieving identity, of facing as adequately as ever we can the question, What are human beings for?

References

1. Kimball Wiles and Franklin Patterson, *The High School We Need: A Report from the ASCD Commission on the Education of Adolescents:* (Washington, D.C.: Association for Supervision and Curriculum Development, National Education Association, 1959).
2. Donald McNassor, "This Frantic Pace in Education," *Journal of Secondary Education* (March, 1967), p. 100.
3. Kenneth Keniston, "Youth, Change and Violence," *The American Scholar* (Spring, 1968), pp. 227-245.
4. *Ibid.*, p. 229.
5. *Ibid.*, p. 231.
6. *Ibid.*, p. 233.
7. *Ibid.*, pp. 233, 234.
8. *Ibid.*, p. 236.
9. *Ibid.*, pp. 244-245.
10. Clark Kerr, "From Apathy to Confrontation." Mimeographed talk given to a conference on "Students and Politics," San Juan, Puerto Rico, March 27, 1967, pp. 16-17.
11. See Tom Wicker, "Wallace Appealing to the Frustrated," © September 19, 1968 by The New York Times Company. Reprinted with permission.

The fact is that George Wallace has a remarkable hold on a sizeable—and apparently—increasing number of American voters because, more than any other candidate in the race, he touches them where they hurt, he speaks in the words they long to voice, and he promises them the release their tensions demand.

If there were not deep and divisive racial problems in America, the candidacy of even so gripping a southern demagogue as George Wallace would be unlikely to get off the ground outside the old Confederacy; but it oversimplifies Wallace's apparent gains elsewhere to suggest that racism is the sole cause.

This, after all, is a frustrating, exasperating, nervewracking time. It is an era of scientific and technological change so sweeping as actually to alter the means by which man perceives and learns, and so profound as to call into genuine question many of the moral and ethical values which have been, if not unchallenged, long dominant.

In such a time, it well may be that Wallace is the only candidate who is relevant, however dangerously, to real American life—to the fear and irritation and bewilderment and the increasing hatred that an unsettled time and an unfamiliar world and a terrifying pace inevitably have produced.

12. Kathleen Nott, "Future-Mindedness," *Commentary* (July, 1963), p. 52.
13. Several of these items are drawn from my earlier article, "How Can Men Become Human?" in *Teachers College Record*, Vol. 67 (1966), 250-259.

chapter 7

Theodore Rice
and
Chandos Rice

The School of the Future—
A Commentary

Although the bases of decisions are not always recognized, individual and group decisions are affected by social goals; the world situation; the condition of the nation; the community setting, the needs, concerns and wishes of youth; and the vision of teachers, administrators, and laymen. From the consideration, formal and informal of these factors, there emerges an image of what the school could be. (From Wiles, *The Changing Curriculum of the American High School*, p. 22.)

In the light of our experiences as curriculum-workers, we are particularly interested in the vision Kimball Wiles had of "The High School of the Future." Not only in his chapter of that title in *The Changing Curriculum of the American High School*, but also in his work as chairman of the ASCD Commission on the Education of Adolescents, and in his work on the pamphlet, *The Junior High School We Need*, Dr. Wiles constantly pushed his thinking and ours into the consequences of the changes taking place in schools. Our concerns are certainly as broad as those of his chapter. However, in this commentary, we address ourselves chiefly to the issue of youth identification in society and to the related role of the adult, especially the educational specialist, in helping youth determine (some might even say "salvage") societal values and manifestations which may be useful in building the future.

SOCIAL FORCES AND THE INDIVIDUAL

Before the recent period of psycho-cognitive excellence in curriculum emphasis, we went through quite a period of examining on the one hand the impact of social forces, and on the other, the need for positing the school program on the needs of youth. The ASCD yearbook, *Social Forces Affecting Curriculum,* was among the foremost curriculum material delineating the impact of society on youth and education. Dr. Wiles reflected this concern. He vividly depicted the conflict between the selected values and concepts "to be taught" and the inescapable fact that youth will select for themselves what they learn. It is this conflict between the old and the new, the tradition of the established society and the emerging values and patterns of the new, that creates a vital need to find a way of uniting the needs of society with the drives and concerns of youth. This must be accomplished in such a way that change serves to strengthen the social fabric as well as to design it.

Events since Wiles' accumulation of data for his chapter and his writing of it point up not only the imperative urgency, but also the immediacy of recognition and utilization of social forces in shaping the school of the future. In the present climate, we are brought squarely into confrontation with the responsibility of educational leadership for selecting those values, undertaking those courses of action which may be most helpful in shaping the world as a desirable place in which to live, and for involving youth themselves in the task.

There are many beliefs in our society which are highly valued at the verbal level, but which are denied in practice because of conflicting ideas as to their application. It is difficult to explain to youth, who frequently see things, fortunately, in sharper contrast than those of us who are older, that we can hold this set of values without taking obvious steps toward their implementation. We find ourselves in accord with the protestations of youth that our society says one thing, but does another. As we examine the current climate of student unrest and the movement toward "student power," we find a realistic approach toward lessening this gap between ideals and performance. To illustrate, let us highlight some of the conflicts:

- How can we profess that education is the most important single factor in the successful operation of our democratic form of government and yet consistently refuse to revise the financial support of schools in order to utilize modern technology and know-how? Schools continue to operate on an economy of scarcity in the midst of a world of affluence.

- How can we reconcile our criticism of modern youth as unwilling to assume responsibility with our own refusal, written into law, to allow them to take any significant social or economic responsibility until they reach the age of sixteen or older?

- How can we reconcile our belief in law and order with our refusal to enact adequate laws for gun registration?

- How can a nation which boasts leadership in scientific knowledge and understanding explain its high infant mortality? the incidence of disease due to air pollution? the water pollution which is bringing creeping death to the Everglades and the Great Lakes?

- How can a country which has, from the days of its very birth, given allegiance to the ideal of equal educational and economic opportunity have permitted the development of the present slum ghettos and pockets of rural poverty?

- How can a country founded on belief in rights of man have allowed the development of the problems described in the Kerner report?

- The inability of our own country to keep out of military engagements matches that same problem in other parts of the world, yet we have not been able to develop a national or international policy which eliminates this futile and archaic method of facing disputes at the national level.

With a technological world which presents young people with choices beyond the comprehension of people scarcely twenty years older, youth are demanding a share in the decisions of policy that bear on the choices they must make. John F. Kennedy's famous sentence, "Ask not what your country can do for you; ask what you can do for your country," has had a response from youth as has no other statement in our time. The school of the future which we envision would meet the needs of the individual within, not apart from, his social setting. It would answer the challenge of youth with a confrontation, side by side with our young people, on such issues as those above—issues which may be a part of our "world becoming." Such a confrontation may help us as educators bring our technical and professional skills into use in a contemporary setting. The school of the future can hardly be a clear pool beside a rushing, muddy stream. The role of the adult as educator is to be involved *with* young people, ahead of them if possible, in seeing to it that obfuscating social forces are brought into the open and that a charter of basic social expectations is foundational in the school, whatever its shape may be.

THE ADOLESCENT AND HIS FUTURE

Still another problem of the adolescent is to understand the world in which he lives. He sees all about him new ideas, new symbols, new ways of living, new values. All of these raise questions about things that he has come to believe as a result of his participation within his own family. . . . How can he find the purpose by which to direct his own life? (*The Changing Curriculum*, p. 55.)

Our concern with the social setting should not be considered as a denial of the importance of meeting the needs of the individual. With the increasing population and its inevitable extension of group controls and narrower societal options, it is increasingly difficult for the adolescent to gain any sense of his own identity, his own range of choices, his own sense of direction and purpose. Traffic laws, collective provision of social goods through taxation, the increasingly specialized definition of vocational channels by both industry and labor, the casual contact with many people that tends to replace intimate contact with a few—all these and many other forces threaten the sense of control of his own destiny which is essential for every individual. The school of the future which we envision will so organize the learning environment that the student will have contacts in small groups where he can gain confidence in himself and in his peer relationships, and close contact with teachers who know him well and encourage him to explore the validity of his ideas and to plan and evaluate his own progress toward the goals which he deems suitable for him.

With the impact of national legislation on education, such as the Elementary-Secondary Education Act, we have undoubtedly made tangible progress and, certainly, widely publicized and overt headway in the manipulation of curriculum materials, resources, and content. We have made some strides toward revision of schedules and toward individualization of instruction. This thrust has been coupled with an increasing awareness that a person sitting in a carrel with programmed material around him is still a person with aspirations, fears, pressures, doubts. So the concept of positing the school of the future on the needs of youth is certainly confirmed in its soundness.

Kim Wiles has consistently supported this position and has been among the more cautious in swinging to a purely cognitive premise. He has, in his writing, placed strong emphasis on the environment for learning and without exception has emphasized the emotional environment as that of highest priority.

The school of the future can scarcely be based on normative surveys of youth or on adult presumptions as to their needs. Whatever the future may be, there is serious doubt that we can back into it from our past experience. Even assuming that for high school youth, the "future is now," adults are wise who are aware of the real or imagined generation gap. Although the personal needs of youth may still deal with finding a personal philosophy, getting along with peers, attaining status, getting along with members of the opposite sex, getting along with adults and finding a place as adults, the contemporary definition of each of these concerns has changed significantly in the last five years, and is still in a state of flux. If the avant garde may be interpreted as an overt expression of the needs and concerns of youth, then it is doubtful whether even "success" in the traditional definition of our culture is as high on the list of priorities for youth as it was at the time Wiles wrote. Is a young person in a contemporary setting striving for success? Or is he seeking, rather, an opportunity to be a significant person—whether that significance lies in 'an effective student demonstration, in outstanding leadership within the establishment, or in some form of esoteric withdrawal? If, indeed, the current development of "student power" movements means a search for significance, then the school of the future must take this paramount need of the individual into consideration.

To be sure, a great number of young people in high schools and colleges continue to try to make the grade which the operation of the present schools demands. And to be sure, that young person would be exceptional who didn't want to share in and exult with his peers over success in sports or other rivalry. But the fact remains that young people are demanding, in Earl Kelley's language, that education become "Education for What Is Real." The signals of success are not adequately phased to youth's needs. Although young people may still conform, they are reaching for confrontation in action toward the solution of social problems. For how can a person become responsible without responsibility. How can a person know that he is a worthwhile individual without an opportunity to participate in action which is worthwhile? How can anyone face reality on a purely vicarious plane?

THE ROLE OF THE SCHOOL

Society and the high school find themselves confronted by the following questions:

1. How to provide a role in which youth feel needed in an affluent society.

2. How to develop a sense of security without conformity.

· · · · · · · · · · · · · · · · · ·

5. How to help children and youth live with conflicts in values and distance between present and ideal status without becoming cynical, cool, and uncommitted. (*The Changing Curriculum*, p. 63.)

In the light of what we have said concerning the relationship of the individual to the society of which he is a part, what would we see as criteria to serve as guides for the school of the future in this area? We would heartily concur with Wiles' picture of the school for the decade of 1970–1980 as a place where there will be a strong emphasis on basic values and rich opportunity for students to consider alternatives, probe into variations, and attain the degree of commitment to implementation of those values which each of them can honestly achieve. We would see this consideration of personal and democratic values as calling for information about the immediate community and the school, the policies of each, and the issues which are inherent. The same would be true on a local and international level.

Active Involvement of the Learner in All of His Communities

In addition to the pattern of information and discussion which Wiles stresses in his vision of the school of the future, we would place a strong emphasis on the importance of actual involvement and participation of students in all of the communities of which they are a part. It is our point of view that values are directly related to the experiences of the individual, and that the development of commitment to the implementation of the democratic idea will develop effectively only as the student is on a par with others in the development of policies and their implementation and evaluation. We cannot assume that a student who has only "talked about" government, social conditions, or jobs can have developed a commitment to values basic to decisions in those areas. As we work with this generation of students, we find them protesting the fact that all they have a chance to do is to talk, talk, talk about problems. They want to "do something." Our vision of the school of the future would give them this opportunity.

Involvement in the International Scene

At any point in time, when there is armed conflict in which their own country is engaged, youth are keenly aware of international involvement. The schools of the present, however, have not been successful in getting the same degree of awareness and concern in times of peace. Students, generally, feel remote from the wide range of international involvement which makes the world increasingly interdependent. In our vision of the school of the future, youth would have direct contact with youth of other countries, through an extension of current exchange programs, through such organizations as the Peace Corps, and through use of modern technology, such as the communication satellites. It is reasonable to envision direct conversations from groups of American students with groups of students in other countries in a discussion of international problems and issues as an integral part of the school program.

Focus on the Present and the Future

In periods of change as rapid as those which we are now experiencing and which will probably characterize the foreseeable future, reality for youth is in the present and the future. They are more concerned with change than with preservation of the status quo. The curriculum of the school, as we see it, would be concerned with the present and with projection of probabilities for the future, and would use the cultural heritage of the past primarily to explore the causes of present practice or of present problems. Familiarity with the past and its traditions would be in relation to concerns and problems which are current and for the purpose of providing a general background. Understanding of other countries would be developed in this same way, rather than through detailed emphasis on chronological events.

Aesthetic and Expressional Valuing and Production

We would add a much greater emphasis to the arts than Wiles has given. In our school of the future, training in the arts would become part of the general education program for all, rather than specialization for the talented only. With the development of a shorter work day, a shorter work week, a shorter work year, there is a shift in values which at present is barely discernible, but which we believe is significant for future education. This is a shift from the work ethic which has dominated this country historically, to a leisure and entertainment ethic. It is readily seen in the heroes or models selected by a majority of our youth; by youth's devotion to their own contemporary music; by the status of TV and film personalities on the national scene. It is also seen in the "do it yourself" movement, which gives the individual an opportunity to find a sense of achievement through his own production.

Formulation of Long-run Personal-Social Goals, Philosophy, and Purposes

We have indicated the need for emphasis on democratic values in the school of the future. We endorse Wiles' statements that the best way to instill democratic values in youth is to have a school environment which is a practicing example of those values. Beyond this, however, is the need for the individual to develop a healthy concept of himself as related to the world in which he lives. Wiles has repeatedly given expression to this need in his comments on mental health. The increased mobility of the population, plus the increasing freedom of expression of the mass media tend to confront the individual at a very early age with a variety of patterns of personal philosophy and moral values. There is little reinforcement outside the home and church of any consistent framework of personal philosophy. For this reason, the analysis groups which Wiles emphasized must deal with this phase of youth needs as well as with values at the civic and political dimension.

Enhancement of the Individual, His Own Sense of Personal Worth

The enhancement of the individual includes ways of helping him recognize his effectiveness in his social setting through his involvement in the assessment of program and progress, through aptitude analysis, and through a program which gives freedom of movement from one special area to another. The present organization of education was designed at a time when higher education and indeed, graduation from a secondary school, were seen as the privilege of the selected few. Evaluation and procedures were used for the purpose of selection. With education now viewed as a continuous life process, such a pattern is obsolete. Program and evaluation must become procedures for helping each individual assess his own progress and examine his own goals.

Continuity of Personnel with Personal-Social Counseling

The school of the future which Wiles envisions and which we see, too, requires a close personal contact and a continuity of adults and students in a personal-social counseling relationship. Although every type of modern technology appropriate to the communication and development of ideas would be used in the program, it would not be as impersonal as the average large high school of the present period. Computers would be used to keep a record of where a student could be found at any given time, but the choices of activity and the timing of those activities would be reached through the counseling contact of the student with his teacher. One of the problems faced in initial efforts to individualize instruction has been the assumption that, given the opportunity, the student would be motivated to choose appropriate activity and work industriously at the projects of his own choosing. Actually, his potential for choice is limited by his own previous concepts of school and school experience. Planning toward goal achievement is a skill to be learned. A relationship with teachers must be set up whereby these skills are developed without jeopardizing the student's own choices and sense of purpose. As Wiles puts it, "Teachers of adolescents should have the ability to move from dominant to supporting roles as necessary."

Continuity in Curriculum Based on Learning Relationships

One of the problems in our age of specialization is the need for seeing relationships between fields of specialization. This is important, for example, in the various fields of science. It is certainly significant in the relationship of science with social sciences and with aesthetics. There are other very natural relationships between fields which the subject by subject organization of schools has left to the student to identify. For example, few schools combine the field of design in art with home science, yet there is an integral relationship. The obvious interrelationship of music, art, and literature is nearly always left to the extracurricular field. With individually designed programs, it should be possible to approach these relationships whenever it is appropriate to do so.

As we stated at the beginning of this essay, we have delimited our consideration of the school of the future to a focus on the individual in his social setting. There are, however, certain assumptions concerning the total school program which are essential in implementing the emphasis we have chosen:

1. Relevance to changing societal patterns means the invention of a far more fluid and rapidly responsive structure of school program and schedule than any which has yet appeared in American education. It involves a basic change in the philosophy of the public school system so that the emphasis is placed on learning rather than on teaching. It means a shift of responsibility to the learner, and a shift in the role of the adult to that of a teacher-counselor.

2. We are assuming an entirely different pattern of the use of time from that which characterizes the present school.

a. Time will not be used as a measure of competence or learning. The criterion in learning a foreign language, for example, will be the ability to use it, not the number of hours spent in studying it.

b. The school of the future will be a twelve-month school, with vacation time planned appropriately for the individuals.

c. Not all kinds of experiences have to be provided for an individual in any one day or week or year. Some learning might best be done in a concentrated period which would take all of the time available. Other parts of the individual's program might best be planned for an extended period of daily exposure.

3. We are also assuming a school completely equipped with extensive materials, beginning with periodicals and books in all fields, and including materials which students can use individually, such as 8-mm film, film strips, tape recordings, both audio and video, and computerized programs of many different kinds.

4. We are also assuming extensive use of television, not so much for the type of direct teaching which is now common, but for lectures, demonstrations, political contacts, dialogue with persons not able to be physically present in the classroom.

5. Although we assume rather complete equipment in the school of the future, and its use by individuals in terms of their own pursuit of learning, we would emphasize the need for "doing" experiences and the imperative need to mature learning through discussion of ideas, conflicts, and uncertainties both with peers and with adults.

6. We would assume a building much like that which Wiles described—but we would also expect to see the civic buildings, hospitals, business establishments, shopping centers, factories, and other community facilities used as a part of the educational setting.

7. One other assumption which we make is that the use of teacher time and the new role of the teacher would recognize the fact now known to every good teacher—that teaching involves far more than the time spent face to face with a student or students. The teacher in our school of the future would spend working time participating in the making of school policies, the evaluation of program, community responsibilities, and extensive inservice programs. All such activities would be included in defining the role of the teacher on his job.

ADDITIONS TO THE MODEL SCHOOL

Recent studies in the field of perception indicate that each person perceives in terms of his background, his purposes, and his needs. (*The Changing Curriculum*, p. 14.)

It is apparent from these criteria and from the discussion which precedes them that we are in agreement with the need for the four areas of curriculum which Wiles has described as essential for his "School of the Future." However, it is also apparent that we would add community service and experience as a fifth area, and a laboratory-studio-shop experience as yet another part of the total program. Wiles' emphasis on analysis groups as the central feature of the program would have our hearty endorsement. However, we would add either additional seminars in relation to the other areas he has described, or include a broader field of reaction than he has assigned to the analysis groups.

The school of the future, as we envision it, and as Wiles has described it, places much dependence on a program of individualized instruction. Implementation of such a program must be done through consultation with advisors who can suggest resources, raise evaluative questions, and help the individual determine whether the courses of action he plans will really take him where he wants to go. The student will need to discuss his program with such a counselor or teacher at least once a week, and sometimes on a day-to-day basis. The student will be faced with many decisions, and a wise teacher-counselor must help him formulate his purposes and develop his program in terms of them. Both through the use of a computerized program and through other forms of programmed instruction, actual learning procedures are predetermined. This cannot be true of the total program of each individual. The truly individualized program must also consist of selecting certain experiences and rejecting others. It is in this larger planning operation that close personal counseling is needed as well as for the purpose of giving the student a chance to *talk* about his programmed lessons.

Central in our school of the future would be a huge resource center consisting of a series of two or three large viewing rooms in which films, lectures, and concerts are continuously in progress. The range of these resources would be determined by the need for a wide background of information in all fields, by stimulating speakers who might be available, by questions or concerns of immediate current interest, by gaps in the community resources available to students, by problems designed to deal with unresolved concerns either of society or the individual. Much of the material which Wiles included in the cultural heritage area would appear here. No student would spend all of his time in this passive, generalized activity, but the schedule would be posted, and such opportunities would be available to all.

Another resource would be the individual study carrel. It would be provided with tape recordings, film strips, 8-mm films, computer programs, and a wide selection of books, realia, and still pictures. These materials might be used for the gathering of information in terms of student interest, for the pursuit of specific development of a project or the study of a special topic, or just for exploration and browsing.

A browsing room would also be included, and would offer displays of all types, changed frequently and designed to stimulate student curiosity, give a glimpse of other cultures or new scientific discoveries, demonstrate techniques of production in the arts and crafts, or call attention to new books or books of special interest. Near the browsing room would be discussion rooms where small groups of students might go to talk about their work, study together, or socialize. Teachers would also use the browsing room and on occasion participate in these small discussions.

The small seminar would be another feature of this school. In the pattern of the analysis groups, it would be a place where continuity of teacher and student would be established so that a student would feel free to initiate discussion of any issue or problem with which he might be concerned. Other seminars would be used as follow-up of some of the programs available in the viewing rooms. Since we are assuming community involvement, some seminars would be used for discussion of experiences and problems relating to that experience. Additional seminar groups might form spontaneously around current issues or problems, then dissolve when the need for them had passed.

There would be many workshops, studios, and laboratories in our school of the future. We assume that at some point in his program, every student would seek experience in some of these areas. These are the "doing" experiences. They would provide research in science, construction in the shops, and production in arts and crafts. There would also be opportunity in music and literature for elective enjoyment of the arts and perhaps, for some, the opportunity for creative endeavor.

Wiles believed in the importance of creativity, but how it would be incorporated into the program was not spelled out. We do not think of creativity as exclusive to the arts; in this school, creativity would be a way of life. In every "doing" experience, in every talking experience, we hope that divergent thinking would be encouraged, that questions would be framed as "How many ways can you find?" rather than "What is the way?"

A large part of each year's program for the individual would consist of actual work in the community. This would be of three types: vocational experience, civic service, and social service. The vocational experience would be designed to give an understanding of the world of work and to let the student find his own identity and relationship to it. Industrialists, professional people, labor leaders, and businessmen would participate in this program. The civic experience would be designed to give an understanding and appreciation of public services and governmental activities and policies. Civic leaders and government officials would be involved. The social service would be designed to help the individual understand and value people from all walks of life, from backgrounds other than his own, and those with problems he might not otherwise encounter. Community activity as a part of the education of youth has proved itself in many ways. VISTA, the Peace Corps, and the distributive education program are examples. The newly vocal student interest in politics and political policies has added dimension to our concerns for this type of experience. We cannot afford in the world of today to keep our students isolated from genuine participation in the problems of our time.

We do not mean to imply that we are totally abandoning the concept of teachers and classrooms. We are sure that in this century, in spite of the emphasis on individualization, classrooms will continue to be a part of the school pattern. However, we look forward to a time when the various specializations represented in the world at large are an integral part of the education of youth. The effort of some schools to have a "poet in residence" is an illustration of such representation. We should like to see a scientist at work in his laboratory inducting students into his research. The program at Harvard for students who have exhibited a previous avoidance of science is, in our judgment, an example of the involvement of students in genuine scientific endeavor which helps them gain an in depth understanding of the world in which they live. Similarly, the contact with a man of letters would do much to foster an appreciation of the ideas and understanding of people and of the world, which is essential to good literature.

We have sketchily described a program which is organized around the idea of individualization of education, but without removing the individual from continuing and meaningful social contact and social contribution. We feel that the school of the future should not only meet the needs of the individual, take into account individual differences, but do this within the context of the larger society in which each person must find a significant place.

We have not talked in terms of hours or credits or grade placement. Indeed, the school we have described would have none of these. It is possible that our present school structure based upon age grouping may have accentuated age status and contributed to the generation gap about which we now hear so much. The school we are talking about includes youth of varying ages in groups based on experience or interest. It also places the teacher, the adult in the community, and the student side by side in the search for answers to real and significant problems of our society. It removes youth from "cold storage" and utilizes their fresh and often creative points of view. Such a school would enhance the individual by giving him an opportunity to become a significant person through undertaking significant tasks.

chapter 8

William Van Til

Alternative Futures of the High School

The invitation to contribute to this volume came to me during the spring of 1968. Regardless of the topic of the book, I would have been honored to contribute because Kim Wiles was my closest national colleague. True, we never taught together on the same staff. Yet, with respect to academic background and occupational roles, commitments and loyalties, and ways of perceiving people and life, we had many relationships as colleagues and friends. So had the Memorial Committee asked me to write on any conceivable topic I would have gladly accepted and tried to make myself competent on the matter. However, the committee proposed to honor Kim through a volume of speculations on the future sparked by a future-oriented chapter he had written. The chapter was one with which I was comfortable.

Kim's speculation on the future of education in 1985 is contained in his chapter, "The High School of the Future," in his 1963 *The Changing Curriculum of the American High School.* My attempt in this essay will be to set beside his speculation my own speculation on the future of education in my presidential address to the National Society of College Teachers of Education, published by NSCTE in *Teacher Education and the Future,* 1968, and my extended version in pamphlet form, *The Year 2000: Teacher Education,* published in 1968 by Indiana State

University. My intent is not to affirm one set of speculations and to deny another, but rather to move toward a synthesis which will draw from both approaches some insights on alternative futures of education, especially high school education.

For orientation of the reader, I need not recapitulate Wiles' chapter. It appears in this volume and it is frequently paraphrased by other contributors. However, I do need to set beside the Wiles projection of 1985 (hereafter called "Wiles" or "1985") the central points made in my speculation on the year 2000 (hereafter called "Van Til" or "2000"). For documentation and sources of 2000, the reader is referred to the above-mentioned pamphlet, *The Year 2000: Teacher Education.*

ALTERNATIVE FUTURES OF THE
LARGER SOCIETY

It is important to preface speculation on the alternative futures of any institution with speculation on the alternative futures of the larger society of which that institution is a part. Even prefacing is not enough; one must *base* such speculation on preliminary speculation concerning the possible futures of the larger society. Clearly, this is true in the case of such a socially sensitive institution as education. When society has a cold, education sneezes. To claim that such-and-such will develop in education without basing that development upon a realistic approach to societal trends and forces is to operate in a vacuum. It is to convert future-planning into a guessing game, played without prior preparation in any parlor where conversation has temporarily lagged.

In any well-based speculation on the larger society in which education exists, two indispensable yet potentially contradictory components must be taken into account. One component can be visualized as curves, sometimes modified and influenced by impinging trends and forces, which can be extended into the future through projection and extrapolation. If this first element of continuing trends and forces were the only component in future-planning, the task of analysis would be simple indeed.

But there exists another component in reasoned speculation. This is the element of surprise, discontinuity, novelty, twist, or turning point. Kenneth E. Boulding calls it the "system break," an expression I will borrow for use through this essay. Perhaps the earliest of "system breaks" was the apple in the Garden of Eden. Among recent system breaks were World War II, the atomic bomb dropped on Hiroshima, the launching of men into space, and American participation in Asiatic land wars during the 1950's and 1960's.

The system break introduces novel elements and often plays havoc with the conventional wisdom based on the arching curves into tomorrow.

Long-term Trends and Forces in Society

As I read them, the American scholars engaged in future-planning toward the year 2000 in the United States suggest that the first component, consisting of predictable and probable trends and forces extending into the future, includes the following:

1. The continuation of the United States as a nation and as a world power.

2. The expansion of world population, with the population of United States rising from the 200 million of 1967 to approximately 350 million projected for 2000.

3. Increased urbanization, with 280 million of the 350 million of 2000 living in urban areas.

4. Increase in metropolitan areas and urban megalopolitan complexes, typified by Boswash (the Boston to Washington complex), Chipitts (the Chicago along the Great Lakes to Pittsburgh complex), and Sansan (the Santa Barbara to San Diego complex) containing almost one half of the American people.

5. A higher United States Gross National Product, and, more important, a higher Gross National Product per capita, estimated at anywhere from two to three and one-half times the 1965 figure calculated in dollars of 1965 vintage.

6. Continuing expansion of scientific knowledge and its practical application in the form of technological development—especially computerized, automated, cybernated, and electronic expansion.

7. An increasingly national society as to such functions as communication, transportation, and production, yet a society marked by creative federalism and even more numerous and influential voluntary associations.

8. Persisting inequality in income distribution, yet a broad diffusion of goods and services among the total population as people on lower income levels acquire their versions of what people on upper income levels have long taken for granted.

9. Less working time required of the ordinary employed worker; unemployability for the unequipped or unable population ac-

companied by subsistence provisions; and extensive investment of time and energy in work by a leadership group which is increasingly intellectual and specialized in orientation.

10. Extension of the knowledge explosion in the varied areas of inquiry accompanied by increasing use of new communication tools for storage, retrieval, and so forth.

11. Extension of the pursuit-of-happiness aspect of the historic Jeffersonian trio of goals stressed in the Declaration of Independence, as a more hedonistic approach to life continues to displace the former puritanical viewpoint termed "the Protestant ethic."

12. Persistence of problems which are social and human in essence rather than technological in nature, including such social-human problems as organized crime, use of land and environment, obsolescent housing in suburbs as well as cities, influential and sometimes irresponsible voluntary associations.

13. Postponement of the arrivals of either the Utopias of Plato, More, and Bellamy or the Infernos of Dante, Orwell, and Huxley.

Possible System Breaks in Society

As I read the scholars of future-planning, the second component emphasizing surprise, discontinuities, and turning points includes the following possible system breaks:

1. Global devastation through nuclear war reducing broad areas of nations to rubble and exterminating large sections of their population.

2. World-wide famine growing out of a tragic unchecked population explosion to which myopia of political and spiritual leadership has unwittingly contributed.

3. Computer-related technology becoming so influential a force in the last third of the century that it revolutionizes technological and social arrangements.

4. A biological transformation of man through transplants, drugs, chemicals, and other means, drastically affecting longevity, potentiality, and behavior of human beings.

5. Sharp reduction of the present widening gap between the developed and the undeveloped nations through marked increases in international support which reduce the living standards of developed nations.

To this list of possible system breaks, any of which has the potential to wreak havoc with the extrapolated trends to the point that all bets may have to be called off, some would add the possibility that a system break toward anarchy may be presently underway in the United States, as well as elsewhere in the world. The word "anarchy" is used here in its dictionary sense, not in a propagandistic sense. Anarchy in the dictionary definition is absence of a system of government and law; confusion, lawlessness. William Butler Yeats described it well in his poem:

> Things fall apart; the centre cannot hold;
> Mere anarchy is loosed upon the world,
> The blood-dimmed tide is loosed, and everywhere
> The ceremony of innocence is drowned;
> The best lack all conviction, while the worst
> Are full of passionate intensity.[1]

Those who suggest that the United States is currently in a system break toward anarchy cite:

- The national inability to escape from the Vietnamese quagmire.
- The problems encountered by the Great Society programs.
- The assassinations of Medgar Evers, John F. Kennedy, Malcolm X, Martin Luther King, Robert F. Kennedy.
- The rebellions and looting in the Negro ghettos.
- The ambushing of police and firemen in the slums; the repressive overreaction of police under boss rule when confronted by demonstrators.
- The revolt on the campuses.
- The alienation of youth and the intellectuals.
- The development of the hippie movement.
- The increased use of drugs such as LSD.
- The avoidance of exposure of the President of the United States to crowds.
- The shouting down of candidates ranging from the radical right to the liberal left.
- The adoption of the Thoreau Doctrine of civil disobedience without willingness to accept consequences.
- The accelerating missile race in the weapons culture.
- The power without responsibility of the industrial-military complex.

- The ineffectiveness of representative government confronted by problems of ghettos, poverty, gun registration, educational inadequacies, obsolete nominating and electoral procedures.

- The encouragement of segregation and the rejection of integration by white supremacists and their ideological blood brothers among the black segregationists.

- The rejection of orderly democratic change by some intellectuals in favor of the revolutionary strategy of encouraging the right wing to assume control in the hope that attendant anarchy will create revolutionary situations.

ALTERNATIVE FUTURES OF THE HIGH SCHOOL

If those of us who speculate on the future recognize that the two components must be taken into account in future-planning—both long-range trends and forces and the possibility of system breaks—we must recognize that speculation on alternative futures is preferable to dogmatically predicting one inevitable future pattern for society or for its institutions. As an illustration, let us consider the alternative futures for the institution called the American high school in a society characterized both by the long-range trends and forces and by the possible system breaks just described. Let us consider first the future of the American high school if such system breaks occurred.

Possible System Breaks and High School Education

If the United States were engaged in global nuclear war, the American high school would become an apparatus in which patriotic support for our side would characterize the value orientation taught. Students would be trained through the content of the curriculum to serve as manpower to maintain the war effort and assure national survival. In the event of nuclear devastation, those high school plants which still stood would be converted into hospitals and refugee centers.

If world famine swept the planet, high school education might be abandoned while youth worked in fields and factories to produce products for human survival. The high school plant, if used at all, might become an attendance center for job assignments.

If computer technology through a sweeping, swift impact revolutionized the school environment, American high school education might be conducted by machines without participation by human teachers.

The high school plant would be a clean and sterile factory in which students received their study assignments from mechanical sources, went to their listening halls and their private carrels to carry out their tasks, and occasionally exchanged words of greetings with a few technicians who fed the machines and repaired any malfunctions.

If biological transformation of mankind were achieved, the behavioral responses of high school students would be changed through a new type of assignment; namely, the administration of drugs and chemicals and the attachment of electrodes to sharpen, for instance, the capacity for reflective thought or for memorization, or to inhibit violence, malice, and destructiveness. Built into the high school plant would be extensive medical and psychological laboratories and facilities for the new medical and psychological personnel supplementing teachers.

If sharp reduction of the gap between have and have-not nations were the system break of the future, younger students would be in simplified basic programs of study with an emphasis upon international orientation, while older high school students would be working, teaching, and learning abroad in a much expanded Peace Corps. If the necessary gap-bridging involved decreased living standards in the developed nations, the American high school plant would reflect a school curriculum stripped to minimum essentials and thus devoid of gymnasiums, auditoriums, shops, and laboratories.

If anarchy overcame the social order and overwhelmed social controls, there would be no high school education. The high school plant, as a symbol of hated establishment and as the embodiment of authority, would first be occupied by mobs, then used temporarily for new and unusual versions of education, then probably pillaged, gutted, and eventually reduced to rubble.

Extreme scenarios, you say. Perhaps so. This is because you assume some changes in our going social organization in these directions, yet nothing as drastic as these full system breaks carried to their logical conclusions with respect to high schools. Probably you are right. None of these system breaks may take place in the years prior to 2000. Yet, these possibilities exist and so these alternative futures must be included in our speculations.

Rather than system breaks, we may find that the long-term trends and forces prevail as the determinants of the future. If so, instead of global nuclear war, we may live in the year 2000 in a period of small, contained wars—or we may even live in a period of peace. Instead of world famine, we may have regional famines similar to those in Biafra in 1968—or we may even have organized world-wide instantaneous famine-relief systems. Instead of the omnipotent, omnipresent computer, we may experience a brisk development of computer technology without teacher displacement—or we may even free teachers for inquiry and creativity while computers do the manual labor. Instead of biological transformation of man, we may experience somewhat expanded use of chemicals and drugs—or we may delay decisions as debate takes place on the ethics of alteration of human behavior and personality. Instead of decline in the living standards of developed nations as the now widening gap between have and have-not nations is closed, we may see a continued widening of the gap—or even some reduction of the gap within the customary and calculated nationalistic frame of reference. Instead of anarchy overpowering our social institutions, we may see the containment of violence and underclass anger within a sufficiently resilient social structure—or even see the elimination of the root social and economic causes such as ghettos, inadequate education, unemployment, and militarism which give rise to the drive toward anarchy. In all the above illustrations, present long-range trends and forces are the prevailing determinants. Substantial changes take place but the sharp system breaks do not occur.

Long-term Trends and Forces and High School Education

So, let us consider the alternative future for an American high school not based on the system breaks described above. Let us examine the future of the American high school if the long-term trends and forces listed earlier in this essay should happen to prevail. Such long-term trends and forces would indicate that the "typical" human high school of the year 2000:

1. Would be located in a United States of perhaps 52 states (including by 2000 Puerto Rico and the Virgin Islands) in a nation which continues to be a world power.

2. Would serve a nation in which the population has grown from 200 million to 350 million.

3. Would be likely to take the form of an urban high school in a nation in which 280 million of 350 million live in urban areas.

4. Would be as likely to be located in one of three giant megalopolises, such as Boswash, Chipitts, or Sansan, as to be located in a lesser population complex somewhere in a still expanding nation.

5. Would have sufficient funds to buy all sufficiently needed plant facilities, supplies and equipment; to pay teachers a professional

wage; and to pay for heavily expanded supportive services out of a U.S. Gross National Product which, per capita, would be two to three and one-half times as large as the 1965 GNP per capita.

6. Would make extensive use of computer technology for flexible scheduling and for instruction as part of an elaborate electronic network feeding into schools, homes, and offices. Simultaneously, would be troubled about what knowledge from the vast explosion to select for transmission by computer and what issues to select for discussion under human leadership.

7. Would maintain a semblance of local control through a local school board, yet would use a curriculum-making process which relies heavily on national curriculum projects; on private foundations; on state, regional, and national government curricular influences; and on the fluctuating social demands and pressures of growingly influential voluntary associations.

8. Would usually take the form of a large city school, often part of an educational park, and with plant facilities and equipment based upon a level below which no school would be allowed to fall.

9. Would be characterized by use of the coordinating teacher as the key person in a complex involving paraprofessionals, clerical assistants, research help, audiovisual technicians, and computer specialists. Such a teacher might work a six-hour day, two hours of which could involve direct instruction by the teacher, two of which could involve coordination of supporting services, and two of which could involve specializations such as leadership of analysis groups, preparation of curriculum material, development of audiovisual aids, and cooperation with computer technicians.

10. Would involve extensive facilities in schools for storage and retrieval through materials centers stressing audiovisual resources and computer technology along with the earlier tools in the way of written materials customarily found in libraries.

11. Would be characterized by lively discussion of value choices and most particularly of how a person should use leisure in a period of multiple competing choices.

12. Would be heavily oriented toward the ever-more crucial human problems which pose difficulties as to survival in a society where the technological processes have solved many of the non-human,

non-social problems. Included in the fundamental problems for study in the high school would be such social-human problems as organized crime and its reduction and control; the intelligent use of land and environment for human enjoyment; the problem of renewing housing in the suburbs as well as in the inner cities; the pressures, demands, and occasional irresponsibility of voluntary organizations.

13. Would recognize that, while plenty has arrived, Utopia is considerably in the future, and that consequently, value-oriented discussion and debate are essential to man.

These, then, are some alternative futures for the American high school, based upon developments in the surrounding society.

COMPARISON OF 1985 AND 2000 PROJECTIONS

Noting agreements and disagreements, we shall now compare these alternative futures for the American high school, reported more extensively and documented in the 2000 projection earlier referred to, with the 1985 projection. This procedure is in accord with Wiles' desire: "It is hoped that these hypotheses will help each reader to formulate his own expectations, which may differ from those of the writer, and to plan his work for the type of change he deems desirable."

Comparison of Authors' Intentions

Two central differences between the intentions of the two authors should first be noted. Early in the "anticipated development" section of his chapter, Wiles makes an assumption which is important to understanding his projection: "Although it is possible that schools in 1985 will be used as instruments of thought control and social classification, the writer is nevertheless optimistic enough to believe that there will continue to be a social commitment to freedom, creativity, and equality of opportunity." This reference is intended to acknowledge the immediate free association by the reader, confronted by Wiles' chosen date, 1985, to the date George Orwell made famous in his novel, *1984*, and to reject that Orwellian alternative future. By implication, Wiles' optimism also rejects other alternative futures based on socially undesirable system breaks such as global nuclear war, world famine, technology dominant over man, negative thought-control aspects of biological transformations, and anarchy. Though he does not specifically deal with such system breaks, it is clear from the projection he makes that he assumes a society in which such negative system breaks have not occurred.

Wiles also assumes that in 1985 the planners will hope that each pupil will have the four types of experience which are the heart of his "anticipated developments" in the chapter. There seems to be a close correspondence between what Wiles himself hopes and what is imputed to the hopes of his "planners for education." The question arises as to whether Wiles' projection is his *"anticipated* development" or his *"desired* development," just as the question must arise as to whether comment on tomorrow's weather is a meteorological forecast or an expression of hope that tomorrow will be sunny and clear. Is the 1985 projection a forecast (prediction of what will be) or a statement of the desirable (description of what should be)? Perhaps Wiles assumed that his forecast and his statement of the desirable corresponded and were thus synonymous. However, the attempt in the 2000 projection, whether successful or not, was to avoid the approach of setting forth the desirable in the guise of speculating on the future. The 2000 projection stresses alternative futures based on analysis of social developments, rather than on the anticipated hopes of the "planners for education." The 2000 projection assumes that the very nature of the hopes of education planners could be heavily influenced by the prevailing system breaks, forces, and trends.

Thus, the 1985 project, which does not describe the larger society, apparently assumes that system breaks will not occur. The 2000 project, which is based on the nature of the larger society, assumes alternative futures and the possibility of system breaks. The 1985 project apparently combines predictions with predilections. The 2000 project attempts to divorce predictions from predilections and to set forth only the former. Recognizing that these differences in approach and intentions do exist between the authors, we can, nevertheless, now determine which of the 1985 anticipated developments seem valid and which seem invalid as examined from the perspective of the 2000 projection.

Examination of Analysis Groups

The first of Wiles' 1985 anticipated developments is "analysis of experiences and values." The "Analysis Group" proposal is an extremely important program component for the high school of the future in the light of the 2000 projection. The alternative future for 2000 based on the long-term trends and forces contemplates an increasingly hedonistic society in which people have increased leisure. It assumes a society in which social problems persist and in which Utopia has not yet arrived. Such a society cries out for opportunities for young people to develop and apply values in situations which afford them multiple choices.

Should a system break toward anarchy threaten to prevail, the analysis group proposal would be even more crucial. Though Wiles wrote in the early 1960's and published in 1963, prior to many of the anarchic manifestations listed earlier in this essay, his comment on the need for value examination is prophetic: "In the late sixties, it will begin to be recognized that unless citizens have values they accept, understand, and can apply, the social structure will disintegrate until authoritarian controls are applied."

In the light of the 2000 social analysis based on long-term trends and forces, any objections concerning the composition of the analysis groups are minor caveats. For instance, in a multi-group society in which interaction with the values of people of many backgrounds is inescapable, educators of the future might think it preferable to vary the membership of analysis groups, including exchanging members among schools of differing social classes and racial compositions, rather than having each group remain "a unit throughout the high school program of its members." Too, in a time of many knowledge sources, the contemplated exclusive focus on "discussion" might be supplemented by the use of multi-media in the groups. Individual reports and sharing might be based on individual study of books, video tapes, films, and computer-supplied data from learning material centers at school and home learning and information centers.

Examination of Fundamental Skills

Equally perceptive and valid as seen from the perspective of the 2000 projection based on the long-range trends and forces is the curricular component termed by Wiles "acquisition of fundamental skills." Envisioned and sanctioned by the 2000 analysis are youngsters learning skills individually through technological resources. Were Wiles writing in 1968 rather than 1963, he would probably have specified computer-aided instruction rather than used the dated and near obsolete phrase "teaching machines." Too, he might have seen a potentiality for computer-aided instruction which goes beyond skills and over into his third anticipated curricular development, the cultural heritage.

Examination of Cultural Heritage

By the cultural heritage, Wiles means "knowledge from the humanities, the social sciences, and the physical and biological sciences." He points out that "the things our effective citizen will need to know in 1985 will be a multiple of the knowledge necessary in 1960." From the point of view of the 2000 analysis of trends and forces, this latter comment is. an affirmation of the continuing knowledge explosion which appears undeniable.

But the crux of any discussion of the cultural heritage (and most particularly of any discussions of a future cultural heritage in a period of multiplication of knowledge, storage, retrieval, long computer memory, etc.) is Herbert Spencer's nineteenth-century query, "What knowledge is of most worth?" well rephrased by Robert S. Lynd for the twentieth century as "Knowledge for what?" The central question is *selection*, and it is exactly the question of selection which is begged by most curriculum theorists who use the large vacuous expression "cultural heritage." Sometimes they describe the cultural heritage through cataloging an array of disciplines and advocating study of their structures, or through categorizing many disciplines into a few broad fields like "humanities" or "sciences." Such catalogues and categories supply no principle of selection. Rarely do those who close discussion of appropriate content with sweeping endorsement of "teaching the cultural heritage" make clear the basis on which content is to be chosen. Yet, content *must* be chosen.

Wiles, too, struggles against the complexity of the phrase "cultural heritage." But he does markedly better than most curriculum-commentators. He writes of the "things that an *effective citizen* will need to know." Thus, he supplies one clue through the concept that content should be selected in terms of *effective citizenship*.

He also writes of the study of the cultural heritage developing for "some" the "desire to enhance further the values on which the society is based." (Incidentally, why only "some"?) Thus, he supplies a second clue through the concept that content be selected in terms of *values*.

One looks for a third essential among clues to selection of content; namely the needs of the individual learner, and finds it in the assumption that ideas "that produce a response" will be discussed not in the large cultural heritage classes but in the small analysis groups. So the third clue to the selection of content, that content which meets the *needs of the learner*, is found in the referral of "ideas that produce a response" to another segment of the curriculum. (Incidentally, of what use are ideas in cultural heritage courses that do not produce a response?)

Thus, somewhat obliquely, Wiles proposes as a basis for selection from the cultural heritage that knowledge which contributes to effective citizenship, value enhancement, and needs of learners. Joining Wiles momentarily in expressing predilections rather than predicting alternative futures, I support the trio as providing a highly useful framework for selection of relevant content. Whether they will prevail in 1985 or even in 2000, when they do not prevail in 1969, is a matter involving more clairvoyance than Wiles and I possess.

From the point of view of an analysis of the year 2000 based on trends and forces, the teaching of the cultural heritage through television, films, and large group lectures, as envisioned by Wiles, is quite probable. But if one is concerned for the best possible communication of ideas, one must quarrel with avoidance of discussion in the context in which the ideas are learned and consequent delay of discussion to the somewhat more random setting of analysis groups presided over by educators with "empathy," "special training in counseling, communication and value analysis" who help "others to feel more secure, to clarify their values." From the 2000 perspective, this type of discussion won't quite turn the trick in that alternative future in which forces and trends include an expanded knowledge explosion marked by highly specialized content and characterized by social problems crucial to survival. More than one-third of the total program may have to be given to a "cultural heritage" component which illuminates social realities, meets the needs of learners, and enhances values.

Examination of Specialization and Creativity

The final "anticipated development" stresses specialization and creativity. The creativity aspect is intended to develop uses of the extended leisure time anticipated for all save the leadership elite in the 2000 analysis of trends and forces. The specialization aspect is composed of seminars in various disciplines or interdisciplinary fields and is intended to provide early specialization for those going beyond high school. Work experience is prescribed for those not seeking a higher education. From the point of view of a 2000 analysis which stresses the complexity of leadership roles and the obsolescence of the unskilled and untrained, the seminars might be a useful introduction to specialization on the high school level. They must, of course, be supplemented on the collegiate level and reach culmination on the graduate level. But it is doubtful as to whether work experience alone will be an adequate training for the work of the twenty-first century for that ever-shrinking minority not going on to the people's colleges.

SYNTHESIS OF 1985 AND 2000 PROJECTIONS

To predict the most likely high school of the future (that is, the high school of the future based on the long-term trends and forces described rather than on the system breaks envisioned as possibilities), we shall now attempt to synthesize the Wiles 1985 and the Van Til 2000 projections. Again, we remind the reader of our weather analogy; the attempt in this synthesis, like the meteorological attempt, will be to forecast the most likely developments, not to express the desire that the weather turn out to be fair and sunny for our vacation or rainy for our crops.

The Most Likely High School of 2000

By way of recapitulation, the most likely high school of the year 2000 will be: (1) within a world power called U.S.A., (2) populated by 350 million, (3) of whom 280 million will live in urban areas, (4) with almost half in the megalopolises of Boswash, Chippits, and Sansan. The nation (5) will be able to finance the facilities, salaries, and supporting services needed for a sufficient educational program, (6) equipped with computer technology for scheduling and for use in some of the instruction which (7) will be nominally controlled locally while, in actuality, will be heavily influenced by national curriculum projects, foundation and governmental funds, and the demands of voluntary organizations. The (8) resultant well-supported urban school (9) will be manned by coordinating teachers with supporting specialized staff and (10) will use versatile resource centers and computer technology. Among the major concerns of this school (11) will be value choices, especially as to leisure time use in an increasingly hedonistic society and (12) the crucial human problems (13) in a society in which neither a Utopia nor an Inferno has arrived.

The Most Likely Curriculum 1985-2000

After examining the Wiles 1985 projection in the perspective of the Van Til 2000 projection, we propose the following new synthesis as to the curriculum of the most likely high school of the future, 1985-2000.

The most likely future high school, 1985-2000, will include as a component "analysis of experience and values," through small groups made up of students of varied social and racial backgrounds who will not only discuss but will also use various media in analyzing the value implications of their individual experiences and of society's social problems. The concerns and procedures of these groups (which may or may not be termed analysis groups) were foreshadowed by the better core curriculum programs of the 1930–1968 period which based content on social realities, needs of learners, and values, rather than overemphasized one of these bases, as did many inadequate core programs.

The most likely future high school will include as a component "acquisition of individual skills" through core-like analysis groups, broad fields, and the specialized and creative approaches. Additionally, acquisition of individual skills will take place through individual study via computers, listening laboratories, and allied technology geared to individual levels and rates of learning. Many old and new skills will be taught at schools within a flexible computerized schedule in carrels and laboratories in which consoles utilizing varied media supply instruction, and at home in learning resource centers including video tape, computer terminal, and visual telephone, which will occupy what was formerly the book-oriented "study" in middle-class homes of the 1960's.

The most likely future high school will include as its single heaviest component carefully selected "knowledge of the humanities, the social sciences and the physical and biological sciences." In addition, this component will include world languages because of the world power setting, and that important universal language used in the knowledge explosion—mathematics. Some of the work in these broad fields will be presented through large group instruction via multi-media. But much of it will take place through moderately sized groups characterized by questioning, discussion, and both individual and small group work directed by knowledgeable specialists in the subject rather than by the empathic generalists in human relations. A persisting problem for the future high school will be the relevance or irrelevance of subject matter (characterized by various principles, structures, and relationships) to the social demands, the personal-social needs of the learner, and the necessity for value formation and clarification.

The most likely future high school will include opportunities for specialization and creativity. Specialization will be less important than creativity at the high school level in tomorrow's society.

Specialization for the leadership group in a society of expanded higher education will be regarded as an indication of incipient potentiality which must be heavily supplemented on the collegiate and graduate level. Similarly, in a society with expanded on-the-job training for the ordinary worker, specialization in high school through work experience or vocational education will be regarded as little more than orientation. Specialization for those who are unemployable in a highly advanced society will be a problem possibly resolved by rotation in undemanding jobs or by new careers in the human-services field which may exist or be created. On the other hand, the creativity dimension, through a variety of laboratory and field inductions into mental and physical leisure pursuits, will be heavily emphasized for the health of the social order and the fulfillment of the individual person in a society providing multiple options for the use of the abundant time on one's hands. Even the leadership group will be urged to develop creative pursuits, if for no other reason than enhanced productivity and more effective cogitation.

ON SPECULATION ON THE FUTURE

With such a book title as *The High School of the Future,* one is tempted to mingle sober descriptions of alternative futures with dramatic and colorful, yet unfortunately facile, vacuous, and empty Utopianism. It would be easy to close this essay with imaginative and gaudy descriptions of a future high school which, strangely enough, would employ one's own current pet forms of organizational wonders, of technological marvels, of curricular spectaculars, and of administrative wizardry. I suspect the educators are going to be exposed to a great deal of this type of astrology. However, I have chosen not to construct a Utopia here.

I have preferred the more sober course of setting forth some alternative futures for society marked by the probable long-term trends and forces in society, some alternative futures for society marked by possible system breaks, and some alternative futures for the American high school in such settings. I have preferred to examine Wiles' 1985 from the viewpoint of Van Til's 2000, and to develop a 1985-2000 synthesis as to the most likely curriculum of the most likely high school of the future based on the most likely of the alternative futures of society —the future based on the long-term forces and trends.

References

1. From *Collected Poems* by W. B. Yeats. Copyright © 1924 by The Macmillan Company. Renewed 1952 by Bertha Georgie Yeats. Reprinted with permission of The Macmillan Company.

part 3

The Individual and His School

chapter 9

Arthur W. Combs

A Curriculum for Learners

Kimball Wiles was a dreamer, a born innovator. That he should write an article on "The High School of the Future" was as natural as sunshine in his home state. One is inclined to think of dreamers generally as an impractical lot and their dreams unlikely of expression in reality. But Kim Wiles was a pragmatist as well as a dreamer. He was given to practical solutions—to making things work. I feel certain that many who read his description of the high school of the future in 1963 regarded some of his predictions with incredulity and others with approval in principle but also with considerable doubt that such things would ever come to pass. As a humanist psychologist interested in the dynamics of behavior, however, what strikes me about those predictions is not their impracticality, but rather their inevitability. If the high school of tomorrow is to meet even the demands of today, it must move in many of the directions forecast by Wiles. If it does not, it will fail us all—we adults, our children, or the nation itself.

The purpose of schools has always been twofold: for the individual, to prepare him to live effectively in the world, and for society, to provide citizens able to cope with society's problems. The schools men create are always determined by what they believe is necessary to prepare for life in those times. So it is in America. From the very beginning, our greatest tasks have been with the control of the external world. We started by wresting a nation out of the wilderness. We were committed to the Protestant gospel of the value of work (preferably hard) as the royal road to salvation. We gloried in our subjugation of nature and in our vast success at the production of things. Providing necessities of life for ourselves and our loved ones was a reason for being; doing it well was a source of pride and joy. The schools we developed were geared to these goals as we sought to prepare our young for productive life. Society needed people who knew what the objective world was like and how to mold it to satisfy people's wants. Information and know-how were the keys to both goals, the individual's and society's, and the high schools we created were designed to that end.

The control of his physical environment has been the major problem of man through all his history. But no more! With the discovery of atomic energy we now have the capacity to control the external world beyond man's wildest dreams. We have at our disposal the means and the knowledge to provide for the physical needs of everyone on earth. Indeed, in America at least, we are embarrassed by our overproduction of things. Control of the external world in our time has become a minor problem. The greatest problems we face as individuals and as societies are no longer questions of food, clothing, and shelter. They are problems of human interaction—how to live with one another and how to find reasons for living in the non-material aspects of human existence. The major problems of man have shifted from the physical to the cultural and psychological; from things to people. This fact, as Kimball Wiles so clearly understood, must inevitably find expression in the schools of tomorrow. The high school Wiles proposed is a deeply human one. Of the twelve questions he posed for most needed research, all but one were concerned with human problems. And the high school he forecast is no pipe dream. While the details may vary, the broad outlines he sketched must surely come into being simply because we are in the grip of events which demand it. That is the thesis of my discussion.

THE NEW ROLE OF MEANING IN EDUCATION

The high school curriculum of the past has, almost exclusively, been concerned with content and information. It saw its task as one of producing informed persons. Learning, however, is more than acquiring information. Learning always has two phases: (1) the acquisition of new knowledge or experience on the one hand, and (2) the discovery of its meaning on the other. Effective, efficient learning requires attention to *both* of these phases. Learning may fail for lack of information or because the student has never discovered the meaning of the information provided him. Just now our high schools are especially bemused with the search for scholarship and excellence. The expression of this striving, however, turns out to be mostly providing students with more information and pounding it home with greater vigor. Current attempts at curriculum reform almost exclusively regard only the information side of the learning process. Whenever we want to reform education, we come up with the same old answers—let us have more! Let us have more science, more math, more languages in the elementary schools, more homework, more physical education, more driver education, more language laboratories, a longer school year, and a longer school day. And, of course, with all our new hardware, we have marvelous new ways to give people more information more rapidly than ever before.

It is a naïve assumption that the acquisition of facts alone will make a difference in human behavior. Few of us misbehave because we do not know any better. We know how we ought to drive, but we don't drive that way. We know we ought not to be prejudiced, but we are. Most of us know what foods we should eat, but we don't eat them. The problem of the dropout is not a problem of lack of information. The dropout was told. His problem is that he never discovered the meaning of the information he was provided. Information without meaning is a mockery. Schools have been preoccupied with the information aspect of the learning equation for far too long. The high school of the future will redress this imbalance and concern itself much more with the problems of meaning. It will do so because it must. A school system which provides information but does not change behavior is a luxury we cannot afford.

There is a second reason why a new emphasis upon meaning must come about. As I have suggested above, the major problems of mankind are now human problems and, if our public schools are to carry out their functions, it is human problems with which they must be concerned. Humane qualities are not likely to be nurtured in dehumanizing settings. A major complaint of our present schools is their depersonalizing, alienating effects upon young people. If our new citizens are to cope successfully with the human problems of our times, education for meaning must necessarily take center stage. Facts do not make people human, but rather meanings, expressed in the form of attitudes, feelings, beliefs, values, understandings, and commitments. In our worship of objectivity and scientific method, these aspects of learning have often been zealously eliminated from the classroom. If we had purposely planned to make our schools impersonal factories we could hardly have done it better.

The school of the future must concern itself with meaning, not fortuitously, but by purposeful design. Kim Wiles understood this and built his proposed curriculum around the "Analysis Group," a continuous seminar led by sensitive teachers in which problems could and would be discussed with no holds barred. "The purpose of the Analysis Group," he says, "will be to help each pupil discover meaning, to develop increased commitment to a set of values, and to offer opportunity to examine the conflicts among the many sets of values and viewpoints held by members of the society." He says further, "The Analysis Group will be considered the basic element of the educational program. In the late sixties, it will begin to be recognized that unless citizens have values they accept, understand, and can apply, the social structure will disintegrate until authoritarian controls are applied. To counter the danger of the collapse of the democratic way of life, the school will be assigned the task of making as sure that each child develops a set of values as it does that he is able to read. The Analysis Group will evolve as the best means of performing the values development function."

Little by little, this prediction is coming into being, albeit more slowly than many of us would wish. At present, we are still engrossed in industrial models and the marvels of electronic means for transmitting information. But this, too, will pass! At the college level, the students themselves are rebelling against the inhumanity such depersonalizing emphases impose. At the high school level, increasing numbers of devoted teachers are beginning to look for ways of rehumanizing the curriculum through increased attention to the meaning half of the learning equation. Such effects must, in time, produce the kind of school Kim Wiles predicted. Eventually, but why not now?

STUDENT RESPONSIBILITY FOR LEARNING

The coming emphasis upon the meaning aspect of learning will contribute to another change forecast by Wiles; namely, an increased dependence upon the student's own responsibility for learning. A school obsessed with information can afford to teach with little heed to what happens to the student. Such a school simply gives people information. If students do not grasp it, they are soundly berated for lacking motivation or thrown out for stupidity or failure to cooperate. Schools honestly concerned about human meaning, however, cannot behave in so high-handed a fashion. Meanings cannot be grasped without the cooperation of the student. Schools concerned with human meaning must be student-centered, not because that is a nice idea, but because it is in students that the process occurs.

Meanings are discovered as students perceive the personal relationship of ideas to themselves and to the world they experience. This calls for schools in which students are actively involved in the process of learning and given major responsibility for its control and direction. They cannot be passive recipients of "the world"; they must get into the act. The emphasis Wiles placed on exploratory experiences in his analysis group and through student self-direction are steps on the road which all schools must sooner or later travel if the discovery of meaning, rather than the mere acquisition of information, is to become a major goal.

There is another reason why increased student responsibility and self-direction must play an important part in the high school of the future. Only through increasing reliance upon the student's own initiative will it be possible for us to cope with the problems of the information explosion about which we have all heard so much. We are up to our ears in information. We have so much that it has become an embarrassment how to handle it, where to put it, and how to find it again when it is needed. One effect of all this is to make it crystal clear that American educators can never again hope to design a curriculum for everyone. This is particularly true at the high school level. While there is some possibility of suggesting at the elementary level a few things that all children "ought" to know, at the high school level there is almost nothing for which that claim can be made.

Students must be prepared to cope with the problems of a society characterized by infinite variety and continuous change. Students who come from our schools must be increasingly unique if they are simply to survive in this setting; even more so, to contribute effectively to it. Since we cannot decide in advance what they ought to be, we have to help them become what they *can* be. The achievement of that goal without student cooperation and responsibility, however, is doomed before it starts. Responsibility and self-direction are learned from experience. You cannot learn to be self-directing if no one permits you to try.

Human capacities are strengthened by use and atrophy with disuse. If young people are going to learn self-direction, then they must be given many opportunities to exercise self-direction in the years they are in school. This means that our schools must get over their pathological fear of mistakes. If young people are to be given opportunities for re- sponsibility and self-direction, we will have to *expect* them to make mistakes. People afraid of mistakes cannot risk trying, and people who cannot risk trying cannot progress. The very essence of creativity is a willingness to go out in the blue, to break with tradition, to risk mis- takes. If the school of the future is to commit itself to self-direction, it must be willing to accept the kinds of frustration that sort of behavior is likely to bring to a nicely ordered world.

To meet the needs of students and the goals of society, schools must necessarily move in the directions of student responsibility and self- direction advocated by Wiles in his "High School of the Future." They will one day because they must. What a pity it is that Wiles had to forecast such schools for the future when we need them so badly right now.

THE GROWTH APPROACH TO LEARNING

To deal with the world of external things, men have invented the scientific method. This intellectual approach to solving problems in- volves attacking them objectively in step-by-step fashion dictated by the tenets of logic. It begins with a careful definition of the problem, proceeds with an analysis of the prevailing factors, determines the de- sirable goal, then sets about controlling forces to bring that goal into being. It provides a systematic, logical approach that has served us well in science, engineering, business, and industry. As a matter of fact, it has helped us so much to achieve control of the world and is so much a part of our everyday lives that we rarely stop to question it. Applied to curriculum problems, the approach had a good deal of merit in times past when the problem of curriculum and instruction was understood as a question of determining the "right" curriculum which everyone ought to take. Now that the curriculum explosion has destroyed any expectation of achieving that goal, the method is no longer so useful. Besides, it is much too slow; before we have even decided what the right goals are, they are almost certain to be out of date. By the time we have decided upon the answers to teach, the problems have changed and we find ourselves in the embarrassing position of teaching answers for problems that don't exist. The objective approach works well in dealing with problems of things; applied to the problems of people it leaves much to be desired.

People-problems call for a humanistic rather than a mechanistic approach to solutions. The growth approach to dealing with human problems does not seek to determine the answers in advance. Instead, it concentrates upon creating the processes for effective search. Instead of deciding what *ought* to be, it concentrates attention upon creating conditions to insure what may be. This is essentially the philosophy underlying the schools Kim Wiles has described. His schools do not decide what people should know. Instead, they surround the students with rich resources of what is known and create conditions designed to assist and encourage the student in the exploration and discovery of meaning. Indeed, as Wiles proposes, the provision of information in the school of the future will be largely a mechanical function. We will turn it over to gadgets and machines. Teachers will use their time for more important things. The genius of teaching will lie in the skills teachers demonstrate in the facilitation and encouragement of student growth. The objective approach calls for manipulating stimulus and response by a doer to a done-to. The growth approach calls for teachers who are only occasionally directors or controllers. Much more often they are participants in a mutual endeavor. Instead of standing outside the process and manipulating it, the growth approach requires "getting with it," getting in the act.

As Wiles has indicated, a humanistic approach to education calls for many changes in roles and functions. The problem of guidance, for example, becomes a quite different question when approached from a humanistic orientation. It is not seen as a procedure for rehabilitation, or for patching up casualties of the system. Nor is it seen as a preventive device to keep students from getting in trouble. Instead, it is an integral part of the educative process of facilitating and encouraging the growth of all students toward maximum fulfillment. Similarly, the high school emphasizing processes of growth and learning rather than knowledge acquired would regard graduation, as Wiles has suggested, as a highly variable affair occurring when students are ready to leave.

The high school of the future cannot hope to provide its students with ready-made answers. Its goal must be intelligent behavior. Intelligent behavior is a highly unique and personal thing having to do with the person's ability to behave effectively and efficiently in the myriad aspects of the world in which he lives. It cannot be taught specifically. It must be nurtured and facilitated in open settings which encourage and aid students to assume responsibility for their own learning and imbue them with the joy and excitement of continuous problem solving. The high schools we have known cannot accomplish such a goal. We cannot afford to keep them much longer.

THE INDUCTION OF YOUTH
INTO ADULT SOCIETY

One of the terrible things that has happened as a result of our highly technological world is the alienation it has forced on our young. Once there was a place for young people in the society of their elders. They lived and worked with them side by side. But no more. The world we have created has little use for young people once they have stopped being babies. They are shunted out of adult society and prevented from dealing with the real world. They are forced to live in an artificial world made up of contrived responsibilities and substitute goals for real ones. Young people are required for the most part to work at things that don't matter in a seemingly endless *preparation* for life. They are almost literally condemned to a life of play. We prevent them at every turn from participating in adult society, then blame them for not growing up! Many adults do not approve of young people in principle. Some adults even delight in hearing of youth beaten by police and advocate more and more rigid controls and punishments. It is little wonder so many young people grow up with a vast credibility gap between themselves and the older generation.

The successful induction of young people into adult society is essential for a stable, dynamic culture. Formerly, this induction took place in the home and community; however, with the increasing technology and diversity of the world we live in, we can no longer count on home and community to ease this transition. No society can long endure the alienation and dehumanization of its young. If the induction of youth is to be properly accomplished, the schools are going to have to do their part. The high school of tomorrow must find new ways to aid our young people to participate in society in a meaningful fashion. I therefore join Wiles in calling for high schools of the future to make much larger use of the resources of the community and find much better ways to give young people *real* experience in the adult world.

Our high schools of the past have sheltered youth, separating them from life while supposedly preparing them for it. The high school of the future must find ways to immerse youth in life to the limit of their capacities. To this end I would go much farther than Wiles has suggested to involve young people in the problems of the real world through concrete responsibilities—a fundamental principle, by the way, in Soviet education. It is difficult to see how the forces of alienation and dehumanization can be counteracted or the yawning chasm between youth and society can be bridged if not by opportunities for youth to be accepted by and participate in adult society. In the training of workers for every profession, provision is made for participation of the student in the practical experience of the profession. In the training of people for the profession of citizen, however, we have departed from this principle, assuming we could turn out citizens in a sterile atmosphere protected and shielded on every side from live participation.

The high school of the future must use its ingenuity to escape from its walls and invade the world, or else bring that world inside. Too much time is currently spent in the endless provision of answers for problems students don't have yet. The high school of the future will deal much more authentically with the real problems of its student body. There will be far greater sensitivity to the world as perceived by the student and a far more flexible structure which will make it possible for him to take advantage of the educational opportunities offered by the world outside his school.

THE NEED FOR A NEW PSYCHOLOGY

The kind of high school Kimball Wiles foresaw would not have been possible in former times even if the goals he set had seemed in those times to be desirable. His high school would not have been possible because the basic understandings of human behavior needed to make it so did not exist. It has always been true that men have behaved toward their fellows in terms of what they believed people were like. Every generation is trapped by its perceptions of the nature of man.

A humanized curriculum needs a humanistic psychology. If we start from a mechanistic psychology, it should not surprise us if we come out with mechanistic answers. For fifty years or more, we have been in the grip of stimulus-response psychology or some of its many variations. This point of view sees learning as a matter of properly manipulating stimuli to arrive at desired results. Looked at in this way, curriculum design becomes almost exclusively a task of deciding what people should know, gathering information for them, and teaching it to them. Motivation becomes a matter of administering rewards and punishments. Learning becomes, quite logically and naturally, a pre-occupation with manipulation of information and an exclusive concern with events outside the learner. Such a psychology concentrates attention on what teachers do to students, or to the content provided. Little or no concern is rendered to what goes on in the student. Pupils are objects to be molded, motivation is a matter of reward and punishment, understanding is taught, and human qualities of emotion, feeling, and caring are largely regarded as obstacles to teaching. Love is not part of such a curriculum.

A mechanistic psychology is totally inadequate to deal with the humane kind of high school Wiles predicted. What is needed for such a high school is a concept of the nature of man and his behavior which helps to see young people more clearly as human beings. We need a psychology capable of dealing with man's experience—a psychology interpretive of students' feelings, values, beliefs, understandings, and personal meanings. These are the things that make us human. We need a psychology capable of dealing with the internal life of the learner, the meaning half of the equation.

Fortunately, this kind of help toward understanding is at hand in the humanistic frame of reference basic to many new approaches to psychological thought. Psychologists working in this new frame of reference call themselves by a variety of names; personalists, self-psychologists, phenomenologists, perceptualists, existentialists, and interactionalists, to name but a few. By whatever name they may be called, however, they are all concerned with the question of what goes on *inside* the learner. This new humanistic approach to the nature of behavior promises much for the development of effective practices needed for fuller development of human capacities in students and teachers alike. Some of the most exciting things it has brought us in recent years include an understanding of the self-concept, new concepts of human potential and self-actualization, and new and more adequate approaches to motivation and learning. Humanistic psychological thought provides criteria and points directions to kinds of solutions required for helping young people to grow in the high schools of tomorrow. As these concepts achieve wide distribution, they may yet provide us with clues which will make it possible to construct the kind of high school Kimball Wiles dreamed of.

As I said at the outset of this paper, I do not believe the high school Wiles predicted is any idle fancy. But what he pointed out for us is not a blueprint but an outline. A blueprint would have defeated his purpose. It would have provided no more than a different set of answers likely to be out of date when the time came to put them into practice. Instead, he gave us the general directions in which he felt we must move. Each of us, of course, can only envision the future "through a glass darkly." So it is with Wiles' descriptions, and each of us must make of them what he can. For my part, I find his directions meaningful and helpful. I feel certain the high school of the future will be very much like what he has described. Our problem is not to find answers to be imposed on the future. Our problem is to apply the growth philosophy to the question—to get with it, participate in the process and see what we can make of it. A good place to start is with the questions Kim Wiles posed for us.

chapter 10

Robert S. Fleming

Needed: Greater Student Involvement

The work of Kimball Wiles has over the years placed great emphasis on the values of youth. He was optimistic about adolescents. He was concerned about the school of the future and wanted educational programs which help each student "to develop a set of values to guide his behavior" (*The Changing Curriculum of the American High School*, p. 301). This paper is an attempt, in part, to implement such a philosophy. It is assumed that the implementation suggested will likewise contribute to positive mental health and to the development of creative citizens.

Education in the late sixties has been characterized as having active students seeking identity and meaning. Projections of things to come in the era of the seventies will doubtless include many more dynamic attempts to relate to the student population in more meaningful and realistic ways.

Young people leaving our high schools today have a new sense of idealism and a new desire for involvement. They seem to have deep insight into social values and want to operate in specific ways and on specific and actual problems affecting them. Certainly, they are not content with any superficial answers. They want a quality of education that is relevant both to themselves and to the world. Robert C. Weaver, former Secretary of Housing and Urban Development, indicates that our students in high school are no longer willing to adjust their lives to fit the framework of established order: "They know already they want something different, something better. They want to be a part of shaping a new order to meet their new needs."[1]

David Mallery writes of an interview with an eleventh-grade boy from a school exploding with curriculum experiments and in which massive homework assignments were given in which the boy said:

> I do the homework to get the grades and get into college, and I try to live it up as a teen-ager and all of this takes a lot of time. But a lot of us think that maybe there must be something more."[2]

Perhaps thousands of our current crop of students are crying out for "something more."

Marshall McLuhan has described today's youth as our first generation of young people growing up in the electronic age. He also relates this age of communications to education: ". . . the school drop-out situation will get very much worse because of the frustration of the student need for participation in the learning process. This situation concerns also the problem of 'the culturally disadvantaged child.' This child exists not only in the slums but increasingly in the suburbs of the upper-income homes. The culturally disadvantaged child is the TV child. For TV has provided a new environment of low visual orientation and high involvement that makes accommodation to our older educational establishment quite difficult."[3]

Edward Yeomans, in his foreword to *A New Look at the Senior Year* discusses the contemporary student as being one, since birth, who has been conditioned by the high-involvement medium of television, yet who is still being taught in school by means of the compartmentalized medium of the written word. He also indicates that the student's dilemma has less to do with the content of either medium and more with the intrinsic message, and its emotional response, that is inherent in each.

Secondary education is currently plagued with problems of youth. Some of these problems relate to the youth themselves; for example, to efforts for emancipation from homes and family. Often, these lead to value conflicts, problems of role perception, and desire for economic independence. These lead to pressure for high marks, excessive homework, and extreme competition. There are problems which are highly personal—they relate to sex, courtship, "going steady," early marriage;

they relate to drugs, narcotics, alcohol, and smoking; they relate to peer relationships, dress, and adolescent mores. There are also academic problems related to perceptions of college admission standards and academic qualifications. There are economic problems related to the buying power of youth and their desire for records, music, hot rods, bizarre dress, and their quest for recreation.

These problems exist at a time at which new curricular programs are being discussed and implemented. Extensive effort is underway with numerous groups and agencies desperately concerned with ways of changing our educational programs. Yet, with all the effort and all the innovative attention, business too often goes on "as usual" in too many schools. The world of today must be in greater evidence in our schools than it is at present.

A systematic observation of groups in our schools underscores that many youth are restless, bored, and victims of poor teaching, lack of vitality in program planning, and inadequate guidance. Conflicts in home and family are numerous and often increase tension, anxiety, and pressure for all concerned.

On the other hand, we find that today's youth are alert, knowledgeable, informed, and dynamic. They are resourceful and independent and creative. Many of our youth have sophisticated tastes in the arts and literature. Many have learned much from television, travel, and communication with world citizens. They have responded to opportunities to learn about electronics, space, rockets, higher mathematics, and other languages. Earl Kelley has called our attention to the dynamic population and has written wisely in their defense.[4] Gardner Murphy, in his classic work, "What Can Youth Tell Us About Its Potentials?" confirms the value of listening to youth.[5]

WHAT DO YOUTH HAVE TO SAY?

In preparing this paper, I have held a series of recorded interviews with high school students in several geographical areas. The boys and girls were asked, "What do you want from high school?" or "If you were to move to another city, what would you want the high school to be like?" Interestingly enough, there is great consistency in the students' answers. There seem to be three recurring themes:

- *We want to be respected.* "Too often our teachers treat us like dirt. They laugh at us, they ignore us, they do not recognize that we too have opinions."

- *We want to be involved.* "School is so dull and we never do anything except follow directions and do our assignments. We have no opportunity in most classes to work except to listen to the teacher, to do our assignments, and to prepare for tests. We would like to do special studies, do some research, make things, and have more responsibility."

- *We want to learn something that is important.* "Why do they spend so much time on stupid things? Why do they think that getting ready for college is so important? How will we ever use the 'stuff' they teach us? Why do we have to learn the same thing?"

The recurring themes seem significant as we think of the secondary school of the future. These young people appear to be highly insightful, ready to plan wisely, and to participate in decision making. Doubtless, such themes give curriculum leaders and teachers unique cues for returning the schools to the students and for the establishment of significant criteria for curriculum design. They likewise may well serve as a framework within which guidance is viewed and guidance and counseling practices are revised. Perhaps our most significant innovations arise from youth themselves. Perhaps it is time now to turn increasingly to young people for their advice, recognizing their hopes and aspirations, and finding more fundamental ways of soliciting their involvement.

By all means, this is not to suggest that all youth are equally skilled or ready for independent functioning. Yet, with our continuing concern for behavioral goals in recent years, the students themselves take us back to basic considerations. To become independent, to assume responsibility, to sharpen work habits, to feel the thrill of accomplishment, youth must have opportunities for independence, for assuming responsibility, and for appraising the consequences for their activities. This will not abandon the need for effective leadership nor will it provide for youth to "take over." Rather, it will establish a climate for responsibility, for growth, for fulfillment, for independence. It will also create a setting within which needs can be assessed more accurately, within which competencies can be better observed, and within which cooperative faculty planning can become focused on youth that need to be served.

We are told that the high school of the future will serve many more students than is currently the case. Projections in the Eight State Project, *Designing Education for the Future,* estimate that by 1980 we will have an increase of eighteen per cent in school enrollment and that sixty per cent of those twenty-five years of age will be high school graduates.[6] Already, we are seeing the beginnings of striking new patterns and conceptions of secondary education. These are made possible through the computer, modular scheduling, conceptions of the extended school year, new emphasis on vocational education, community college opportunities, new developments in technology, new conceptions of independent study, developments in the arts, and new emphasis in various national curriculum projects. New organizational patterns will continue to emerge. Doubtless, many developments will occur which maintain and extend the philosophy of core curriculum. Team planning, cooperative teaching, and many aspects of team teaching will be maintained and extended. But this is not enough.

The most far-reaching and penetrating opportunities for educational advancement lie in continued and renewed emphasis upon the human potential: humanizing teaching and instruction, designing opportunities for the ego to be enhanced, maintaining positive mental health, emphasizing the development of competent men. It is here that the voices of the adolescent tell us in specific and fundamental ways that they seek opportunities to develop competence. They require a quality of leadership and guidance that "turns them on" in meaningful ways.

To enhance adolescents' feelings that they are respected, there are no ready-made answers or models which are universal or "foolproof." It is clear, though, that today's adolescent knows a "phony." He cannot be kidded; he is both child and adult with acute sensitivity and keen awareness. In emphasizing academic competence, many teachers overlook important opportunities to respond meaningfully to the needs of particular importance to these adolescents.

RESPONDING TO STUDENTS

It is felt that the high school of the future should place greater priority on the concerns of youth. This means the particular youth in a particular school. Earlier, the three themes suggested by students were given. These themes seem important for specific suggestions for future developments in all phases of secondary education.

"To Be Respected"

To be respected is of unique importance. It is not enough to have a "number," to "sign in," to appear for a fifteen-minute counseling session at an appointed time on a given day. It is not enough to be referred to as "you in the blue dress." It is human to want to be known, to feel a sense of belonging, to develop strong personal ties, to feel that someone cares. To be known is not a superficial thing; it must have depth, maturity, and quality. To know a student calls for an overall assessment of him, using numerous sources of data concerning status, interests, values, activities, aspirations, accomplishments, responses, needs, health, family, perceptions. The goal is to develop quality relationships based on trust and acceptance. To realize this goal, school personnel need time, support, and unlimited resources. Such relationships likely are continuing ones and emerge as relationships over the span of years. They require teachers to study previous records, to identify additional sources of data needed, and to compile information from other teachers.

What do we mean by guidance? How is the guidance function to be achieved? Certainly, it is more than establishing a program (schedule). Certainly, it is more comprehensive than course selection. Certainly, it is not limited to counseling those having difficulty. Certainly, it is not limited to college selection and college admission.

To be known is to be wanted, respected, encouraged, helped. Such a simple aspiration should be understood by any teacher, in any content area, in any organizational plan. The following techniques, although not new, have proven useful and still illustrate important ways of relating to young people and getting to know them:

1. *Encourage pupils to write about themselves.* Numerous projective devices have been used including:
   a. Unfinished sentences;
   b. Paragraphs on specific topics such as "Me," "My School," "Things I Consider Important," as well as such topics as work, friends, race, war, money;
   c. Answers to specific questions encouraging pupils to project their ideas;
   d. Themes on topics selected by the pupils;
   e. Autobiographies;
   f. Logs or diaries kept over a period of time;
   g. Descriptions of work experiences.

2. *Encourage individuals to talk.* In friendly interview situations—informal, seemingly casual, teachers secure important information *if they listen.*

3. *Encourage group conferences* with small groups of students in which they are encouraged to talk about themselves, school, and ways they can be helped. Students' perceptions, aspirations, difficulties, and questions are considered and help is provided.

4. *Encourage an attitude of relating to individuals.* Illustrations include: "Stop by for a chat," "Let's have lunch together," "How may I help?"

    a. Write an occasional note, make a phone call or inquiry;

    b. Use communications which congratulate, extend good wishes, or suggest awareness of an individual or his situation.

5. *Encourage individuals to express themselves* in ways appropriate or unique for a particular individual.

6. *Acknowledge and/or attend an event, work situation, or school affair* to demonstrate interest in the student.

7. *Read thoroughly and with critical sympathy what a student writes,* discuss this with him, and provide situations for the individual to get help, advice, and encouragement.

8. *Engage in opportunities for value clarification* by providing actual situations which enable students to feel that they are important.

    a. Use a student's writing to identify things or qualities which the student accepts and those which he rejects;

    b. Confront a student with a situation and get him to discuss it;

    c. Use conflicts or dynamic experiences in history, literature, or drama as a basis for discussion;

    d. Provide many opportunities for role playing.

"To Become Involved"

To become involved is a fundamental ingredient in learning. Youth are eager, alert, and energetic and they want to expend their energies in constructive and meaningful ways. As they are passive, as they are fulfilling "ready-made" assignments or activities determined by the teacher, as they are consumers and not actively engaged in planning and decision making, they are robbed of significant learning. By and large, youth are not indifferent to learning and to the development of skills. They do want to see themselves treated as mature and thinking individuals.

Over and over again, the young people I interviewed said, "I like to be challenged. I want more freedom to pursue things which are important to me." Such clear and reasonable requests from our student population have far-reaching teaching and curriculum implications.

Suggestions for greater involvement of students have been made over and over in the literature, but the current scene offers greater potential than ever before. At this point, we have greater quantities of materials, more resources of technology, and an increasingly favorable climate for independent and small group work.

Perhaps we must now give greater and greater attention to diagnostic activities, provide more time for counseling, and listen more closely to students' concerns and purposes. Some illustrations which appear to hold great promise for active involvement of students in a mature way include:

1. *Have students participate in many types of discussion groups.*
   a. Seminar and small group discussions provide for students to probe, to share, to clarify, to analyze values, to search for leads, "to give and to take." Such sessions may emerge from any of the content areas as well as from general concerns of youth;
   b. Use less "teacher talk" and more group discussion. Following a lecture, film, dramatic episode, trip, work experience, or youth activity, young people might be helped by discussing the situation. Such discussion situations should increasingly provide challenges to assumptions, create need for new or additional data, challenge fallacies in thinking, or provide for all sides of an issue to be presented. The use of open-ended procedures by the teacher with keen sensibility to qualities which make such sessions productive appears fundamental;
   c. Help with discussion techniques, human-relations considerations, as well as with the development of skill in logical thinking. It should be kept in mind that youth problems, youth needs, and youth situations should provide many opportunities for discussions within the confines of a subject discipline.

2. *Provide opportunities or freedom to pursue an idea or a study in depth.*
   a. Many young people want not only to read widely but they often are highly motivated to build, repair, construct, or analyze. This might include constructing a garment, building a model, arranging a study, or designing a piece of equipment. Whether it is in the area of shop, homemaking, literature, science, or history, the impact is great. Young children often express themselves by saying "Look what I can do." Such a quality likewise is valued by a high school student;
   b. Use of long-range assignments rather than day-by-day piecemeal activities is often appreciated. For example, if an individual could follow the developments of a session of Congress, or the General Assembly of the United Nations, his reading, listening to news, and following daily events in the press would eventually give unlimited information to be organized, summarized, interpreted, and presented;

    c. Increasingly, research activities are being carried on in science. Local history, an analysis of early traditions of a community, or studies of local problems might also provide opportunities for important research. Unlimited opportunities exist in any community for significant studies of local problems, local needs, and local situations.

3. *Provide opportunities for creative work.*

    a. Young people are often starved for creative expression. Writing a novel, a play, a symphony, or arranging an art exhibit, or presenting a drama is not beyond the creative efforts of alert high school students. Opportunities to become involved in various art areas and to create a major production have lasting personal and academic potential;

    b. The related arts are increasingly of interest to youth. As they are helped to see relationships between color, sound, and movement, and released to create out of each area, another challenge is provided. Modern dance, dramatics, art, and music hold rich possibilities. Each student can carve out his own niche which evokes the charm and unique expression of a maturing self;

    c. To make a movie, to prepare a television program, to arrange radio programs, to sponsor or arrange exhibits, or to provide for local talent often leads to creative work or to a quality of involvement which helps students to "unfold."

"To Learn Something of Value"

To make it possible for young people to learn something of value is the continuous responsibility of all working on curriculum. Our youth today want to learn; they want to probe in depth, and they want to share, discuss, clarify, and apply their understandings. Too often, we underestimate their ability to deal with new, difficult, and abstract ideas.

As young people feel that they are on the frontier of new knowledge, or as they feel that they are creating new or novel sets of principles, they become enthusiastic. Creative teaching which gives responsibility to students, which gives them an opportunity to plan, communicate, and evaluate is welcomed.

Perhaps the most wholesome attitudes toward self and school emerge out of intensive work, carrying out an important study, receiving genuine help, needed direction, recognition, and mature praise. The following suggestions are illustrative:

1. *Approach adolescents as mature individuals living in a complex world and listen to their concerns as a basis for developing depth studies.* This immediately replaces unrelated curriculum activities with topics of concern to students such as power, money, sex, understanding current youth activities, understanding the peoples of the world, and identifying ways for youth to "fit in."

2. *Provide opportunities for social service.* To work on real and vital problems in real and dynamic places is of value. The hospital, the recreation center, the factory, the city hall, the bank, the laboratory have characteristics which are real, tangible, and important. Youth want to work; they often are impatient in classes which "study about," but do not provide opportunities "to do."

3. *Provide rich learning opportunities which make full use of many media.* Using products of modern technology, extending uses of photography, developing television programs, analyzing television, reviewing new films, setting up exhibits, sponsoring recreational opportunities for younger children, engaging in dramatics, painting, participating in musical activities, and writing poetry are illustrations of dynamic experiences that young people crave.

This is not to suggest that the curriculum of the future has no roots or that it is without continuity or sequence. It is to suggest that young people must have many more opportunities to participate in planning and following through their plans in specific ways. At once, this generates new modes of organization of "subjects," of schedule, of guidance, and of evaluation. It recognizes current uses of technology both in scheduling and in data retrieval. It also highlights creative uses of technology to make learning real and dynamic.

The illustrations given likewise suggest the need for a complete overhaul of the entire evaluation program. The students interviewed constantly referred to the inadequacy of the testing programs now in operation. They were conscious of teachers teaching for tests, of students being pressured to make high scores. Such limited evaluation activities are rejected by the student group. They are not at all reluctant, however, to provide evidences of accomplishment on work which is relevant to them as citizens in today's world.

Current efforts to describe the educational program of the future give much attention to uses of technology, to organizational changes, and to updating the content of the curriculum. Perhaps the most important factor which is missed is enunciated by the adolescents themselves when they say that "something more" includes "being respected," "becoming involved," and "learning things of value." Such responses are likely not separate, they may be a part of a general syndrome or a characteristic of teaching which must be highlighted if Wiles' projections are to be realized. He says that the quality of the program will be determined by the wisdom of decisions made by "you and me."

References

1. *New York Times,* September 21, 1968, p. 36.
2. David Mallery, "Something More," *Saturday Review* (June 18, 1966), p. 70.
3. From *Understanding Media,* 2nd ed., p. x, by Marshall McLuhan. Copyright © 1964, by McGraw-Hill Book Company. Used with permission of McGraw-Hill Book Company.
4. Earl C. Kelley, *In Defense of Youth* (Englewood Cliffs, N.J.: Prentice-Hall, Inc., 1962).
5. Gardner Murphy, "What Can Youth Tell Us About Its Potentials?" *Bulletin of National Association of Secondary School Principals,* 50:10-34 (May, 1966).
6. Edgar L. Morphet and Charles O. Ryan, *Prospective Changes in Society by 1980* (Denver, Colorado: Eight State Project, 1966).

chapter 11

Earl C. Kelley

Humanizing the High School of the Future

There are a few educational principles which seem obvious to me, and I think that Kim would want me to state them. I do not know where I got them, but some most certainly came from Kim. I have known him for many years, and have read and enjoyed his writings.

I do not see myself in the role of a prophet; therefore I cannot say what the high school of the future will be like. I can only say that no operation, business or public, can go on forever while losing thirty or forty per cent of its product without either changing or going out of business. And dropouts are only part of the problem. Actually, most "dropouts" are still in school, having lost all track of what is going on, held there by social and parental threats, and believing that they will never amount to anything without that precious diploma. And so they stay in school long after it has lost all meaning for them, just to get that piece of paper. They may have to cheat and lie in the process, but they did not ask for the situation, they had no part in making the rules, and the diploma is their only profit. Good young people, who in no case would take anything from anybody, feel justified in cheating in a situation not of their own making, in which pressure is inexorably applied.

WILL THE HIGH SCHOOL SURVIVE?

During the economic depression in the 1930's, the high schools were in process of being supplanted by the federal government. We had the CCC (Civilian Conservation Corps) in which our young men were transported far away, and eventually put in the hands of the military. This is not intended as any deprecation of the military, but only to point out that it was really not trained to educate the young. There were very few teachers to be had; we had not nearly enough even to staff the schools. This was primarily caused by our policy of starving the teachers, so that few saw teaching as an attractive way of making a living. It was looked on as a temporary way of earning a living, until something better came along. The military personnel were always available.

Another threat to the high school was the NYA (National Youth Administration). This was set up so that the young people who stayed at home (mostly girls, as I recall) could earn enough money for survival. They worked in offices, assisted professors, and went to school part time. I believe that the federal government had no intention of doing away with either of these institutions had we not become engaged in an expensive war. Men, women, and materials were all urgently needed, and such non-essentials as education were quickly forgotten. So the high schools were saved by war.

The high schools got along during and after the war without public scrutiny. But then the Russians sent up a satellite which humiliated the American people. Everybody knew that Americans were the smartest people on earth and were expected to be the first in space. The public did not look to the Pentagon, or to the Congress, or to the President, but they had to have a scapegoat. They therefore attacked the most helpless group in the society—the children and their teachers. The rationalization was that this awful thing had happened because "those damned kids were not studying enough physics and chemistry." The teachers, a frightened lot at best, responded in many peculiar ways. They "cracked down." Some of them raised standards by lowering grades. People were driven out of school in droves. And so we come to the present, with many teachers still taking pride in how tough they are, while many students leave them. Some of these students become delinquent, some withdraw into mental illness, some just sit around waiting for something, God knows what.

I believe that it is time that we lose faith in pressure as a way to bring up our young. We have tried it long enough, and it has brought a holocaust of violence and crime. It has come to pass that it is no longer safe to walk the streets of our cities. In fact, it has come about that there is no place to hide.

It seems to me that the whole organizational pattern of the school, set up to serve adult purposes, will have to be abandoned. There is nothing in the nature of the child to justify our venerated system of putting all children of the same age in the same group. It is done so that adults can conveniently keep track of everybody. It is well known that when we have children of the same age together they do not get along as well as when we have children of different ages together. There is less rivalry and more mutual aid when the children are of different ages.

Every time a discussion is held, the marking system comes up. Publicly, there is general agreement that it is bad for both children and teachers. It delimits the learning, rather than promoting it. Furthermore, the mark is unscientific. There are data showing that when a considerable number of teachers are asked to grade the same paper, the marks given vary all the way from failure to perfection. Each school will have to work on this in its own way, but surely something better than an abstract symbol can be found to describe a living, breathing human being.

These marks are a way of applying pressure on our young, although it has been pointed out that it works only on the most conformist, least creative people. And it does not always work on them. The influence of the peer group is very strong, and often the most conforming prefer to be like their fellows, rather than meet adult standards. If it is fashionable to get a "C," these people will stop studying when they think they have achieved that goal.

Pressure causes sickness, and I believe we must abandon it if we are to learn how to live with our young. Pressure is an authoritarian device for bringing about our own adult purposes regardless of the ideas, feelings, or needs of our young. It is the road to rejection with all its accompanying evils. Of course, I realize that everybody is under some pressure, but it is best when self-induced. It is a matter of who is doing what to whom.

We Have Not Changed Significantly

The whole secondary school system has failed the American society almost completely. It has failed to take into account the changes that have taken place in our society. It has failed to profit from the many studies that have been made. It is out of step, and therefore doomed.

Surely, some who read this will say that it is not so, that there have been many changes, and that the high schools are indeed different. One can see this simply by examining the offerings of any large school. But in spite of this, our youth are presently in rebellion. They are trying, through violence, to accomplish what so many of us have tried to bring about through exhortation. How much of this rebellion is due to the use of computers for making out student programs and the many other mechanical devices that take the person out of the process cannot be determined. It is likely, however, that the remoteness of the teacher from the learner and the demands of adult society for spurious diplomas have a great deal to do with it. At any rate, these are exciting times for those of us who have been pleading for change.

No matter how many courses have been added, there is one basic ingredient lacking in our present educational system. That is the involvement of the learner in the planning of what is to be done. Without the learner having a part in the planning, he will never feel part-ownership in what has been planned. We can argue all we want to that young people do not know what is best for them, but the fact remains that nobody does anything with much enthusiasm or verve without having some part in deciding what is to be done. A person does not necessarily have to want to do what is agreed upon, but he feels quite differently if he has been consulted about it.

We have known this for a long time. This understanding brought about the core curriculum in the early 1930's, almost forty years ago. What has happened to that is well known. There are many junior high schools that profess to have a core curriculum. But more ways have been invented than I can relate to defeat the real purpose of the core which is student planning, the planning of outcomes, student evaluation. The adults do not really believe that the students will plan "what is right," and so they keep interfering until the students' true feeling for having done something is gone. I once knew a teacher with considerable reputation as a successful teacher-pupil planner. But on examination, it came about that his students always planned to study radio, a matter in which this teacher had considerable knowledge and skill. It would have been more honest, it seems to me, if he had come right out and said "Now you kids are going to learn about radio, because that is what I want to teach." Of course, there are a few of us who keep plugging for the core curriculum because it is the only method which has inherent in it the consultation of the learner about what is to be learned, but the outcome does not look very encouraging.

One wonders why, if core is good for junior high school students, it is not good for senior high. The fact is, I fear, that we do not believe that core is good for anybody. It is put into the junior high school in response to the demands of the people who know that involvement is a necessity. In senior high, however, life is real and earnest, and it is felt that we can't fool around with anything scientific because we have the time-honored curriculum to inject.

Tradition has an enormous grip on us all. It is hard to change just because the society we are supposed to serve has changed. Tradition is probably the main obstacle to change in our high schools. In order to take on a new idea it is necessary to get rid of an old one. We cannot keep our integrity and keep both.

We Continue to Reject Our Youth

Pursuing a policy of inflicting an unwanted and uncomprehended curriculum rejects a large proportion of our young and has a great deal to do with the so-called generation gap. Our young do not understand us, and in many cases they flee from us. I believe that we have no right to reject anyone. To reject is to try to make over the society which sponsors the schools. I realize that many people are very exasperating, but that is the way our society is, and educators had best make the most of it. Rejection leads to hostility and alienation from self and others.

THE HIGH SCHOOL OF THE FUTURE

So we come to the high school of the future. I cannot say that I actually predict certain changes, but only that I believe that no institution can survive forever while losing such a large proportion of its people, not to death, as in a hospital, but to life as antagonists of society. And so I hope that some of the changes suggested below will occur. I have devoted my life to this cause, and I am hopeful that events will be more persuasive than talking or writing.

We Need More Money

I believe that we must have more money so that classrooms can be reduced in size to a point where every teacher can know every child. In order to do this, the teachers may have to strike. Those in power have created the idea that it is immoral for teachers to strike, but they have done so for their own convenience. It makes it easy for them to withhold money from the schools. And, unfortunately, the schools are not so good that missing some classes constitutes an emergency. It is an emergency only to the parents, who then have to take care of their own children. That is the teachers' great strength. It is what would cause adults to vote money quickly.

I hold that this rich country can afford a good classroom, ample materials, and well-educated teachers for each group of twenty-five children in our society. There is nothing sacred about the number, but with twenty-five a teacher has a chance to know each child. Lengthening the time that a teacher is with each group would reduce the number of groups, so that it would be possible for the teacher to know even more about each individual.

We Need Changes in Teachers

Lack of money, however, is not our greatest need. We need a change in the hearts of teachers so that they will be more humanly oriented. Our problem would be fairly simple if all we had to do were get money. But we could double the salary and reduce the number of students by half and a hostile, youth-hating teacher would still be hostile. I believe this is not understood by many. The federal government has recently increased the amount of money sent to the schools, in the apparent belief that the money would make the difference. But then they have tied it up on the basis of the old curriculum, and many of the people who are getting these grants are completely unable to use them in a humanitarian way. Even if the federal money went directly to all teachers, it would only compound the evils of hostility and rejection on the part of those who feel hostile.

What we need is a new breed of teachers; this is only possible, I think, by changing the standards we hold for admitting students to the profession and by centering our teaching around the nature of the human organism instead of on those things which lie outside him.

We are often charged with being materialistic, but this term is usually misunderstood. It is true that we have a few in our society whose basic motivation is to make money, and having made plenty, to use all their energies for making more money. But there are not many of them. There is nothing wrong with a person wanting a better wage, a better house, a chance to take a few trips. It is when a person cares more about things outside than he does the person affected that he becomes truly materialistic. To cite an example from the teaching profession, if a teacher cares more about reading, or mathematics, or geography than he does about the learner, this is materialism.

The high school of the future will have to have teachers who concern themselves with the whole child. This is a cliché, but we cannot abandon it because it has often been mentioned. We shall have to keep at it until it has come into action. We shall have to come to the realization that the learner has emotions—fears, wants, needs, and so on. We shall have to abandon the old idea that this is none of the teacher's business and that his function is only to crowd in as much subject matter as possible. There is no such thing as a cognitive self apart from the rest of the organism. Stuffing in the subject matter without regard to the rest of the learner simply does not work.

Each child has his own set of fears, hopes, and needs. Each individual is unique and therefore acquires knowledge on his own basis. This has been provided by nature; it is the human being's real reason to be. Nature cherishes uniqueness, while the schools have been trying to repeal it. The fact that no two people can learn exactly the same thing and come through with the same answers has been the despair of teachers as far back as teaching has existed.

We Need Education for Citizenship

Our schools, in order to survive, will have to come to a new understanding of what it means to teach citizenship. One of the primary purposes for founding and supporting the schools is based on the belief that an uneducated electorate cannot support a democracy.

We now, however, interpret good citizenship as doing what the teacher wants. The student who always does exactly as he is told, who never does anything creative, who is a complete conformist is the one who gets the best grades in citizenship. But these people do not see themselves as good citizens, only as people who know how to get along with the teacher.

In order for one to learn to be a good citizen, he has to see himself as a citizen. This calls for his having some part in the operation of the school. This calls for a genuine system of student participation in school government. This is not so hard to achieve as may at first appear. It means that the adults in the school have to have real confidence in the general rightness and goodness of young people.

The great obstacle to the achievement of this condition is the teacher or administrator who takes pride in the fact that he has always run things his way with no interference from anybody. The young people do not want especially to interfere, but only to feel that they have been respected and consulted. Most student governments are shams. We try to make the students believe that they are having something to say about the curriculum, or the rules, without this actually being the case. This is doomed to failure, as anyone ought to know. To undertake to fool a whole schoolful of young people is rash indeed.

When I was working on my doctoral thesis, I visited a school which was nationally famous for its student government. I was given royal treatment and spent the whole day going to council meetings and meeting with the students and the teachers involved. When I left at the close of the school day, the principal said that of course the reason for their success was that he wouldn't stand for any nonsense.

Teachers and administrators have invented many ways in which to see to it that nobody but the "best" people can aspire to office in their student council. They have not hesitated to disfranchise people. Sometimes, the adults in the school prepare lists from which the students must choose council members. More common is the grade requirement. So that a group of really "nice" people gets into office.

The school is a natural place for young people to practice being citizens. It has many of the complexities of a modern society. The school has the opportunity, provided the adults in it have the courage to use it, of giving every young person a genuine chance to practice being a good citizen, and to see himself as such.

If we grant suffrage to all who have reached the age of eighteen we will take another big step in the direction of making young people active citizens. If we assume that our present methods of teaching citizenship do some good, it certainly does not help for the young person to go for three or more years in a void. This argument, it seems to me, is far more potent than those so often advanced. For example, I do not think the argument that "if he is old enough to fight he is old enough to vote" has much validity. Nobody should ever have to fight, but when it becomes inevitable, there is no connection between fighting and citizenship.

We must have, in the high school of the future, a new concept of the meaning of freedom. I do not mean freedom to do just as one pleases; nobody has that, or ever can have it as long as he lives anywhere near anybody else. Even the hermit has to go into town once in a while for supplies made and marketed by other people. And it is getting harder and harder to find a place to be a hermit. What I mean by freedom is the opportunity to make choices.

In many of our present-day high schools, the young people have no choice but to follow the teachers' orders. The young person who does his homework, however inane it may be, is not exercising freedom but simply following orders. Each human being is uniquely purposive. But there is no point in being purposive in the absence of freedom. Plato said centuries ago, "A slave is one who gets his purposes from somebody else."

It seems to me that in society, and in the schools in particular, freedom is currently in a bad way. The routine method of textbook, assignment, recitation, and examination does not provide for freedom. It can only be provided through consultation and through learners having a chance to work on matters which make sense to them. There is no shortcut, no economy, in the education of our young. Adults will squirm and try to avoid this fact, but to no avail.

We Need a New Curriculum

Many of our young people are now in rebellion. Most of their hostility is directed toward schools of all kinds. And the major complaint is that the old curriculum has no meaning, no appeal for them. When they sabotage, they usually pick a school to destroy. We have long known this, but we do not seem to get the message. It seems to me that the high school of the future will have to take this matter into account.

Adults will have to acquire a new concept of the nature of subject matter. They will have to see the difference between subject matter and skills. The three R's, for example, are skills, not subject matter. Reading, penmanship, and some mathematics are good things to know. They are not, however, absolutely essential for survival. I cherish them for everyone, but they are not worth the destruction of the personalities of our young. It is better to come through with a whole, well child than to have young people who are frightened, rebellious, and hostile. I contend that our frenetic attitude toward our young causes most of our reading problems. This is just one item in the whole adult compulsion to inject what, for centuries, has been called education.

We shall have to come to realize that the proper subject matter for each individual consists of the things nearest to him and/or those matters of most concern to him. For example, the child may have someone who means a great deal to him in the armed forces in Vietnam. He is likely, then, to be interested in that war, its causes and consequences. When this is the case, it is difficult indeed to interest him in the wars of the ancient Greeks. Adults often attach too great an importance to chronological order of events and so inhibit learning.

It is not only history that is taught backward in these times, but many other subjects. For example, geography is taught without considering people; only climate, imports, exports, and so on. We shall have to get an entirely different view of subject matter, individualizing it as much as possible, using textbooks as resources instead of bibles, and finding as many ways as possible for our young to do things, rather than just talk about them.

We shall have to lose faith in the lecture method of instruction. It is possible, of course, for an occasional lecturer to be so fascinating as to hold the attention of most of his listeners. But in a captive audience, which is universal in school, there is nothing to prevent minds from wandering far afield while the lecturer drones on.

WHAT HUMANIZING EDUCATION MEANS

Our young are leaving us in great numbers with nowhere else to go. And they are doing this in spite of all our urgings, protestations, and warnings. Recently, there has been a good deal of federal money spent in an effort to get young people who left school to come back and finish what they already rejected. A good many were talked into coming back, but few indeed remained more than a semester. The trouble was that they could no longer tolerate being containers instead of people.

Much has been said recently about humanizing education. I do not need to quote references here to show what research has come to show. There was a large conference of educators recently, the principal topic or theme of which was "To Humanize Education, The Person in the Process." Many school people understand the meaning of this theme and believe in it, but few seem to know what to do about it. The old blinders are still on, and holding them fast.

I shall now attempt to say what humanizing education means to me. We must first of all look to the learner to see what he is like before deciding how we can best help him. And we must see ourselves as helpers, not as people who are going to do things to people whether or not it makes any sense to them. "This will be good for you, whether you like it or not, I, in my infinite wisdom know best." This is what too many of us have been saying for too long. Now we must say "I am here to help you. What can I do?" This makes a vast difference in how a teacher behaves.

When we look to our students, we learn many things. In the first place, we see that there are no two alike. They can be grouped on the basis of similar interests and they can happily work together, but this does not mean that they do not need personal attention. Some need more than others, but they all need some. It has been said that no child ever became delinquent who had one adult who really cared about him and in whom he had confidence. This adult usually has to be the teacher. Teachers too often say that "caring" for children should be the function of the parents. But there is too much emotional content in the parent-child relationship. The attitude of teachers who like to proclaim that they are there to teach and not to wet-nurse the young must be abandoned; primarily, because it will not work.

When we look to the learner, we are apt to find some who have been so badly damaged psychologically that it is difficult to reach them. This calls for patience and reconciliation to the fact that all teachers, including our most authoritarian ones, have their losers. Some teachers like to boast of how many successful people they have taught, never asking themselves how many of their former students are in jail or in mental institutions. We shall, in the high school of the future, learn to count our losers along with our winners.

When we look to the learner we shall find that he is seeking love from an adult. The kind of love that involves caring about what happens to our young in a way that shows enough so that the love-seeking youth can really feel it. The teacher may have to be the one person in the life of a learner who can fill that role. Of course, not every young person needs personal attention from the teacher. The ones who do need it are readily identifiable. I think that those who need special attention can be listed, and the faculty of any school can divide them so that no one person will get special attention from every teacher.

All of this precludes any form of mass education. Mass education implies, or requires, that the learner give his full attention either in listening or looking. This can never be achieved on account of the uniqueness of each individual. We have invented various tests and quizzes in order to pass out praise or blame. But it takes more than these to make the unique individual look or listen.

The form of education advocated here will be expensive from the point of view of the first outlay. But it would be a great economy in the long run when we consider what our society spends because of the penny-pinching educational system we have at present. There would be a great reduction in our expenditures for all of the agencies that try to combat hostile youth. Think of what we spend for police, social workers, courts, and jails, to say nothing of our great loss in human resources. From a purely economic point of view, people are our great resource, and when a life is rendered useless, it is impossible to estimate the loss to everybody. We are all bound together, and when we lose the potential of one of us, we all lose.

This is how it looks to me. I have spent my whole life trying to make the high school keep up with the times. And I hope with all my heart that it will do so. We need, however, to have more than just better facilities, lower class loads, and better pay. We need a change in the hearts of teachers, so that they will become aware of the responsibility they have assumed and will try to do something about it.

part 4

The Program of the School of the Future

chapter 12

Morton Alpren

The Curriculum in
"The High School
of the Future"

This essay attempts to be both personal and deal with ideas. My memorial writing to Kim Wiles is based upon the fact that Kim cared for both people and ideas. He never shirked from the dialogue that led to agreements and disagreements. I would not wish to write about the man or his ideas without the two being in some kind of joint context—and neither would he wish it.

In order to view Kim's curriculum thoughts, the approach used will be to first examine how he viewed schools and society, then how he viewed curriculum in general, and, finally, how he viewed curriculum through his "High School of the Future" chapter.

SCHOOLS AND SOCIETY

Kim Wiles was a practical writer. He got down to cases promptly and spent little time answering the question, "What are schools for?" This does not mean that he did not raise the question of himself, answer it in many ways through his classes and, indirectly, in writings. I think it's safe to say that Kim had a primary concern for the individual in a democratic society. This pervaded his work. To Kim, an ever-improv-

153

ing, participatory democracy was a desired school focus. The individual guidance (non-directive) of each youngster was paramount. And all of this was of one piece.

In a formal, philosophical sense, Kim was a reconstructionist. The school's role as he saw it was to help reshape its society by its open, up-to-date learning challenges. The school was not only to be a democratically run organization but was to serve as a model laboratory for the society. To Kim, an individual's intellect was not to be divorced from his values. He pioneered a new perspective in supervision by placing the job's content into a human context rather than a task-oriented one. Witness the table of contents of the text *Supervision for Better Schools* which reveals a writing organized about the five skills of a supervisor: (1) Leadership, (2) Human Relations, (3) Group Process, (4) Personnel Administration, (5) Evaluation.[1]

In effect, human values either supercede or incorporate intellect. The writing makes almost no mention of the knowledge, if any, that a supervisor should have of the content that teachers should be responsible for in helping pupils learn. It is more important, in Kim's view, that an educational leader be concerned about human values than about any prescribed learnings (for teacher or pupil).

Kim accepted William H. Kilpatrick's thesis that it is most important that supervisors work with teachers in the same manner as the latter work with pupils. The process is more important than the product. This has vast implications for curriculum and curriculum development.

Those who either knew Kim or read his works would never dispute his desire to influence our society through formal schooling. Few can berate the societal and individual values to which he aspired. If one wishes to find fault, he can do so more by questioning the attainability of the dream—less, its desirability. Kim dealt with a school and society that he wished to see—not the school and society of today.

THE CURRICULUM

To Kim Wiles, the school's job is to provide for all kinds of growth: attitudes and values, intellectual, physical, moral, and the like. Furthermore, one does not separate or give priorities to a particular kind of growth because all are important. (I suspect that if we had to guess which was most important to Kim, it would have been attitudes and values.) In this light, Kim defines curriculum as all the school experiences provided for children and youth under the guidance of school authorities. These experiences would then include what a given society, school, and staff deemed most appropriate to serve all kinds of growth.

My own definition is at variance with Wiles' and most others associated with curriculum writings. This is because I do not see the school reconstructing its society so much as being a forward-going part of its society. These views were stated as such in my own curriculum writing[2] and I repeat them here so that the reader will know my bias in this attempt to review Kim Wiles' orientation to schooling and curriculum. I fully realize that neither of us is right or wrong—but we differ on this important point.

To state that Wiles' views on supervision are in one book, on curriculum in a second book, and on teaching in a third is only partially accurate. Kim Wiles' thinking was too wholistic to be so neatly compartmentalized, even though these books are devoted to their separate subjects.

As stated earlier in this essay, his supervision text does not refer to curriculum in the table of contents—nor does it appear in the index. The same is true of the original edition of his text on teaching.[3] As with his supervision book, the table of contents is devoted to the human role of a teacher, with skills in human relations, group work, evaluation, individualizing instruction, cooperation, and self-improvement. The index does not contain reference to curriculum.

And yet we know that Kimball Wiles saw curriculum development essentially as a teacher function. This is stated explicitly and is implied in all his writings and speeches. Why not? If human values, involvements, and participatory democracy are to grow, authority must be decentralized. In effect, democratic values supercede disciplinary content, and this is consistent with Kim's gestalt.

"THE HIGH SCHOOL OF THE FUTURE" AND THE CURRICULUM

In treating these ideas, it helps to begin with the recognition of two major movements that have occurred since the writing of Kim's last book. One is the curriculum movement reflected in Bruner's *Process of Education*.[4] While the movement's origins existed prior to Bruner's writing, the writing gave both rationale and impetus for the subject curriculum changes of the present decade. The second movement is the black, poverty disadvantaged concern. This, too, had its origins prior to Wiles' curriculum book, but the main thrust belongs to the 1960's.

In terms of Bruner's work, one might wonder why Kim chose to ignore it? Kim's bibliographies include other 1961 writings (Bruner's publication date). It could well be that his rejection of the importance of the disciplines for the school curriculum did not permit his objectivity to prevail. It does seem safe to state that this educational-curriculum direction was not one in which he was interested.

On the other hand, the social-educational concern that has led to the current interest in curriculum and instruction for pupils in ghetto schools is one that Kim Wiles would have cherished and shared leadership in. This movement contains all the ingredients that he stood for, viz., decentralized curriculum controls, participation and involvement of minority groups, and the need for an unprejudiced kind of society and schooling. To those who knew him, racism was anathema to Kim Wiles. He fought it with every breath.

In summation, to the movements that followed Kim's major writings, I would say that he would tend to reject the disciplinary curriculum movements forwarded by Bruner and be wholly at home with the present curriculum advocations for disadvantaged and black youth.

In "The High School of the Future," Wiles' introductory remarks refer to the knowledge we need "about learning, adolescents, the social trends, the new technology." In other words, we need to know and use our knowledge about educational psychology, sociology, and instructional applications of newer media. To my orientation, only in the realm of the last notion do we approach the content of the curriculum and, even here, Kim shows more concern for curriculum development and its implementation than for the very substance or content of the curriculum itself.

In discussing needed research, he refers to "the type of secondary curriculum needed" as requiring research in twelve areas of study, noted as questions, and ranging from mental health to assessing pupil growth. The closest his concerns come to the curriculum itself are in questions dealing with the differing perceptions of teachers and pupils about curriculum content, skills needed by all who receive diplomas, and the content and skills which can be taught by teaching machines and mass media. In reporting on this, I do not mean to denigrate the importance of the research areas advocated. However, I believe that his failure to wish to research the contributions of concepts and disciplinary structures, or Bruner's hypothesis that any subject can be taught to any child in some intellectually honest way, was because he preferred to relegate this task to the academic community.

Kim hoped to see high schools of the future foster development through (1) values, (2) skills, and (3) understandings that would (4) allow each individual to make a specialized contribution to society. It is indeed a tribute to the man's well-organized mind to note how he develops these ideas.

For value development, a specialist teacher will work with pupils for six hours weekly in "Analysis Groups." When the specialist teacher is not working with his three groups of 33 pupils each, he will use his time counseling each individually and/or meeting with parents. The demands on the talents of this teacher go beyond his skill in personal and group relationships. He is also responsible for following up on the knowledges and concepts to be learned in explorations of cultural heritage. Does this not call for a super-teacher? Yes, it does. It is part of Kim's dream for our youth and the society.

For developing skills, technicians and librarians will make use of technological hardware. (Note that Kim does not trust even skill learning entirely to non-humanized curriculum implementation.) In addition, skill expectations are prescribed and must be mastered, although the pace is child- rather than adult-determined.

Whereas Kim does not provide specific curriculum prescriptions about values and attitudinal learnings, he does come closer to this in skill development. The skills include specific expectations, and mathematics, foreign languages, and grammar are cited to reveal curriculum content. He also cites inclusion of skills in scientific processes, and I suspect that this would lead to questioning by some science educators who do not accept hardware applications for the learning of their subject's skills.

A third of the proposed program is to provide each high school student with the basic knowledge of the culture. The notion of *basic* knowledge is enhanced by discouraging discussions relating to cultural heritage learnings and relegating the function to analysis group specialists. The knowledge presentations take place in very large groups with specialist lecturers and the use of newer media.

While one may question the idea of placing so much significance on the role of the analysis group specialist and the value orientations of the concepts and ideas derived from the knowledges, it is hard not to admire the thoughts about school personnel preparation.

In this plan, one who prepares for teaching decides on the kind of interest he has, specializes in one or two kinds of functions he is to perform for youth, and, while having much demanded of him in such performance, is not expected to be the jack-of-all trades typical of today's teacher. While I question the departure from subject emphasis, it is hard to dispute the beauty of methodological expertise in this organization of personnel. There are few goals for youth that are left unexamined. One may question the attainability or the priorities—but hardly the worthwhileness or the organization of the ideas.

The three elements discussed above are supplemented by the need to prepare specialists. Wiles here calls for helping youth diagnose their directions as vocational or academic (these terms are my interpretation rather than Kim's). Specializations provide for work experiences for some, intensive academic-intellectual learnings for others. All will graduate without ceremony since individual rates of learning will be respected to allow for completion of high school at age fifteen or twenty. However, graduation will not be whimsical. All will be required to complete experiences in the four elements of the program outlined.

In retrospect, Kim Wiles did not neglect curriculum content when he dealt with his program. On the other hand, his lack of comment on the newer programs and neglect of curriculum content in needed research does appear paradoxical. Is it that Kim was disrespectful of intellectual concerns? I think not. Is it that he was so obsessed about a better democracy and better world for people that some of his intellectual concerns were submerged? Perhaps. Or is it that intellect and emotions were all of a single piece to Kim? Most likely.

I think it most important to note that his analysis groups required that the teacher be expert in values and attitudes as well as in knowledges and concepts from disciplinary learnings. These entities are not to be separated in the learnings of our youth.

To repeat, the desirability of Kim's ideas is most difficult to question. Their attainability can be questioned. On the other hand, even this most legitimate area for questioning must be left in doubt. Progress requires dreamers. Progress of the kind that is designed to benefit man requires dedicated dreamers who have the ability to organize and communicate their ideas.

References

1. Kimball Wiles, *Supervision for Better Schools* (Englewood Cliffs, N.J.: Prentice-Hall, Inc., 1950).
2. Morton Alpren, ed., *The Subject Curriculum: Grades K-12* (Columbus, Ohio: Charles E. Merrill Books, Inc., 1967).
3. Kimball Wiles, *Teaching for Better Schools* (Englewood Cliffs, N.J.: Prentice-Hall, Inc., 1952).
4. Jerome Bruner, *Process of Education* (Cambridge, Mass.: Harvard University Press, 1961).

chapter 13

Robert H. Anderson

Is the Wiles 1963 Model Still Futuristic?

The essays in this volume will all have been prepared during the middle months of 1968. In view of the time lag that almost invariably occurs between the first-draft writing and the actual publication of a book, it would seem that Kimball Wiles wrote his chapter on the high school of the future sometime between mid-1961 and mid-1962. Something like six or seven years has, therefore, elapsed since Kim offered his forecast. In that interval, of course, Kim continued to sharpen his thinking on the issues he raised and we know that he had begun to move in some new directions before February, 1968. Furthermore, his 1963 chapter obviously had an impact between 1963 and 1968 on prevailing secondary school practice and, therefore, some of the ideas with which we were comfortable in 1968, but which were by comparison new and unfamiliar when Kim first wrote them, seem upon reexamination less bold or creative than indeed they once were.

So it has been for every forward-looking educator in these times of remarkable change. We are told, and we see little reason to deny, that knowledge in all fields is being generated at such a pace that half of what we now know (in the aggregate) was not known a decade ago. This would suggest that a very substantial portion of a book written six or seven years ago would under ordinary circumstances be signif-

icantly outdated. In the face of this awesome probability, it is remarkable that so much of Wiles' chapter remains useful and authentic. That
a few of his points now seem less tenable, by contrast, is scarcely to be
lamented but rather to be construed as evidence that even the best of
our leadership (and Kim surely belongs in that group) has at times
been puzzled or even misled by the events and the feelings of our
time.

It is hard to imagine a time in which educational change has occurred more rapidly or in a greater variety of ways. In October, 1967,
editors of the *Phi Delta Kappan* offered the opinion that "the current
decade is undoubtedly the most yeasty period in educational history."[1]
Other commentators have consistently used adjectives like "revolutionary," "unprecedented," and "radical" in describing the components
of educational reform and the societal upheavals that have inspired
or accompanied them. Often, the described changes proved better on
paper than in practice; but nonetheless it seems fair to say that few if
any moments in history have seen such significant changes in the ways
of schooling children as have the years which preceded Kim's death.
As one of the most respected voices of his time, Kim contributed to
these changes in countless ways, and even now his chapter offers more
sound and practical advice than do the majority of more recently published statements on secondary education.

FROM AN ELEMENTARY SCHOOL POINT OF VIEW

As one who works primarily in the field of elementary education, I
find a number of ideas and convictions in Kim's secondary school fore-
case that are relevant as well to the world of younger children. With
the possible exception of number eight, for example, his list of twelve
items of needed research (*The Changing Curriculum of the American
High School,* p. 300) is perfectly applicable to the elementary school
situation. If anything, some of these items probably deserve to be
given even greater emphasis in research dealing with pre-adolescent
children than in research dealing with youth of high school age. The
fostering of mental health, for example, is a function for which society
increasingly holds the nursery school, the kindergarten, and the early
primary period particularly responsible. Similarly, there is growing
evidence to the effect that unless the teachers of young children help
them to develop and to release their creative potential, it may be virtually impossible for teachers in the secondary schools to develop or
to restore this creative spirit.

Going down Kim's list of twelve items, we find that essentially the same argument may be offered with respect to self-direction and the ability to deal effectively with change. On the whole, it seems fair (although regrettable) to say that in the typical American classroom, youngsters have all too few opportunities to make decisions concerning what they will study, the way they will go about their work, or even the criteria against which their performance will be judged. For the most part, children do in the schools as they are told, and the unwillingness of teachers to permit unorthodox exploratory activity or deviations from the usual pattern of seated, indoor, verbal learning activities tends to press children into a mold with little chance to conjure or to practice alternatives.

Even the opportunities for person-to-person communications are peculiarly limited and controlled in the typical elementary or secondary classroom. There is no need here to review all the studies which show that teachers do too much of the talking, that what passes for teacher-pupil interaction is often little different from an oral-testing situation, and that children have too few opportunities for small group interaction in situations where they set the rules. Happily, there has been a healthy spurt in research and discussion concerning the group process and person-to-person interactions within classrooms. However, we still have many unanswered questions in the general field of communication and interpersonal relationships.

Sixth on Kim's list is a provocative question about the differing perceptions of teachers and pupils concerning the curriculum and the transactions within the classroom. Professors in the universities, no less than the students whose rebellious actions have captured headlines through the past year, recognize all too well the significance and pertinence of Kim's question. We are even told that the rebellion of college students is only a foretaste of rebellion that will soon be spreading into the secondary schools as well. Invariably, the confrontation between teacher and student, whether in a college or secondary school setting, grows out of dissatisfaction not only with general management policies, but also with the curriculum itself and the general environment of the classroom within which the curriculum is experienced. Although political and other issues undoubtedly have a central significance when students revolt, and although many teachers have labored mightily to produce better curricula and improve the classroom situation, it seems nonetheless fair to comment that, for the most part, one's sympathies must be with the students rather than with the teachers when the relevance of curriculum is being questioned.

This leads to an acknowledgment that Kim's seventh area for investigation, concerning the essential cultural heritage, remains a knotty and unsolved question in our time. Similarly, his eighth area involving the skills that all youngsters should have before passing along to the next level of education is one deserving of continuing study. Though these were raised as questions related to the secondary school, it can easily be seen that even in number eight, as worded, we find a question relevant to the elementary school.

In items nine, ten, and eleven, Kim raises questions about the appropriate role of technology and mass media in the educational program, and about those things that are better done within a person-to-person tutorial or group situation. Again, these are questions as vital to the work of elementary teachers as they are to the teachers of adolescents; and in these categories, it is a pleasure to report, we now seem much closer to some workable answers than we appear to have been a decade ago.

The final item in Kim's list of research topics has to do with the measurement of pupil growth. This too, is a universal question and one on which some valuable work has been reported during the past few years; and yet, for all the progress that has been made in educational research, it would seem that all too little is still known and too much of present practice is based upon incomplete or inadequate evidence.

CONTINUOUS PROGRESS:
A CONSISTENT IDEAL

Although Kimball Wiles rarely used the vocabulary which has been associated with the movement toward non-graded schools, and although he was even a bit skeptical that organizational changes are or can be a significant part of a more fundamental educational reform, it would seem to this observer that the high school of which Kimball Wiles dreamed would be essentially a non-graded school. Through his emphasis on releasing creative potential, through his almost obsessive concern with the development of human values in children, and through his eagerness to provide young people with opportunities for self-direction and for meaningful interaction with fellow students, Kim was at least indirectly endorsing the type of organizational environment within which each individual youngster is accepted for what he is and given an opportunity to become whatever his inborn potential permits. Especially in urging that guidance and teaching functions should be brought closer together, and in his insistence upon concern for mental health, he joins himself both spiritually and operationally with those who have advocated a loosening of graded structure and the creation of a more open, fluent environment within which each child's continuous progress is more easily insured.

In one section he argues, in support of such arrangements, that youngsters would spend more or less time in the secondary school depending upon their success in reaching certain desired stages of development. Throughout his book, he is consistently reminding us that youngsters will be different in their needs and talents and that the program he describes is in no sense intended to affect all children in the same way. Though he says relatively little about the actual basis of evaluation, it is quite clear (especially from his other writings) that the application of conventional grade-level-expectancy standards to the work of all children must be abandoned in favor of tailor-made evaluation programs. In much of what he says about the need for re-vamping teacher education programs, it is also clear that he hopes and expects that future teachers will pay little heed to the conventional strictures and the dangerous assumptions associated with gradedness.

THE PROPOSED "ANALYSIS GROUP"

One of the most interesting propositions in Wiles' chapter has to do with the so called "Analysis Group" comprised of eleven pupils and a skilled teacher-counselor. The "Analysis Group" is described as the basic element of the educational program, and Wiles commits himself with what seems like exceptional fervor to the notion that this arrangement will evolve as the best means of performing the values-development function. This intriguing idea probably deserves partic-ular comment by those of us who have had a special interest in various patterns of pupil grouping.

Certain assumptions underlie the proposed arrangement. One of these has to do with the optimum size of a group, another has to do with the composition of that group, and a third has to do with the question of the group's continuity over time. From my experience, I would judge Wiles is on stronger ground with reference to the size of the group than he is with reference to the other two assumptions. Ex-perience in both elementary and secondary schools over the past fif-teen or twenty years tends to confirm that a discussion group in order to be viable and productive should be limited in size to a dozen or so persons, certainly fifteen at the absolute maximum. Some researchers have even commented that the number twelve, which is associated with the jury system, may have been selected in primitive societies over centuries of experience as the best number (at maximum) for groups which are obliged to make decisions. By proposing that there be eleven pupils and one teacher, Wiles was either intentionally or accidentally honoring this observation. There is every reason to believe that the analysis groups would indeed be the right size for the functions Wiles has proposed.

One runs into problems, however, when considering the suggestion that each analysis group should consist of pupils all the same age. Granted that youngsters of the same age have numerous problems and needs in common, one wonders nevertheless whether there might not be greater value in belonging to a group which includes not only some other youngsters of one's own age but also a few youngsters who are either older or younger, or both. One problem of the conventionally graded school, which has become all the more evident as educators have experimented with multi-aged classes, is that the present system tends to lock children of the same age into a rather closed society which lacks perspective (in some respects) and tends to isolate itself from the adjoining age groups. Certain intellectual as well as social disadvantages obtain in a narrowly defined age group, the evidence suggests, although few really safe generalizations are possible at this stage of our profession's experience with pupil grouping alternatives.

Especially since Kimball Wiles wants his analysis group to remain essentially permanent over time, I would at this juncture incline to recommend that some schools experiment with analysis groups on a multi-age basis, in order that some of the assumptions and assertions in the foregoing paragraph might be more adequately tested. In schools where the analysis groups have already been created in response to Wiles' recommendation, it should by now be possible not only to assess the practicality of the general idea, but also to engage in some productive speculation concerning the optimum membership arrangements for such groups.

On the whole, it should be acknowledged that the analysis group as a major arrangement within the high school is a creative idea worth developing. That teachers should be recruited for the relatively exclusive purpose of dealing with analysis groups and for individual counseling with the pupils from three such groups (and their parents) is another creative idea which deserves to be implemented and evaluated.

OTHER ORGANIZATIONAL FEATURES

Several other dimensions of the proposed high school, particularly those that relate to organizational structure, deserve special mention in this brief review of Kim's thinking. Already noted is that many of

Kim's ideas are consistent with the viewpoint of those who would eliminate the philosophy and the machinery of the graded school. Now we may observe that although Wiles was generally silent on the topic of team teaching, indeed even inclined to be a bit skeptical of its merit, much of what he proposes is consistent with the earlier work of Lloyd Trump and others who sought to break American secondary education away from the customary pattern of autonomous teachers working in classrooms of uniform size and with class groups numbering somewhere between twenty and thirty youngsters. In fact, so much of the argument in his chapter is hostile to this conventional pattern that it is quite clear that Kimball Wiles at this stage of his thinking was no longer loyal to the conventional pattern of horizontal school organization.

Only a few examples are necessary to confirm this argument. For one, the analysis groups are a significant deviation from the conventional pattern. Acquisition of skills with the help of mechanical equipment in materials centers under the librarians and their mechanical technicians is another example of deviation from the conventional. The use of large classes (for example in the cultural heritage program) taught by television, films, or highly skilled lecturers in person is yet another deviation. Although all too little is said about the school plant (see p. 9 of this text), the building as described would have rooms of many different sizes. Virtually none of the teaching would be done in conventional-size classrooms, and seminars and individual research would emerge very early in the evolution of the new high school. In short, virtually all of the proposed arrangements are substantially in accord with the recommendations that are ordinarily associated with the advocacy of cooperative teaching.

It is probably significant that, in spite of his commitment to large group and small group arrangements, Kim makes scarcely any reference to the possibilities for and the desirability of cooperative planning and cooperative evaluation within the high school staff. For the most part, his chapter seems to assume that teachers will be autonomous, that they will tend to specialize in one or another types of teaching functions proposed. To this observer, it is a flaw in the Wiles proposals that there is no direct reference to teacher-teacher interaction as one of the most important elements in the life of the new high school. By implying that each teacher will have his special and separate role to perform, and by failing to suggest that (as in the case of the pupil) there is great potential value to themselves as persons and as developing professionals in working more closely with other teachers, Wiles neglects or at least overlooks one of the most important arguments that has been offered in support of cooperative teaching. Quite apart from the greater flexibility (for example, in using school resources or in grouping and scheduling pupils) that results from teacher cooperation, the opportunity for continuous interchange of professional ideas and criticisms is one of the most significant benefits that teachers may expect when they work together in teams.

Again, it should be remembered that Wiles' chapter was written in a time when cooperative teaching was a relatively undeveloped idea with an inadequate literature, and when most of the authority figures in the "Establishment" were inclined to be skeptical if not hostile. Though development still proceeds slowly, it seems significant that at this time the discussion of organizational alternatives is much more peaceful, and there is growing acceptance of the probability that various patterns of collaborative teaching (planning and evaluating) will predominate in the future now being planned. Wiles must have come to this conclusion himself toward the end, for in this 1963 sample he has already set down a series of recommendations with which the conventional definition of horizontal school organization is incompatible.

One other development which has grown in importance since 1963 is the inclusion of various non-professional and paraprofessional personnel in the work force of the school. Although Wiles makes only one or two references to this trend, it seems quite clear that he anticipated it and that he would have given strong support to the idea of supplementing and augmenting the work of regularly certified teachers.

Finally, I would add that although Kim's chapter happens not to include it except by implication, the need for expert and sophisticated supervision in the high school of the future is particularly great. The school of which he dreamed would be an exciting, invigorating, constantly changing place, and the people who work in it would generate questions and create problems much more interesting and challenging than those on which secondary school principals and supervisors now tend to concentrate. It follows, therefore, that these leadership people will have to be selected more carefully and given more excellent training, both pre-service and inservice, than their predecessors. This is a job that would have appealed to Kim—and he would certainly have done it well. His work and his writing in this field will inform us for a long time to come. For those of us who remain in the battle, this is a most welcome source of strength.

References

1. *Phi Delta Kappan*, XLIX (October, 1967), p. 66.

chapter 14

Hollis A. Moore, Jr.

In Search of Self

Predictions and prognostications are commonplace in our educational literature. Even a little guesswork crops up occasionally. One remembers, also, impressive statements of the Educational Policies Commission which outlined desirable future courses of curriculum development and school organization. Through the 1930's and 40's special ad hoc commissions with predictable regularity published projections of five-year or ten-year "plans of action" for professional associations. A few writers and a great many speech makers have found a convenient rubric for startling audiences by predicting changes in our way of life—the description of what life will be like at a certain point in time: everything from disposable clothing to selective genetic strains.

Common as futuristic approaches have been, the forecast of "The High School of the Future" presented in 1963 by Kim Wiles has an unusual quality. Probably for several reasons. For one thing, he differs from the speech makers by passing up the opportunity to startle the audience with predictions which border on science fiction. The forecasts make sense—have a believable quality. Moreover, he makes his forecast in sequential terms; he seems not so much to vault into the future over the heads of fifteen years but rather to move logically from present discernible trends. And finally, he sticks to the subject: the high school.

There's bound to be a rather special, poignant quality to the Kimball Wiles forecast, because unlike his colleagues' predictions of changes in

167

the coming years, this one will now stand as his firm and final forecast. He will not be privileged—as will some of us—to explain away the near misses or alter published speculations in the light of later, unpredicted developments.

WILES' FORECAST OF THE LATE SIXTIES

It may very well be that in 1975 some other part of Chapter 15 will appear to be the more significant contribution, but as I read the chapter in the fall of 1968, the most meaningful section to me is the one on the analysis of experiences and values. Without historical perspective it would be easy for one to miss how great were Wiles' powers of perception when he predicted:

> In the late sixties, it will begin to be recognized that unless citizens have values they accept, understand, and can apply, the social structure will disintegrate until authoritarian controls are applied. To counter the danger of collapse of the democratic way of life, the school will be assigned the task of making as sure that each child develops a set of values as it does that he is able to read. The Analysis Group will evolve as the best means of performing the values development function.

Remember, this effort to help students in search of self was written prior to the start of the current five-year period of violence. This chapter was written before the murder of either of the Kennedy's, the riots in Detroit and Newark, the assassination of Martin Luther King, or the confrontation in Chicago in August of 1968. Wiles sensed the seriousness of our problem before it became acute.

I suppose it's an open question whether the analysis group as described by Wiles is the organizational vehicle of the high school which is most useful for accomplishing the purposes described in his chapter. But there certainly can be no question as to the need for some concerted effort to bring about a new moral tone in our society. The need is unquestionably greater even than it was five years ago when Wiles identified it. In the last half-decade, we have seen the phenomenon of violence reach crisis proportion—from napalm in Vietnam to night sticks in Grant Park. And the nation is unlikely to let the schools slip by without accepting a share of the responsibility for such immoral behavior or its causes or both.

There is today in our nation a deep concern with the phenomenon of violence and brutality—expressed in some quarters as a need "to return to law and order"; elsewhere as a matter of controlling "crime on the streets"; on Sunday morning (and in my part of the country on Sunday night and Wednesday night as well) as a need to return to the fundamentals of the old-time gospel. But whatever the parameters of its definition may be, the core issue is clear: there is a crisis of confidence in our system of justice and a need for new moral and spiritual tone to our corporate life.

Clearly, violence is too much a part of our life. Sections of cities have been burned; stores have been looted and burglarized; students as well as their out-of-school contemporaries (younger and older) have rejected customary mores of sexual behavior and thus far have found no substitute morality; the entertainment establishment—especially TV—serves up a never-ending diet of violence and combat; students in some of our colleges and universities have thrown in the towel on improving the present structure of education and have chosen to destroy rather than to reform. I could go on, but the case is a strong one that something is obviously wrong. Can the educational system find acceptable answers?

One explanation for current stress and tension is described in several articles by Toffler as "future shock."[1] This he defines as a time phenomenon, brought on by volcanic dislocations, twists, and reversals —not merely in our social and economic structure, but also in our value standards and in the way individuals perceive reality. Such changes crush many people, bewilder and disorient others. We have seen it with each announcement of new nuclear weaponry, organ transplants for prolongation of life, genetic discoveries, population control, jungle warfare. It's like culture shock in your own home town.

McLuhan explains it this way: A pre-school child grows up in a twentieth-century world of adult, international experience—watching TV from his playpen. (Later, of course, he is "contained" in a nineteenth-century school and curriculum.) "And this interface," says McLuhan, "between TV and school is a frontier that generates violence because it forces the child to mold a new image of himself. Violence, then, is the quest for identity inspired by technical innovations. Wherever there is violence, by definition there are people who feel that their images of themselves have been endangered or effaced."[2]

It is our conditioning that is all wrong. We still think of goals and identity as some nineteenth-century literate version of privacy and separateness. Yet, we are technologically creating a microscopic togetherness by removing all the spaces between the people on the planet. It is out of this type of situation that violence becomes the quest for identity, inspired by technical innovations.

It is worrisome that we have few clues as to what kind of behavior is rational under the circumstances. Obviously, our problem of counseling and assisting pupils to mature emotionally is a complicated one.

One approach is addition to the curriculum—planned ways in which we can simulate life in the future, create opportunities to speculate freely, even fancifully, draw on science fiction and "way-out" predictions in order to cushion the shock which seems inevitable. Another avenue is a planned effort to achieve maturity and emotional stability in spite of stress and tension.

WILES' "ANALYSIS GROUP"

Such an invention for the high school of the future is Kim Wiles' "Analysis Group." It would consist of ten pupils of the same age and with relatively equal intellectual ability but with quite varied social and economic values, plus a skilled teacher-counselor. Such groups, according to Wiles, would meet six hours a week in the school to discuss "any problems of ethics, social concern, or out-of-school experience [which would] help each pupil discover meaning, develop increased commitment to a sense of values, and also receive opportunity to examine the conflicts among the many sets of values and viewpoints held by members of the society." It was anticipated that the group would remain a unit throughout the high school program of its members. Wiles expected the teachers of analysis groups to be specially prepared. Teacher-counselors assigned to analysis groups were expected to have no other school responsibilities, probably meeting three such groups on a regular basis and spending the remainder of their time in individual counseling with parents and pupils.

In a somewhat subtle way, the analysis group is a kind of latterday homeroom with considerable change in organization and much clearer articulation of purpose. It seems to have great promise.

If we accept Wiles' general outline of the analysis group, what can we say about the scope and extent of the idea and of the vehicle?

It seems apparent that one of the greatest needs for the adolescent is to establish a feeling of confidence in an authority figure of the next older generation. The crisis of confidence between generations is a deeply serious matter. Adolescents quite obviously are impatient with our adult hypocrisy. They are asking us to tell it as it is, they are asking us at least to try to keep our actions consistent with what we express as our values and our purposes, and they have a suspicion of the establishment which goes beyond the age-old adolescent attitude toward elders.

I have recently been reading essays written by some of the most militant college students of the last few years. Their view of the educational diet served them in elementary school, high school, and college is a disturbing picture. One young man wrote, "School for me was always stuffy, crowded, tightly scheduled—an authority center where questions were slaughtered quickly and efficiently with brilliant little answers from teachers. We all know how unnecessary and redundant many teachers are—how they never quite come alive before their classes as if the administration were controlling their oxygen supply. Most classrooms are merely a recital of the text you read last night. But every now and then, one sneaks through and holds the class on his own, which balances off the entire history of inadequate teachers. But isn't it unfortunate that the clothesline of education droops so low between the occasional giants!"[3]

At Peabody College, we have had some experience in re-educating for confidence in teachers. Our project has dealt with emotionally disturbed children. "Project Re-Ed," originated in 1960, has been built on the premise that rebuilding confidence in an authority figure is a part of the re-education of children and adolescents who are unable for emotional reasons to function effectively in the school setting. In a less extreme form, this may very well be the problem of a great many adolescents approaching the exit of our high schools today. And the teacher-counselor proposed by Kimball Wiles (also a term and a function used in our Project Re-Ed) is perhaps the best type of school employee to bring about renewed confidence.

There is a divisiveness in many schools which accentuates the normal generation gap between teachers and pupils. Paul Dodson, head of New York University's Center for Human Relations and Community Services described it to the Commission on Civil Disorders this way:

> A divergence of goals (between the dominant class and ghetto youth) makes schools irrelevant for the youth of the slum. It removes knowledge as a tool for groups who are deviant to the ethos of the dominant society. It tends to destroy the sense of self-worth of minority background children. It breeds apathy, powerlessness and low self-esteem. The majority of ghetto youth would prefer to forego the acquisition of knowledge if it is at that cost. One cannot understand the alienation of modern ghetto youth except in the context of this conflict of goals.[4]

The importance of something like the analysis group is intensified in the schools where children of minority groups attend. For the question of values and self-image is a crucial one in these situations. James Farmer, Assistant Secretary of H.E.W., told it with feeling:

I looked through a stack of pre-school books several years ago to see what kind of self-image my little girl would get—how she would see herself. Well, I found that in most of those books she would not see herself at all unless she was cleaning somebody else's house, carrying somebody else's bag or was in some ridiculous position with a string tied around her toe and other kids poking fun at her and laughing. Not an acceptable self-image. But this is what those books, and I've been through a million of them, would have told her that she was. And furthermore, horror of horrors, this is what the millions of white children who read those pre-school books are told that my daughter is.[5]

The self-identity problem is clearly still a serious one if a textbook is still in use in Washington, D. C. which makes the following statement: "Negroes made ideal slaves. They fitted admirably into the slave system. They thrived under the paternalistic love and care of their slave owners. They enjoyed nothing more than sitting under the magnolia trees, strumming on their guitars and singing sweetly of the hereafter." While the children from racial minority groups struggle to preserve ego in the face of unrelenting discrimination, middle-class adolescents fight the "punch-card syndrome," the anonymity and loss of individuality.

Howard Mumford Jones has argued that the only way in which we can effectively combat the facelessness of our society, which he sees as one contributing factor to violence and irresponsible behavior, is to elevate the humanities to a position of top priority at all levels of education. But he rejects the easy way out—tinkering with the curriculum. To him, the fundamental difficulty lies not in machinery but in men. He says, "Even our teachers in the humanities find it too easy to study processes, too difficult to enunciate purposes. The question is not whether teachers are capable of aesthetic analysis—which some of them do brilliantly— but whether they are capable of ethics in . . . the democratic culture." Perhaps what we really need is what Jones calls a "revival of belief in man":

> But, if in the matter of humanity, the best lack all conviction, the worst, then, are bound to be full of passionate intensity. After Dachau and Buchenwald, after two world wars and the threat of total destruction through the passions of little men, if we do not re-establish a belief in the greatness of man, what is to save us? Not science, too quickly misused by men not scientists; not social science, too glibly misinterpreted by propagandists not scholars; but only a second renaissance of belief in the human spirit.[6]

As I read the analysis group section of Wiles' Chapter 15, the message which comes through is that high school experience which follows only the route of subject areas is inadequate. Only if we break apart the crust of present arrangements and create a structure for analysis of ethical problems and personal identity shall we achieve the renaissance of the human spirit.

THE TEACHER-COUNSELOR

Of course, a major part of the problem is suggested by Wiles when he talks about the need for emotionally mature people to serve as teacher-counselors—people "selected early in their teacher education program because they display a high degree of empathy and are warm, outgoing personalities whom other people like. They will be given special training in counseling, communication, and value analysis. Each person will be taught to see his role as one of helping others to feel more secure, to clarify their values, and to communicate more effectively with their colleagues."

What a different kind of teacher education experience this implies! Quite the contrary today, our present teacher graduates find their preparation so book-bound and campus-contained that rarely do they have an opportunity to examine alternative values and to take clear positions on issues of significance.

One must fight an immediate feeling of discouragement in contemplating the number of such teacher-counselors needed, and the extensive revision of present teacher education programs in so many colleges which would be necessary to make this condition come true. We can at least speculate that if the role of the teacher-counselor were defined and training programs were available for persons interested in this, some new resources would come to the forefront, opening up a pool of adults (perhaps some of them part-time) not presently attracted to teaching. There are enough isolated examples in pilot programs today for us to know that some young adults who have themselves had problems of adjustment and resolution of conflicts with society are attracted to the Teacher Corps, VISTA and the Peace Corps. Hopefully, new opportunities and a fresh approach to teaching will release new sources of manpower.

NEEDED: LABORATORIES TO AID
THE SEARCH FOR SELF

One would be false to the curriculum ideals of Kimball Wiles if he were to suggest that the return to a classical curriculum full of moral preachments or literary excerpts would be the most appropriate response to the needs of our current society. The essential purpose of the analysis groups cannot be gained that way. Why should we find the basis for value discussions principally "in school"? We can instead find laboratory situations out of school which can serve to provide the setting for discovering the full meaning which is lacking in our curriculum—the relevance of which the student speaks—laboratory situations in which the contradictions of our own society and the essential elements of conflict and violence between the individual, his so-called neighbors, and his society come into clear focus.

We know that mode of inquiry should really be the heart of content. We are told that to discover meaning rather than to be given conventional wisdom from the next older generation is the essence of learning. There is today a genuine readiness for learning in the area of moral values on the part of youth in our society. We are getting students now who are concerned enough to ask crucial questions about human existence, identity, meaning, the existence of values, and the good life. As Arrowsmith has said, "We have a student generation blessedly capable of moral outrage in a morally outrageous world, but almost without exception the response of the school has been parochial, uncomprehending or cold."[7]

It may be possible in the years ahead for our students to spend significant amounts of time in laboratory situations in which solutions to social problems and personal identity can be incentives. Certainly, we cannot provide individual counseling for every pupil in our schools. We should try to individualize as much as possible, but we must recognize the logistical difficulties of the purely personal curriculum and should form groups which will continue together throughout the high school career. These groups we must hope can provide for the individual an understanding of values and ethical concepts through wrestling with community problems in actual settings. I can imagine many of our students participating as VISTA-type volunteers, assisting with tutoring and personal counseling of younger pupils in disadvantaged areas of town. This is not easy to do with the present daily schedule, Carnegie unit high school program, but one can only hope that present roadblocks will soon dissipate.

Instead of adopting intellectualized, compartmental approaches to learning, the experiences implicit in a Kimball Wiles' "Analysis Group" involve the total person, intellectual and affective, and can be deep and personally meaningful. Who could say that genuine achievement along this line will not reduce friction, restore an effective working morality, and obviate the need to further arm ourselves for internal social warfare?

References

1. Alvin Toffler, "The Future as a Way of Life," *Horizon*, VII (Summer, 1965), 108-115.
2. *The McLuhan Dewline*, No. 1 (July, 1968).
3. Otto Butz, ed., *To Make a Difference* (New York: Harper & Row Publishers, 1967), p. 18.
4. *Report of the National Advisory Commission Civil Disorders* (New York: Bantam Books, Inc., 1968), p. 436.
5. Cited in *The Community School and Its Administration*, Vol. VI, No. 11 (August, 1968).
6. Howard Mumford Jones. From an address delivered at the Honors Convocation, The University of Arizona, December 1, 1961.
7. William Arrowsmith, "The Future of Teaching," in *Improving College Teaching* (American Council on Education, 1967), pp. 57-71.

chapter 15

Galen Saylor

A Complete Education
for Adolescents

Inasmuch as Kim in his introductory statement invited readers to formulate their own plans for the high school of the future which, he recognized, might differ from his plan regardless of how solid and valid one might regard it to be, I will agree wholeheartedly with two aspects of his proposal and present additional ideas; disagree with one aspect; and discuss two aspects of the high school of the future which I feel that Kim failed to consider or just mentioned in passing.

RESEARCH NEEDED FOR DEVELOPING THE
HIGH SCHOOL OF THE FUTURE

I agree wholeheartedly that there is urgent need for undertaking greatly expanded programs of research and for conducting research investigations that will give answers, if at all possible, to some urgent problems in educational planning and provide data essential in planning the development of the high school of the future.

It is my belief that we must devote in this country vast sums of money for thoroughgoing, systematic, imaginative, and comprehensive research investigations in the general area of education and schooling.

Research in Basic Curriculum Data Sources

A large part of these greatly expanded research efforts should be devoted to the advancement of knowledge about the two basic data sources for all curriculum planning—the pupils to be educated and the social values, mores, traditions, and beliefs to be perpetuated and the nature of group living for which the schools are to prepare the young. Although an extensive body of research on adolescents and young adults is available, greatly expanded efforts are needed in basic areas of human motivation; the formulation and role of self-concepts and self-images in behavior and learning; the basis for the formulation of aspirations, career goals, and goal expectations; the nature and role of perceptions of self and the basis for perceptualization by an individual; the nature and character of human capabilities and potentialities in a broad conception of what constitutes talents; and the nature and influence of basic factors that shape the human personality.

A related aspect of these investigations is, of course, the bases and conditions for learning and the factors and conditions that facilitate learning. Research of this kind should not be conducted solely in the abstract, constituting what is often referred to as "basic" research, but rather should be related to curriculum planning, instruction, teaching, and learning in school situations. Teachers, curriculum-planners, and administrators need a much more definitive and greatly expanded body of principles, concepts, and generalizations in the whole area of human motivation, learning, and character development directly related to school learning situations.

The Nature and Character of Social Behavior

The second basic data source—the demands and character of social life and of individual and group living in a social environment—also should be subjected to greatly expanded investigations of a definitive nature. The educational planner is probably much more seriously deficient in reliable knowledge in this area than in the one previously discussed. In the first place, we need studies of what really constitute the basic values, beliefs, socially approved modes of behavior, traditions, and the social structures and institutions that should be perpetuated through the education of the young. These, obviously, are difficult matters to investigate scientifically, but how can the schools be expected to inculcate social values, for which Kim makes an eloquent plea, unless teachers have some rather clearly defined conception of what the social group really wants to have perpetuated or what it is willing to accept and defend as its system of social values?

And, furthermore, the educator needs a great deal of tested conclusions on the nature and character of the conditions of individual
and group living that result in the greatest measure of self-fulfillment,
self-actualization, and human satisfactions for each individual in a
complex, industrialized, technological society.

The much discussed Coleman report[1] is an example of the sort of
research that is needed. Whether we are willing to accept fully the
conclusions of this investigation or not, it certainly illustrates one kind
of research that does need to be carried on extensively and definitely
so that curriculum-planners will have conclusions from investigations
that even the most critical researcher will accept as valid and that have
been replicated in many different situations and sets of variables.

Another segment of research needed in this basic data source is the
predictable or the alternative sets of conditions that will face the young
people in the decades ahead. Unless research agencies are continually
investigating the changing nature of society and the possible kinds of
conditions that people probably will face in future years, we are seriously handicapped in at least some aspects of planning for the high
school of the future.

The Attainment of Educational Objectives

A third major area of research should concern thoroughgoing, comprehensive, and valid measurements of the extent to which adolescents
and young adults are achieving the full range of major and significant

objectives of education. Measurement of educational outcomes of the
schools of this country is woefully inadequate, flimsy, and inconsequential. For the schools of the future, we need much more accurate
data on the extent to which each boy and girl is achieving to the highest measure desirable all of the proper and valid objectives in the
cognitive, affective, and psychomotor skill domains of behavior. And
these measurements should not just cover the first levels of objectives
in these three domains but should extend to full and complete measures
of attainments at the highest levels of conceptualization, generalization,
analysis, synthesis, evaluation, and valuing.

The measurement of behavioral attainments in this broad sweep of
objectives seems almost an overwhelming undertaking, but it is one
to which the educational scholars of this nation must devote unprecedented efforts and resources. Not to do so is to continue to plan without adequate and reliable information and tested results which could
result in serious miseducation or non-education of boys and girls, a
serious waste of human resources, and, undoubtedly, the serious un-
der-development of our national life.

The Development of Value Systems and
Modes of Behavior

A fourth area in which curriculum-planners need a great deal of help from the researchers is on the process by which people develop their systems of values—on all of the cultural factors which affect the building of character, the development of personality, and, particularly, the formulation and establishment of a value system and modes of social and individual behavior.

Obviously, these are very difficult areas to research, but we certainly won't even get preliminary answers until vast sums of money and tremendous efforts are devoted to these matters that are of utmost concern to educators, parents, and citizens.

The Establishment of Research Agencies

The research tasks and projects envisioned will obviously have to be financed. It is my belief that the federal government should provide most of the money needed, and should, in fact, be largely responsible for the establishment of the research agencies that would be required for these efforts. I envision three principal types of research agencies: At the top, as a super-agency that would not only conduct research of its own but would assist other agencies and groups in research, would be National Institutes of Research on Human Affairs. These would be in the pattern of the great National Institute of Agricultural Research at Beltsville, Maryland and several specialized ones throughout the country; the National Institute of Health at Bethesda, Maryland; or similar to some of the research efforts conducted by the Defense Department and the National Aeronautics and Space Agency at various locations.

The institutes of educational research would be staffed by the most outstanding people that could be employed and be provided with ample funds for building the kinds of facilities needed for such research, for conducting major research projects themselves, and for supervising and consulting with other educational research agencies. These institutes may also sublet research projects, providing funds for other groups and agencies that could carry out particular parts or aspects of major investigations.

In addition to the National Institutes of Research for Human Affairs, there should be state or regional institutes of a similar nature but operating on a somewhat smaller scale or specializing in particular aspects of research. These institutes would of course be established in conjunction with a major university or a consortium of universities and state departments of education. These state or regional institutions would, obviously, be modeled on the present system of agricultural experiment stations established in conjunction with each of the land-grant institutions throughout the country. Staffing and research coordination would be on much the same basis as in these stations. The institutes would establish and maintain close working relationships with the school systems and other youth-serving agencies, just as the experiment stations work with the agricultural interests of the state. This model is used for the very reason that agricultural research produced through a system of research institutions has been eminently successful in advancing our knowledge of agriculture in all of its phases.

If research on beef and swine production, grains, tobacco, fruit, and vegetables merits the hundreds of millions of dollars appropriated annually by the federal government, surely major research efforts in the area of human affairs merit even more governmental support.

A COMPLETE EDUCATION FOR ALL
OF THE YOUTH

Kim Wiles was very perspicacious in delineating the four aspects of a school's functions and purposes: to enable each pupil to "develop a set of values to guide his behavior; acquire the skills necessary to participate effectively in the culture; gain an understanding of his social, economic, political, and scientific heritage; and become able to make a specialized contribution to the society." This is a valid and meaningful categorization of the functions and purposes of the secondary school.

But I disagree sharply and, in fact, reject summarily many aspects of Kim's proposals for fulfilling and carrying out these four functions. To be quite blunt about it, as Kim presented his proposals in his short chapter on the high school of the future, it seems to me that he has divided the program into discrete parts with little acknowledgement that education is a complete act within itself, that experience is a broad, inclusive act of learning in most of its aspects, that each major learning activity or enterprise should contribute (and usually would) to a number of important and significant goals and purposes of education, or that behavioral outcomes are not achieved in single, isolated bits of experience unrelated to the total act of behavior. It seems to me that the program of the school cannot be segregated and subdivided into four such sharp aspects, each designed to serve primarily if not solely in isolation one of these major sets of functions.

The integrated nature of learning experience is, of course, self-evident, and the concept enunciated by William H. Kilpatrick many years ago of concomitant learnings is valid today. In fact most of us would not make even a distinction between primary and concomitant learnings, as Kilpatrick was wont to do, but rather regard all learning resulting from a set of experiences as being significant in the education of pupils. The self-concepts and perceptions of himself in relation to his environment that a pupil acquires in a large lecture section in American history is as important a part of the learning act in that history class as is the acquisition of some knowledge of a minor aspect of the cultural heritage. Actually, knowing Kim well, I am sure that he did not intend to propose a multipartite program of secondary education of this type —each part being designed primarily to serve a particular set of objectives—for this concept simply doesn't square with his own teachings, writings, and practices in the field of education. Hence, my purpose here is not to disagree, essentially, but rather to discuss the nature of a complete education for adolescents.

The Development and Refinement of Values

I agree wholeheartedly and enthusiastically with Kim's emphasis on the necessity of helping youth develop a set of values to guide their behavior. The American secondary school for much too long has acted too largely on an assumption that either children and youth will acquire their systems of values and modes of individual and group behavior outside of the formal school program, or that there isn't much the school can do anyway to develop values, change basic modes of behavior, or even refine and extend systems of values of individuals.

The school long ago rejected the bland, moral platitudeness of the McGuffy Readers; and the Supreme Court has even prevented public schools from using Bible readings or prayers as a means of moral inculcation. But it seems to me that the schools have gone much further, and have carefully avoided any significant and overt efforts to inculcate moral principles or to examine and consider systems of values. Kim is to be highly commended for setting as the first major responsibility of the high school of the future that of helping pupils to "discover meaning, to develop increased commitment to a set of values, and to offer opportunity to examine the conflicts among the many sets of values and viewpoints held by members of the society."

The difficulty in teaching values and modes of moral behavior, or even of modifying or refining those the pupil brings with him to school, particularly at the secondary school level, is obvious to any educator. Bloom and his associates who have done such a tremendous service to educators in developing a taxonomy of educational objectives discuss these difficulties rather extensively. In their first handbook, in which they describe their project and the development of the three domains of objectives, the authors describe their difficulties:

> Much of our meeting time has been devoted to attempts at classify-
> ing objectives under this [affective] domain. It has been a difficult
> task which is still far from complete. Several problems make it so
> difficult. Objectives in this domain are not stated very precisely; and,
> in fact, teachers do not appear to be very clear about the learning ex-
> periences which are appropriate to these objectives. It is difficult
> to describe the behaviors appropriate to these objectives since the
> internal or covert feelings and emotions are as significant for this
> domain as are the overt behavioral manifestations. Then, too, test-
> ing procedures for the affective domain are still in the most primi-
> tive stages.[2]

Eight years later, when this group published their *Handbook II, Affective Domain,* they pointed out that "under some conditions the development of cognitive behaviors may actually destroy certain de-sired affective behaviors and that, instead of a positive relation between growth in cognitive and affective behavior it is conceivable that there may be an inverse relation between growth in the two domains."[3]

However, these scholars do point out rather obvious aspects of ed-ucation for values:

> The evidence suggests that affective behaviors develop when ap-
> propriate learning experiences are provided for students much the
> same as cognitive behaviors develop from appropriate learning ex-
> periences. . . . If affective objectives and goals are to be realized,
> they must be defined clearly; learning experiences to help the stu-
> dent develop in the desired directions must be provided; and there
> must be some systematic method for appraising the extent to which
> students grow in the desired ways.[4]

It is obvious that if particular patterns of moral behavior are to be developed and a system of values accepted, the pupils must have an extensive body of experiences in the desired conduct and in identifying, understanding, and applying sets of values to be incorporated into character. Whether the school can provide adequate sets of experiences for these sorts of things is a moot question. But, as Kim pointed out, this should not deter us from making efforts to assist pupils with their value education.[5]

Kim's proposal for an analysis group seems to me to be a highly commendable one and constitutes an aspect of secondary education that educators should set about immediately to incorporate in the school program. Support for Kim's proposal for analysis groups comes from a quite unexpected source (at least unexpected for secondary public school educators)—the report of the Select Committee on Education of the Academic Senate at the University of California.[6] After student disturbances and protest movements occurred on the Berkeley campus, this committee was appointed for the purpose of finding "ways in which the traditions of humane learning and scientific inquiry can best be advanced under the challenging conditions of size and scale that confront our university community."[7] The report is cited here in support of Kim's proposal for the analysis groups, for surely types of educational programs appropriate for freshmen at a university would not need to differ radically or drastically from programs appropriate for high school students.

One of the principal recommendations of the committee is that "every undergraduate should be offered the option of close faculty contact at any and all levels of instruction. As one step towards this goal, we are submitting a formal recommendation for a program of freshman seminars and it is our hope that this program will be expanded and supplemented rapidly."[8]

Furthermore, the committee states that "seminars are not the only alternative to the essentially passive experience of a lecture course; and they may fail to meet the demands of the exceptionally gifted or idiosyncratically talented student. We feel that the campus as a whole has not made sufficient use of field study, and the flexibility and independent study which are afforded by Honors Programs"[9]

With regard to the freshman seminars, the University of California Committee stated almost verbatim Kim's proposal for his analysis group: "Such freshman seminars should consist of groups of no more than twelve students, taught by members of the faculty in whatever areas of intellectual discourse a faculty member is inclined to meet with entering students. The subject matter of all such seminars need not be strictly determined as long as the orientation is one of dialogue and the spirit of inquiry. Each faculty member offering a freshman seminar would act as academic adviser to seminar students."[10]

One of the most promising and worthwhile developments in secondary education during the 60's has been the small group and independent study features of the "Trump" plan to which Kim makes bibliographic citations. But rather extensive observations in schools that have adopted these plans in some form or another, reveal, in my opinion, a quite inadequate and often perverted use of the small seminar-type of grouping. On one hand, too much time is often devoted in many of these small groups to chit-chat and inconsequential matters, resulting in simply an exchange of existing points of view, prejudices, or opinions; or, on the other hand, the procedure becomes highly structured and the teacher really continues the lecture or recitation methods he traditionally used in the regular class program.

Hopefully, these small groups will all become highly significant and challenging educational activities in which pupils will really come to grips with fundamental issues and problems facing the American people and the world today. Hopefully, the groups will foster penetrating, definitive, and meaningful analyses of the character and nature of the values represented by the conditions that give rise to the issues, of the extent to which various groups of people (particularly those of minority racial and ethnic groups and culturally and economically disadvantaged groups) suffer because of the inability and failure of American people to make the American dream come true for all of the people, and of changes needed so that there may be better implementation of democratic values for all people in the years ahead.

Many of the topics and problems studied in depth in the seminar groups should arise from content studied in other courses, but the type of analysis group that I think Kim envisioned and that was envisioned by the Muscantine Committee at Berkeley is not simply an avenue for further study of the same subject matter, but rather one by which students will have opportunities to come to grips realistically with matters that trouble them, problems and issues about which they are concerned, and conditions in the world today that need to be corrected. The seminars should be truly interdisciplinary; their purpose should not be confused with that of the small discussion groups now prevelant in the Trump plan that are simply extensions of classroom activity for a particular course or subject area.

In brief, I subscribe wholeheartedly and recommend complete adoption of Kim's plan for small analysis groups, but I do suggest that perhaps the matters that constitute the organizing elements of the seminar group be somewhat more systematically planned and be more concerned with fundamental issues and problems than Kim implied.

The Acquisition of Knowledge and Understanding

It is in his proposals for classes in the cultural heritage aspect of the high school program that I disagree most sharply with Kim's vision of the high school of the future. It appears to me that his discussion of this aspect of the program almost completely ignores the totality of the learning act and the organic nature of educational experiences. I believe that you cannot acquire a knowledge of the cultural heritage in isolation, separate from the development of values, the acquisition of fundamental skills, and the total development of human personality.

Kim proposed that the cultural heritage be "acquired" through large group instruction. His plan calls for very large classes and he flatly states that "only one teacher and an assistant will be needed in each subject-matter field in each school. The teacher will lecture or present the material through an appropriate medium."

I am violently opposed to large group instruction as a regular, systematic aspect of the secondary school instructional program. This is the one feature of the "Trump" plan that I reject. I fervently hope that the secondary school in its efforts during the present period to evolve new and more effective methods of instruction will not be lulled into an imitation of the colleges and universities in the use of large group instruction for the presentation of knowledge. I believe this would be a serious mistake that secondary educators should avoid in all circumstances.

I recognize that the school schedule should enable departments of the school or the entire school staff to bring together large groups of pupils on occasion, but this is different from regularly scheduling one to three periods a week of systematically planned instruction in the major subject fields, with these large group classes being the only vehicle for presenting much of the important and significant knowledge. Our psychology of learning, it seems to me, would cause any of us to repudiate completely this approach to instruction on a systematic basis.

Fortunately, based on my observations and conferences, I judge that some of the "second-generation" schools that are experimenting with new types of schedules and pupil groupings are not rigidly and systematically following the original "Trump" plan of devoting thirty to forty per cent of the school week to large group instruction. Some departments in some of the schools I have visited recently do not use large group instruction at all, although occasionally they will assemble a considerable body of students in some subject field for some special presentation or instructional project.

One of the most significant developments in instructional methods in recent years has been the emphasis placed on the generalization of knowledge and the organization of knowledge around basic principles and basic structural systems. Few schools have yet done a thorough and imaginative job in moving to this mode of organization for instruction in the academic subject fields, but some very promising and significant efforts are in evidence.

One of the reference points here is the taxonomy developed by Bloom and his co-workers. These scholars have presented a hierarchy of essential aspects of the acquisition of knowledge. From a mere acquisition of facts, as essential as this is as the first step, the taxonomy then recommends instruction that leads to comprehension, application, analysis, synthesis, and evaluation. Unless instruction enables each pupil to advance through these six steps, instruction is seriously deficient. The fact that much of our instructional program in secondary schools of the past has ended for the most part at the first step, the acquisition of knowledge, does not justify continued perpetuation of this inadequate procedure in teaching in the high school of the future.

Hilda Taba, in her outstanding developmental program with teachers of the Contra Costra county school systems in California developed a whole process for helping youngsters advance to the more complex and higher levels of learning in the cognitive field. In terms of the acquisition of the cultural heritage, I am frank to say that I think she set the pattern much better for the high schools of the future than Kim did in his brief presentation in the final chapter of his book.

But I still emphasize that learning must be a complete and total process in which the child must integrate the many things he learns in schools and build it into character and personality. This process cannot properly be broken up into isolated aspects of learning.

THE EDUCATION OF THE DISILLUSIONED, THE DISENCHANTED, AND THE FRUSTRATED ADOLESCENT

The most serious omission I find in Kim's description of the high school of the future is his failure to deal overtly and directly with the problem of high school dropouts—those alienated, frustrated, disillusioned, and sometimes rebellious adolescents and young adults who have not found enough value or significance in the secondary school program of today to entice them to remain until graduation. Although probably only about twenty-five to twenty-eight per cent of the total youth population of this country today are school dropouts, obviously the ratio is much higher, perhaps running as high as fifty to sixty per cent, among the young in the congested, overcrowded, disheveled slums of our great urban cities. The congregation of alienated young people in these slum areas has produced what Conant in 1961 had already labeled "social dynamite".[11]

The Situation

In my opinion, the most serious problem facing the educational agencies of this country in the decades ahead is the development of programs that will serve effectively, meaningfully, and significantly the educational, economic, social, physical, and emotional needs of young people who are frustrated and disillusioned. As a nation, we cannot continue to pile up a slag-heap of rejected, discarded youth at the rate of one-half million to one million persons a year.

At our present population level, even a twenty-five per cent dropout rate means that almost a million young people a year are not completing the programs of secondary education we now offer them. It is not to be presumed that all of these million youngsters are necessarily disillusioned, and certainly all are not alienated. Students drop out of secondary schools for a number of reasons. But it would seem to be a safe assumption that at least half of this group could be properly classified as disenchanted and frustrated. In due time, of course, a considerable number of the group work out of this social malaise and establish themselves as productive, upright citizens, although often economically destined to a life typified by inadequate standards of living in all respects.

The factors typical of the secondary school today that give rise to frustration and disenchantment have been extensively discussed by citizens and educators alike. But the recent report of the Task Force on Juvenile Delinquency of the President's Commission on Law Enforcement and the Administration of Justice has stated these conditions rather forcibly and clearly:

> The school, unlike the family, is a public instrument for training young people. It is, therefore, more directly accessible to change through the development of new resources and policies. And since it is the principal public institution for the development of a basic commitment by young people to the goals and values of our society, it is imperative that it be provided with the resources to compete with illegitimate attractions for young people's allegiance.
>
> .   .   .   .
>
> Recent research has related instances of delinquent conduct to the school-child relationship and to problems either created or complicated by the schools themselves. First, in its own methods and practices, the school may simply be too passive to fulfill its obligations

as one of the last social institutions with an opportunity to rescue the child from other forces, in himself and in his environment, which are pushing him toward delinquency. Second, there is considerable evidence that some schools may have an indirect effect on delinquency by the use of methods that create the conditions of failure for certain students. Mishandling by the school can lower the child's motivation to learn. It can aggravate his difficulty in accepting authority and generate or intensify hostility and alienation. It can sap the child's confidence, dampen his initiative, and lead him to negative definitions of himself as a failure or an "unacceptable" person.[12]

The Task Force Report and a special study for the Task Force by Walter E. Schafer and Kenneth Polk[13] spell out in considerable detail what they feel to be school factors that create resentment and disillusionment among young people who eventually drop out of school, often turning to delinquency or even open rebellion against society.

Possible Lines of Solution

What the nature and form of the educational program of the nation should be to forestall and avoid these conditions that result in dropouts, I am unable to envision fully, and I regret to say that I feel Kim's plans for the high school of the future equally fail to come to grips with this problem; in fact, the kind of school he portrays, may, in the long run, even add to the seriousness of the problem.

In general, however, I think that we will have to move to a really thoroughgoing and soundly developed program of individual school progress, repudiating the present models of rigidly structured, ungraded school programs of both the elementary and secondary schools as they have evolved so far. We now must truly individualize programs of instruction in terms of the educational needs of the child. Individualized instruction in the secondary schools certainly does not mean individual work, for there would indeed need to be a large amount of class and group activities of various kinds, particularly the small discussion groups or seminar groups that Kim so wisely propounded. Furthermore, the fourth part of Kim's program, "acquisition of fundamental skills," should, of course, be made a major function of the individualized instructional programs.

One of the principal responsibilities of the entire school system beginning with kindergarten and nursery school and progressing clear through the twelfth grade is the development of the basic skills so essential for all other types of learning and also for effective citizenship, home life, and the like. The schools of this country cannot afford to continue to build up the frustration, the sense of failure, and the concept of inadequacy among many pupils, particularly those in the slum areas of our cities. The Task Force Report states that by "asserting demands for performances the child cannot meet, the frustrated teacher may become hostile and the child indifferent, apathetic, or hostile in return. If the child is also rebelling at home, the effect is more immediate and the confrontation becomes intolerable to all. The too-usual result is that the child turns to other things that has [sic] nothing to do with the academic learning, and the school finds a way to ignore him or push him out so the rest of its work can continue."[14]

The schools will have to adopt a rigid policy to ensure that no child fails in acquiring his basic skills. All children must continually progress in the acquisition of skills at rates that are appropriate for them. Secondly, the high school of the future, if it is to effectively educate the types of students who now constitute our dropouts, must make the entire program relevant and meaningful to these children. The typical high school of today is offering a program and engaging in modes of instruction that are meaningful and significant for some adolescents, particularly those who aspire to a collegiate education and to entrance to the professions or the learned occupations. This is not to say that the present program of education for these children is necessarily the most relevant, but at least they find meaning and significance and engage with enthusiasm and alacrity in the program of the school. At the other extreme is the group about whom we must be more concerned—the frustrated and disenchanted.

But before I continue with proposals for the dropout problem, let me insert at this point that Kim was one of our educational leaders who had serious reservations about the school's program for the in-between group. During the time it was my privilege to serve on the Executive Committee of the Association for Supervision and Curriculum Development with Kim, he frequently advocated that the schools must become concerned about what he designated the intellectually and academically average and below-average portion of our secondary school student body. He strongly urged us in our planning sessions to formulate plans and projects that would bring this inadequacy in our program of secondary education to the attention of the profession in dramatic and forceful ways and also to propose programs that would improve and enhance the program for this particular group of adolescents. Unfortunately, neither the Executive Committee then or later nor Kim himself ever developed an encompassing, visionary, far-looking program of secondary education for this large group of students who remain in secondary schools until graduation but who find little of real significance or meaning in the program in which they participate often half-heartedly and certainly unenthusiastically.

The dropout, on the other hand, simply becomes so frustrated that he just chucks the whole thing and casts himself adrift from the one social institution that could really help him establish himself as a self-actualizing individual. Hence, the second aspect of the school's plan for challenging the dropout is to make the instructional program much more meaningful and significant to him. The Task Force states that "to the youngster, the instruction seems light years away from the circumstances and facts of life that surround him every day. . . . Too often, as a result of the virtual absence of relation between it and the life he is living or will live, the school can not hold the slum child's interest."[15]

A third aspect of the program for the non-academic student is an extensive vocational and prevocational educational program with a co-ordinated work-experience program. The slum child needs to establish himself as a self-sufficient individual, as a person who has status and standing certainly with his peer group and probably also with the residents of his neighborhood. In addition to a meaningful instructional program within the school, the opportunity to engage in productive and satisfying work in businesses, factories, offices, and the like is an important part of his requirements.

The secondary schools of the future must find significant ways in which to provide these opportunities for self-development, self-fulfillment, and the establishment of status and prestige on a basis that looks to a productive life of the future, rather than on the basis of a student's standing as a member of a group of juvenile delinquents or rebellious youth.

THE EDUCATION OF TEACHERS FOR THE HIGH SCHOOL OF THE FUTURE

In forecasting the high school of the future, Kim dealt only incidentally with a few points concerning the education of teachers for the high school he envisioned. It would seem appropriate to set down at this point some of my thoughts about the preparation of these teachers.

In the first place, I think the preparation program for entrance into the profession must be at least six years long but hopefully seven. Although I would not advocate that colleges of education blindly imitate colleges of medicine, I think that many aspects of their preparation programs should be similar to those of medical schools. Certainly, as a basis for planning teacher education programs for the high school of the future, college staffs should analyze thoroughly and critically the programs of education for members of the other scholarly professions.

The undergraduate years of teacher preparation would be devoted primarily to general education and specialization in the subject field to be taught. Part of the senior year would be devoted to the first phases of professional education. Basic and significant reforms are badly needed in both the areas of general education and subject-matter specialization for teachers. I certainly do not advocate a continuation of the typical program of general education that now prevails in our colleges and universities. The program should be one in which interdisciplinary seminars and depth studies in seminar, discussion-type classes are held for a specific field as well as for areas of general interest. Moreover, as a part of the program of general education, considerable opportunity should be provided for actual involvement in community field work, participation in community and national affairs in a significant and meaningful manner, and depth studies revolving around field situations.

And the student's program of course work in his subject field of specialization, similarly, should be redesigned and restructured. Considerable work in systematic types of courses that would provide not only the knowledge but the basis for scholarly investigations and research in the field should, of course, be offered, but the student should also have ample opportunity for deep and penetrating studies in his specialized subject field. At the advanced level, probably as a part of his senior-year work in his subject field, he should have opportunity to carry on original research, or prepare a scholarly investigation or thesis on some topic in which he is greatly interested.

In the senior year, the student would take his first course work in professional education. Courses would include those in the general areas of history, philosophy, and sociology of education but, again, not taught in the typical course manner, but rather as integrated seminar-type discussions and penetrating studies of topics, problems, and issues significant to these three fields of study. It is through this program that the student should gain a thorough understanding of the purposes, aims, objectives, functions, character, and nature of the schools, and an understanding of some of the basic issues and problems confronting the educational system in the United States.

In the fifth year, the perspective teacher would devote about a half of his program of studies to professional education and the other half to advanced studies in his field of specialization. Work in this latter aspect would be designed to develop his scholarship and to establish him as a neophyte scholar in his major field.

The professional program should be a fully integrated program, combining observation of school practice in many different situations, penetrating studies of problems and issues related to teaching and education, and considerable attention to the organization and methods of instruction, making use of all of the technology now available for educational purposes.

The student would spend his sixth year as an intern in the schools, but he would not devote full time to teaching or to school responsibilities. About two-thirds of the week could well be devoted to actual instructional activities in his cooperating school, but there should be ample opportunity for seminar and group work, in which a considerable variety of people would participate, such as representatives of many community agencies that also work with children and youth, scholars from the subject fields in which the candidate has specialized, and people who have something to discuss about major social, political, and economic conditions of relevance to our program of education itself. During this year, the student should have considerable opportunity to visit other types of youth-serving agencies, particularly facilities and programs for exceptional children of all kinds and voluntary programs for youth of different backgrounds and character. I envision the sixth year as much like the internship for the medical student, but including somewhat broader and more comprehensive opportunities for learning about, observing, and becoming more thoroughly familiar with the work of a considerable number of agencies outside of the school that are concerned with the problems of youth.

At the end of the sixth year, the candidate would be fully certified as a teacher, eligible for full-time employment in the secondary schools of the nation. Beyond this, of course, there would need to be extensive provisions for continued education, for such a teacher would have thirty-five to forty years of professional service ahead of him. It is quite obvious that elaborate programs would need to be established to enable the teacher to keep abreast of developments not only in his field of specialization, but also in professional education. Challenging opportunities for continued study in depth of many aspects of the world about us should be available. Study for advanced degrees would be one aspect of this program, but there should also be programs of much broader scope and design for different purposes than the typical program of graduate work now in vogue in our colleges of education.

Kim Wiles, of course, was one of our most insightful and most visionary leaders, and he performed an outstanding service to the profession in forecasting the kind of high school we need in the future. His proposals are fundamental, and I am sure that if he himself had chosen to add thirty to fifty more pages to his exciting book, he too would have presented in much greater detail ways in which the secondary school could effectively carry out the four basic functions that he defined.

References

1. James S. Coleman, Chief Investigator, *Equality of Educational Opportunity* (Washington, D.C.: Government Printing Office, 1966).
2. Benjamin S. Bloom, ed., *Taxonomy of Educational Objectives: Handbook I, Cognitive Domain* (New York: David McKay and Company, 1956), p. 7.
3. David Krathwohl, *et al.*, *Taxonomy of Educational Objectives: Handbook II, Affective Domain* (New York: David McKay and Company, 1964), p. 20.
4. *Ibid.*, pp. 20-23.
5. Robert C. Angell, in his scholarly and helpful study, *Free Society and Moral Crisis* (Ann Arbor: University of Michigan Press, 1958), presents a model in which he identifies the factors that determine a society's moral code (p. 17), and discusses the process by which the young build a system of values (Chap. 4).
6. Charles Muscantine, Chairman, Select Committee on Education, The Academic Senate, University of California, Berkeley. *Education at Berkeley* (Berkeley: The Regents of the University of California, 1966).
7. *Ibid.*, p. iii.
8. *Ibid.*, pp. 124-125.
9. *Ibid.*, p. 125.
10. *Ibid.*, p. 135.
11. James B. Conant, *Slums and Suburbs* (New York: McGraw-Hill, Inc., 1961), p. 2.
12. Task Force on Juvenile Delinquency of the President's Commission on Law Enforcement and Administration of Justice, Task Force Report: *Juvenile Delinquency and Youth Crime* (Washington, D.C.: Government Printing Office, 1967), p. 49.
13. Walter E. Schafer and Kenneth Polk, "Delinquency in the Schools," *op. cit.*, pp. 222-227.
14. Task Force on Juvenile Delinquency, *op. cit.*, p. 49.
15. *Ibid.*, pp. 50-51.

part 5

Teachers and Teaching for the School of the Future

chapter 16

Glen Hass

Instruction Theory and the High School of the Future

In its responsibility for teaching values and critical thinking, the high school of the future will need teachers who can use knowledge from many of the behavioral sciences in planning with and for learners. So we shall have to plan for changes in teacher education as much or more than for changes in organization of the school or the content of instruction, as we plan for the high school of 1985. In learning to deal in better ways with problems of teaching, we must give attention to the development and use of instruction theory. Kimball Wiles would have been a vigorous leader in working for changes in teacher education; since he is not to be with us, others must work harder to prepare the necessary concepts, theories, and plans.

When Kim published his predictions about "The High School of the Future" in 1963, like so many others, I found his ideas worthy of careful consideration. Some of his predictions I hoped might come into being; other I hoped would not. Actually, I believe that Kim felt that the less desirable features of the school he described were inevitable, or were necessary to gain other advantages.

Now predictions which are based on understanding, knowledge, and long experience as Kim's were, can be useful. If one can foresee the potential nature of the future, he can work to bring about those aspects of it that he favors and hope to develop forces which may prevent the realization of those features which he considers undesirable.

ANALYSIS OF KIM WILES' PROPOSALS FOR THE HIGH SCHOOL OF THE FUTURE

To support a social commitment to freedom, creativity, and equality of opportunity, according to Kim, 1985's high school must provide time and opportunity for every learner to examine and develop values to guide his behavior. To "discover meaning" and resolve value conflicts, learners must have time with a group of their peers and with a warm, emotionally mature, and outgoing teacher. The "Analysis Group," with no curriculum set in advance, meets these and other requirements, and is the most attractive and important feature of the future high school as Kim describes it. He calls it the "basic element" of the educational program of 1985. It will bring the guidance and the teaching functions together.

The high school of the future will, for most learners, not be the institution where they terminate formal education. Most will continue formal learning in a community college or university. But the high school will still contribute to goals related to citizenship, self-realization, vocation, and critical thinking. In this framework, the self-selected activities including creative activities, work experience, individual investigations, and special seminars which Kim predicts have special significance for the self-realization of learners. With increasing technological development, such learning opportunities will be even more necessary than they are today.

The portions of Kim's program about which I have doubt are those in which he suggests how the fundamental skills may be acquired and the cultural heritage explored. The use of teaching machines to teach the skills and television films and skilled lectures to present the cultural heritage have much merit. I believe they should be tried in some schools in the manner described. But these are the areas which are to be the *minimum essentials* and on which the learners are to be tested. I suspect that individual interests, differences, and needs cannot be suspended in these areas any more than they can be in an analysis group or in the creative, self-selected areas of study. In my opinion, the large group instruction approach may be used and may be effective for many learners in the cultural heritage program; for some, the same may be true of the use of teaching machines for the acquisition of fundamental skills.

But in planning for the high school of the future, we will have to think about changes required in teachers and teaching as well as changes in organization, content, and presentation of school subjects. In all areas of the program of the high school of the future, skilled teachers will be needed who can provide for learner differences, who can diagnose needs, and who can aid learners in functionally relating themselves to content and experiences.

To perform these functions, teachers in the high schools of 1985 will need to be skillful in their understanding and use of curriculum and instruction theories. They will need to be hypothesis-makers about learners, about society, and about the curriculum in the practice of diagnostic teaching. To understand how this may come about, one must understand the development of curriculum and instruction theory.

SEVENTY YEARS OF CURRICULUM THEORY

Three approaches to curriculum development during the past seventy years can be identified: the subject matter to be taught in the school, the society to be served, and the learners to be educated.

When the learning of subject matter was the high school's major emphasis near the beginning of this century, it was thought that the chief function of the high school was to transmit this knowledge. The curriculum was a body of content to be learned by those who came to high school and its mastery at one grade was usually the basis for moving into the next grade, for graduation, and for college preparation.

The decades following 1900 saw many important changes in the social forces influencing the high school. Industrialization and urbanization increased very rapidly, immigration increased, and the high school students increasingly included the children of the working classes. With these social changes, knowledge from sociology and anthropology seemed more pertinent to the development of the high school curriculum. A classical content curriculum would no longer do. In the 1930's, with the rise of totalitarianism, arguments urging the use of democratic processes in the classroom gained in relevance and significance. Thus, the social forces influencing education were increasingly recognized and became a generally accepted basis of curriculum theory, even though the high school program was not generally affected. Those who emphasized society as the basis of the curriculum saw the needs of the social order as having the highest priority in determining what was to be taught. With this point of view, *Dare The Schools Build A New Social Order?* was written by George Counts and published in 1932.

To the subject matter to be taught and the society to be served was now added the third emphasis in curriculum development: the learner to be educated. Those who emphasized the learner and his nature, particularly during the 1920's and 1930's had increasing support for their views. The extensive studies of human development clearly showed the uniqueness of childhood and adolescence and the sequential and ordered nature of development. The learner was seen by some as the source of educational means and ends. He was not to be sacrificed either to the demands of subject matter or to the needs of the state. Standards which stifled his creativity had no place in education. In this emphasis, the curriculum was to serve the learner. It was to be what was termed a "child-centered curriculum."

Changing Views About Man's Nature

These concepts about the preferred nature of the curriculum were related to ideas concerning man's nature which were developed and which also changed several times during the past seventy years. In the nineteenth century and in the thirty years following 1900, there was the "Rational-Economic Theory of Man" in which man was considered a passive being to be manipulated and primarily motivated by economic incentives. All men were classified in two groups: the untrustworthy mass; and the trustworthy, broadly motivated, moral elite. This view of man's nature was supported by the stimulus-response, conditioning theories of learning. Since the kind of assumptions any teacher makes about learners largely determines his teaching methods and strategies, the Rational-Economic Theory and the S-R learning theories supported the development of a high school curriculum which was a body of content set forth to be learned.[1]

But scientific evidence accumulated in the 1930's and 1940's that showed the importance of social motives in organization life. This, as illustrated in the Hawthorne studies, showed that man is basically motivated by social needs and is responsive to leadership to the extent that the leader helps to meet his needs for acceptance. This research led to a new set of assumptions about the nature of man and to the view known as "Social Man."[2]

In the 1940's and 1950's, a number of psychologists studying human behavior in large organizations came to the conclusion that organizational life, particularly in industry, had removed meaning from work. This group of psychologists, however, believed that this loss of meaning was not related so much to man's social needs as to his inherent need to use his capacities and skills in a mature, productive way. Maslow and others developed the assumptions which state that man's motives fall into hierarchical classes with the needs of survival, safety, and security at the bottom of the hierarchy, moving upward by way of social needs to ego and self-esteem needs, needs for autonomy and independence, and, finally, to self-actualization needs in the sense of the maximum use of one's resources.[3] This view of man's nature is known as "Self-Actualizing Man." Perceptual and cognitive learning theories have been associated with this position.

Curriculum Difficulties Related to Separate Views About Man

Now the difficulty has been that curriculum-workers and teachers have tended to be guided by one or another of these views of the nature of man or of the bases of curriculum construction. Persons committed to self-actualization and to the child as the focus of the curriculum have often tended to reject or neglect subject matter and society as major guiding foci. But today we know from the behavioral sciences that all human behavior is a product of complex patterns of interacting forces. We know and can prove that behavior changes are produced by psychological and sociological elements currently present. On the other hand, there is increasing evidence from research in biology which indicates that powerful physiological and biochemical processes influence learning, behavior, and personality. For each study pointing to a biological or physiological determinant of learning or specific behavior, we can find evidence pointing to sociological and psychological causes. Such variables as level of aspiration, self-concept, and role expectations have effects as significant as enzymes and genes. A "multidimensional" approach to the planning of teaching is necessary, and the high school of 1985 should be based on such an approach.

Another View of Man: Complex Man

Empirical research has consistently found some evidence for each of the conceptions of man's nature including the rational-economic, the social, and the self-actualizing views. Man is more complex than he is considered to be in any one of these positions, and is highly variable as well. Learners have many motives arranged in a hierarchy of importance, but this hierarchy is subject to change, from time to time, and from situation to situation. Man is capable of learning new motives through his group and organizational experiences. And in any group, the needs and motives of different members will vary and must be treated differently. Viewed collectively, this evidence leads to a new view of man as "Complex Man." In this view, we cannot understand human behavior if we look only to man's knowledge, or only to the individual's development or motivations, or only to environmental or group or social conditions and practices. These influences interact in complex fashion, requiring us to develop theories for the high school of 1985 which can deal with systems and interdependent phenomena. Teachers will use these multidimensional views of "Complex Man" in planning for individual guidance and instruction. They will do so because teacher education programs will prepare them to utilize theory in analyzing individuals and in planning teaching; they will do so because the importance of the complexity of man's nature will be better understood by that time.

TEACHERS OF THE FUTURE WILL USE INSTRUCTION THEORY BASED ON RESEARCH

The term "theory" has been employed in education in two main senses. A distinction must be made between the two. One usage falls within the area of the philosophy of education. Philosophies of education may include statements about the nature of man, society, knowledge, as well as statements concerning the proper aims and goals of schooling. Such philosophies are not necessarily consistent with the descriptive findings and theories of the behavioral sciences.

The second usage of the term "theory" refers to descriptive scientific theory which is based on established empirical data. A scientific theory is an organization of empirical data to make them meaningful. There are several sources of descriptive educational theory including the analysis and description of peculiarly educational phenomena, and the use of theories of human behavior from the behavioral sciences.

In 1985, high school teachers and curriculum-makers will make use of many descriptive scientific theories developed in the 1950's, 1960's, and 1970's based on a recognition of man's complex nature including his rational-economic, self-actualizing, and social nature.

Teachers as Hypothesis-Makers

Many public school teachers in the United States now hold to the theory of teaching which considers it to be continuous, intelligent inquiry or problem-solving behavior. This is the concept of teaching which was developed by John Dewey in *How We Think* in 1933.[4] This does not mean that it is generally well understood, or that its implications for teaching practice are generally correctly interpreted. It was Dewey's hope that a theory of teaching based on findings from science might become possible as the various findings are "linked up" and confirm one another.

Teaching, in this view, consists of four aspects: (1) the purposes, objectives, or criteria aspect of teaching (2) the knowledge aspect (3) the procedures aspect (4) the evaluation aspect.[5]

In the purposes aspect, the teacher develops a clear awareness of the kind of changes he desires to achieve with the learners. He must be sure that the objectives are clearly stated so that he can be aware of what the learner is to be like or to be able to do when he has successfully completed the learning. The learners also should be aware of the objectives so that they can be aware of their own progress and so that they can organize their own activities to be relevant to the goals which they share. When the goals are not clearly defined by both teacher and learners, there is no sound basis for selecting materials or content for study, or instructional methods. Too much of the time, teachers function in a fog because they do not clarify their goals for the learners.

The knowledge aspect of teaching leads the teacher to conclude, correctly or incorrectly, that certain knowledge, experiences, and procedures will be effective in generating the particular kinds of behavior changes he is seeking with and for the learners. This includes knowledge about the learners concerned, about human development in the particular age group, about how learning is likely to occur in the given situation, about the nature of knowledge, about the community and the society, about the sub-culture of which the learner is a member, and the teacher's personal knowledge gained from previous experience in similar situations. It also includes the content which it may be hoped that learners will henceforth include in their cognitive structures.

In the procedures dimension, the teacher and the learners both perform actions in the light of the information and knowledge utilized to accomplish the changes that the purposes propose. The teacher makes materials available, he plans with the learners, he arranges the physical environment, and he selects his teaching procedures with the conscious expectation that they will produce the kind of changes of behavior and thinking he is seeking with the learners.

The next dimension of the teaching cycle is the evaluation aspect. If teachers are hypothesis-makers, then they must assess the extent to which the goals sought and the knowledge, experiences, and methods utilized appear to result in the behavioral or cognitive changes which they seek. The professional significance of measuring school achievement is that the results enable the teacher to evaluate his own planning for changes in and with learners, and modify it. The cycle is then repeated in light of the changes.

In this way, the teaching act can be thought of as a continuous act of inquiry. Today, too many teachers see no relationship between their purposes, knowledge, procedures, and evaluation. In the high school of 1985, this will no longer be the case.

Fragmented Instruction Theory
Limits Teaching Effectiveness

A lack of understanding of the process and the fragmented nature of the theory utilized have led many teachers to reject the total process. Teachers either do not make use of theory based upon empirical study, or when they do make use of such theory, they use fragments which describe only a portion of the learner's action, such as theories of human development, theories of child study, theories about the nature of knowledge. The use of fragmented theory about human action makes it unlikely that a teacher's predictions can be successful ones.

What we need for the high school of 1985 are comprehensive, multi-dimensional theories of human action, curriculum, and teaching based on the Complex Man view as presented earlier in this chapter.

Instruction Theory and the
Analysis Group Teacher

The analysis group teacher will be aware of the complex nature of the learners he teaches. He will hypothesize regarding the purposes he seeks with them in terms of their needs for self-actualization, their desire to cope with problems, and the values of peer groups, subcultures, and society which they share. This will be necessary if, as Kim Wiles suggests, "guidance and the teaching function will be brought closer together" in the high school of 1985. Teachers and learners will select content and procedures based on their joint purposes, and the knowledge assembled. They will evaluate together in the light of the jointly planned goals. And they will repeat this cycle as goals are partially achieved or as new objectives are selected.

Instruction Theory and the
Learning of Skills

In the acquisition of fundamental skills in the high school of 1985, Kim states that machines will teach basic skills as "effectively and efficiently as a teacher." I do not believe that this is possible in the manner proposed.

I believe that the complex nature of learners and learning is such that teachers of the fundamental skills will be required to aid the learners in diagnosing their own problems so that goals will be clear to them, and appropriate choices of materials and procedures can be made. Drill, of course, can be accomplished on teaching machines, but the understanding and use of skills requires much more than drill.

Instruction Theory and the
Cultural Heritage

I am similarly concerned about the teaching of the cultural heritage as Kim describes it in the high school of the future. The steps he describes are important: basic knowledge from the essential fields must be prepared in the "most easily understood media" and presented "dramatically and forcefully." But classes will be five hundred to a thousand in a section in his proposal, and the knowledge covered will include the physical and biological sciences as well as the humanities and social sciences. This method of teaching the cultural heritage depends too heavily on the Rational-Economic Theory of Man, described earlier in this chapter, and ignores Social and Self-Actualizing Man.

To hope that the analysis group and its teacher can provide the needed discussion nullifies our knowledge of instruction theory. It seems to suggest that relating the knowledge presented to the learners is unimportant. And the assumption that only those areas that particularly appeal to the learners require discussion assumes too much. The idea that the analysis group teacher could serve as a resource to the students in any or all of the disciplines included—biological, physical, and social sciences as well as the humanities—is impossible. Our knowledge of the nature of man and instruction theory emphasizes that teachers of the various disciplines included in the cultural heritage will be needed to meet learners in discussion sections and on an individual basis to make this knowledge meaningful. These teachers must make use of *adequate* instruction theory if they are to be effective in aiding learners to achieve understanding of the cultural heritage and their own relationship to it. Multi-media, dramatic presentations in large groups cannot do this teaching which is necessary in achieving goals of citizenship, self-fulfillment, and critical thinking.

Individual Differences and Instruction
Theory in The High School of the Future

Planning for the high school of the future requires much more than planning for changes in organization and content of the curriculum. Kim Wiles started our thinking in these directions and challenged the profession to go on from there. In addition, we must plan for and think about changes needed in teaching. Better planning for teaching is needed and this can be greatly aided by the understanding and use of research-based instruction theory. If the teacher uses the concepts of Rational-Economic Man, Social Man, Self-Actualizing Man, and Complex Man presented here, he will: (1) regularly test his assumptions about his teaching and seek a better diagnosis; (2) value individual differences and vary his professional decisions accordingly.

To prepare for the high school of the future, we must learn to value difference and develop the diagnostic processes which reveal difference to make appropriate instruction possible. Research-based instruction theory will be necessary and will be used to aid in accomplishing these goals in the high school of 1985.

References

1. B. F. Hoselitz, *A Readers' Guide To The Social Sciences* (Glencoe, Illinois: Free Press, 1959).
2. Elton Mayo, *The Social Problems of an Industrial Civilization* (Andover, Massachusetts: The Andover Press, 1945).
3. A. H. Maslow, *Motivation and Personality* (New York: Harper & Row, Publishers, 1954).
4. John Dewey, *How We Think*. Boston: D. C. Heath, 1933.
5. Arthur P. Coladarci, "The Relevance of Psychology to Education," in George F. Kneller, *Foundations of Education* (New York: John Wiley & Sons, Inc., 1963), pp. 308-404.

chapter 17

Vernon E. Anderson

Teacher Education for the High School of the Future

As I examine Kimball Wiles' proposed steps for the development of his vision of the high school of the future, I am impressed by the fact that we are on our way. Another conclusion, one that Wiles clearly recognized, is that teacher education will need to change in order to attain all of these goals. We can move only so far in secondary education with an antiquated system of teacher preparation that seems to belie the future.

I am sure that Wiles realized that his vision was an open-ended one, for he chose to take the evolutionary steps to 1980 instead of 1985, the year for which the high school program was described. The deliberate five-year gap speaks volumes; no one in 1960 or in 1969 could safely predict what a rapidly changing world might bring twenty-five years hence. Now we are about fifteen years away from that vision. Yet, the current riots, race conflicts, and value conflicts make even more essential that basic part of the proposed program: the analysis and development of values.

The inevitable conclusion reached from the study of Wiles' concept of the high school of the future, as well as from trends that have accelerated considerably since 1960, is that the high school youth will have to be taught how to cope with an uncertain future. Both the accelerated pace of technological change and the precariousness of international peace make this indispensable. In itself, the ability to help people deal with uncertainty points up the need for a new breed of teacher.

Moreover, these are certain assumptions regarding the future which are pertinent to both a secondary school curriculum and a teacher education curriculum:

- That technology will make individual progress at one's own speed not only possible but practicable.

- That greater depth in specialization will be required—specialization of all types, not only in the academic disciplines.

- That high school students will be better prepared when they enter college, both in general education and in some specialty within the school curriculum.

- That instructional groups in public schools will vary in size from one to one hundred.

- That refinement of selection procedures for teacher education students will occur.

- That the supply of teachers will increase.

- That a greater number of aides of all kinds will be used in the public schools.

INVENTING THE FUTURE

How does one teach young people to "invent the future"? Will more or less of the same pattern of teacher education, of methods, educational psychology, social functions, and student teaching do the job? Sometimes I wonder if we are so bankrupt of ideas in teacher education that the only curriculum change we can conceive of is deletion or addition of courses, reduction in the number of education courses, or placement of the professional courses at a different level in the student's progress in formal education.

Whatever gave us the conception anyway that in a college or university, the only way to change the curriculum is through addition, deletion, or shuffling of courses and credits? A perceptive college student knows better. He knows very well that courses of the same name and number, taught by two differing personalities, are not the same. He chooses—especially if he is a graduate student—a section or a course for the particular professor with whom he wants to work. If we are really honest with ourselves, we will admit that usually the student has registered for three courses of Wiles, when the choice was his. I am convinced that three courses of Anderson would be too many for a graduate student, no matter which of the Andersons in teacher education was teaching. And pity the poor fellow if he should have to suffer through three courses of Whiffleznoozer, who droned on through stale notes day by day either in history or in education.

No matter what the catalog says, the college student knows that content and method differ in different sections. The student seeking a significant educational experience, and who is not too hemmed in by prerequisites and program requirements, seeks the ideas and the contacts with a dynamic personality. All we have to do is to contrast the undergraduate student's use of the "course guide" that evaluates professors and their courses with his use of the college catalog.

A teacher education program that is relevant to the times will bring the student into close contact with stimulating faculty in education, in the behavioral sciences, in the humanities, or in whatever field he chooses in order that he can interact with teachers in both the college and the secondary school. I am sure that the influence on both my students and me will be greater if I can have personal contact with them in my office, in my home, and in small seminar discussions over a period of more than one year. One of my most fruitful experiences as an undergraduate teacher education student was through my contacts with a great scholar in American literature in an honors seminar; in my graduate education, through my contacts with a great scholar and human being in secondary education as his graduate assistant.

Invention of one's own future, learning to cope with change, uncertainty, and eventualities will not come about by sitting through courses. Those of us in teacher education have to be more inventive than that.

COMPETENCIES OF THE TEACHER OF THE FUTURE HIGH SCHOOL

Kim's dream of a high school in which students would spend six hours a week in an analysis group and in which the teacher of such a group would have three small groups a week for a three-year span would necessitate a different kind of teacher for a function markedly dissimilar from that of the typical secondary school teacher. Probably, this teacher would be most similar to the teacher of the advanced seminar and the honors section or the consultant for independent study. He would deal with value conflicts, controversial issues, and examination and analysis of values in a culture group—what many teachers tend to shun for the safer, more stable content. He would discuss in-school and out-of-school experiences, ethics, and youth concerns in a world somewhat foreign to the adult who grew up in a relatively stable and unchanging society. His functions would be somewhat similar to those of the much-maligned core teacher. If "the exploration of questions, ideas, or values advanced by group members will constitute the primary kind of experience," the teacher's behavior indeed becomes radically different. Development of a child's set of values never was the teacher's long suit.

Evidently, in Wiles' high school of the future, the proportion of teacher specialists needed in a secondary school would be approximately the following:

- Specialists in value and experience analysis: 52%
- Specialists in the subject fields and in areas such as reading, evaluation, materials, etc.: 40%
- Librarians prepared for the use of new media: 8%
- In addition, each school would have a number of technicians or aides

What kind of competencies would these specialists in analysis and specialists in the subject fields and in varied skills need to have? As one examines the kind of program visualized, the following appear to be the common and more specialized competencies needed in order to implement the program:

Common competencies:
    Independent study and self-direction
    Inquiry and research procedures
    Evaluation based on individual progress
    Adjustment of program to individual differences
    Communication
    Use of materials including newer media
    Development of creativity
    Mental health

Common to all teachers, of course, would be a broad base of general education.

Special competencies:

1. Analysis Teacher

        Individual and group counseling
        Individual and group planning
        Group discussion and process

Value analysis and examination

Value conflicts, ethics, and social concerns

Community involvement

Parent contacts

Self-evaluation

Cultural backgrounds and values of inner city, suburban areas, rural areas, foreign countries

Broad in-depth cultural background especially in the behavioral sciences, social sciences, and humanities

2. Specialist Teacher

Lecturing

Visualizing concepts

Dramatic ability and speech

Communication via mass media

Depth in the field of specialty, either one of the subject fields, the cultural heritage, library, diagnosis, work experience, disadvantaged children, special education, reading, writing skills, vocational skills, urban development, media, international education, or other

In addition, I am assuming that in junior colleges and in institutions of teacher education, or in cooperation between the two, we shall be developing specialized preparation for technicians and aides to the teacher.

The analysis teacher will be a new type of specialist whose major responsibility will be helping youth to put together the pieces learned in other portions of the secondary school program; to look at what is happening in their society in relation to change; to deal with the conflicts and tensions they see about them; to channel their interests, energies, and concerns for social justice; and to initiate them into adult civic activities. This specialist will need to have far different skills from the traditional social studies teacher, who in many cases succeeded more in developing distaste for social studies than in involving youth in social concerns. As Kim has said, these teachers will be selected "because they display a high degree of empathy and are warm, outgoing personalities whom other people like." Far more important to this teacher than a typical major is a broad cultural major.

If these are the competencies demanded, in general terms to be sure, what kind of program in teacher education is needed to develop them? It is assumed that the teacher-educator will define them in behavioral terms, one of the essential skills that will be taught through cooperative teacher-student definition.

DIFFERENTIATION OF PATTERN AND TIME

Kim's vision of the pattern of teacher education for the high school teacher of the future was that different patterns of teacher education would be planned for the varied teaching functions. That the teacher's role in the school of the 1980's will be different from what it is today can be safely predicted. More of the total teacher time in a school staff will be spent in analysis, diagnosis, leading discussion, conferring with individuals, evaluating, making parent and community contacts, and planning with pupils. These will be the major types of pupil-teacher-community relationships of the analysis teacher and the specialists who work with advanced seminars, clinics, materials, other centers or laboratories, and the specialist in the teaching of disadvantaged children.

The types of specialists that need to be prepared for the future high school will be many and varied. No longer can the major-and-minor teacher preparation concept serve a school system or a society in which specialty is required. The teacher with a conglomeration of credits in a subject field, no matter what quality, will be outmoded, for the measurement of competence by credits can no longer be countenanced when the possibilities of learning will be enhanced far beyond that ever dreamed of in the 1950's.

Some teachers will be specialists in both a subject field and the learning of a subject. My own institution, for example, has currently between forty and fifty joint appointments who are such dual specialists on the College of Education staff. Some will be television teachers, programmers, technological and media specialists, librarians. Others will be specialists in evaluation, in reading, in diagnosis of learning problems, in research, in vocational education, and in the inner city problems and in urban development. In fact, the distinction between the teacher and supervisor or other specialized consultant personnel will be diminished. These are the kinds of specialists who will form teams together with aides, technicians, and intern teachers.

Surely, we will have realized by then that the principle of individual differences in teacher education does not mean that all students will need to spend an equal amount of time in a course or in an activity. Why should a student who comes well prepared from high school and who has learned mathematics and science to an increased depth in elementary and secondary school spend four or five years in his original preparation as a teacher? What rationale has led us to decree for each student teacher a like sixteen weeks in one teaching situation with one teacher?

Not only will each of the specialties demand some variation in preparation time, but so will the backgrounds and the abilities of individuals. Differentiation in the nature and length of laboratory experiences will become a necessity so that a student intern may spend some time with a specialist in history, some with a specialist in cultural heritage, some with a specialist in urban development in a community center, some with a research or evaluation specialist, some in the materials center or in the technology center. The student's program will depend on his goals and purposes planned with his analysis teacher and with his teacher education coordinator in the school.

The all-or-none theory will no longer be tenable in a teacher education program, any more than it was in secondary education twenty-eight years ago.[1] Yet, Wiles in 1963 still found it necessary to predict that graduation would be eliminated in high schools and that students would move into a job or college when they were judged ready for the initial experience. Moving from full-time teacher education to full-time teaching will be a gradual transition. For some, it may mean a half-time paid internship under the guidance of a master teacher for a year or more as the progress of the intern demands. For others, the full-time paid internship with a team guided by an experienced, expert teacher will furnish the optimum kind of induction into the teaching profession.

Teacher education admission and completion will be independent of the bachelor's degree requirement. Selection will become more important and objectively carried out. In fact, the selection process will be interwoven with preparation, planning, and decision-making toward specialization in some area of competency. Undoubtedly, imaginative school systems, in cooperation with teacher education institutions, will find ways of giving secondary students pre-teaching experiences in the laboratory of the school, which is one of the most easily provided without additional cost. The secondary school student's experience in working with the handicapped and disadvantaged as a tutor and guide, in or out of school, could be one of his most fruitful high school experiences.

As such a concept of continuing teacher education in place of the all-or-none idea is implemented, inservice education will also assume the characteristics of a planned program, with built-in provision for individual differences, rather than a mass accumulation of credits merely because a course is offered conveniently in the teacher's back yard. The change that has been gradually coming will be seriously recognized by professional teachers' associations and by school systems: the continuation of teacher preparation throughout life. For there can be no stopping of the learning process of the teacher in the rapidly changing age of the future. Even the changing social conditions—to say nothing of what knowledge is being accumulated in a speciality or in the teaching-learning process—demand it.

INDEPENDENT STUDY AND SELF-DIRECTION

The expectations of the secondary school in which independent study and individual progress will be common will demand that a teacher's experience in a teacher education institution be of the same genre. Secondary schools have advanced considerably in recent years in providing genuine independent study opportunities to the extent that students can profit by it. Surprisingly enough, these schools have found that far more students respond positively to this kind of learning freedom than they had suspected. Why then does a doctoral candidate in a university, who supposedly is selected for his ability to become an independent scholar, take ninety or more credits in a doctoral program, most of them in organized courses? If we have to be slaves to a credit system, then let us be sensible about it and allow credit for important accomplishments whether in a classroom, a laboratory, a community, or in a library. We have done this with student teaching and with internships. As a teacher advances to graduate work, we should assume that he is being selected because of his capability of continuously engaging in more self-directed study with competent advice and assistance when needed or desired.

Such a concept of progress toward self-directed study would not be too difficult to effect. The means are there at our disposal. Over the past few years, those of us in teacher education institutions have assisted in placing and providing more adequate libraries, new computer centers, counseling centers, and audiovisual service centers on college campuses. There are also the dormitories, the science laboratories, the industrial arts shops, the music and art laboratories, the home economics laboratories.

At the University of Maryland within the College of Education itself are the industrial arts laboratories, a counseling laboratory, a reading center, a science teaching center, an educational technology center, a nursery-kindergarten school-research laboratory, a bureau of educational research and field services, an office of laboratory experiences, an institute for child study, a curriculum laboratory, a statistics laboratory, a comparative education center, a special education classroom-laboratory, a home economics education laboratory, and a mathematics education center. Each of these facilities includes special types of materials, equipment, services, or personnel. Each lends itself to independent study for the undergraduate student, the graduate student, and the teacher in service. Some of these service centers are utilized extensively. In the case of others, we have yet to realize their potential.

The Educational Technology Center, for example, provides equipment, facilities, and personnel for programmed instruction, micro-teaching, video-taping, teaching by television, computer-based instruction; laboratories for constructing audio-visual aids, for independent learning of the use of projectors, and for research in the instructional media.

The teacher preparation program for the high school teacher of the future will undoubtedly center its instruction around facilities and services such as these, plus others now either undreamed of or a gleam of an idea in some inventive educator's mind.

THE PUBLIC SCHOOL LABORATORY

The best laboratory for teacher education is the public school. In the past few decades, teacher education has advanced most rapidly in the area of providing laboratory experiences in the public schools. The progress has come about through the combined efforts of the schools and the teacher education institutions.

I believe we have long recognized that the teaching process and the duties associated with teaching are best learned in the laboratory of the classroom and the school, working with children. The laboratory school was a product of this concept. Now the media, such as video-tape recorders, make possible even more effective directed observation and analysis of teaching as a supplement to observation within a school building.

The public school as a laboratory for teacher education is an outgrowth of the campus laboratory school, while the latter has moved in the direction of developing experimental programs and research. In the future, the public school will receive direct support from the state for teacher education in order to provide time for teachers to perform this function in which the profession should play a significant part. The school system itself will be an integral part of teacher education for all types of laboratory experiences from the person's high school days throughout his teaching career.

The teacher education center is not new, but it has taken on a new vitality and a different orientation in the past few years. No longer is it thought of merely as a place in which student teachers can receive their practice teaching. The focus in more recent developments is on the experiences and content of the teacher preparation that occurs in the center.

The Teacher Education Center program cooperatively developed by the University of Maryland, the public schools of Maryland and the District of Columbia, and the Maryland State Department of Education is one example of an emerging partnership in teacher education. The planning for the center is done together from the beginning to encompass one or more contiguous schools in an area. Financial support comes both from the school system and the University. A key feature is the joint employment of a teacher education coordinator who is located in the center but who is also a faculty member of the College of Education. The salary of the coordinator is paid jointly. He is cooperatively selected. In essence, he is the leader for teacher education experiences in that center, having full time to devote to this function. He works with the college students in their student teaching and their laboratory experiences, and plans with the teachers and each student the type and length of experience that the student is to have. He also works with the principals and the University faculty in providing inservice education for the teachers in that school who are especially selected for their competency and for their interest in teacher education.

Students from the University are assigned to a school, not to a teacher. The entire school, in other words, has responsibility for teacher education. The university supervisor's function becomes that of an inservice educator and consultant who works with the teacher education specialists (the teachers) in the school.

Funds provided through the University are used for inservice workshops, materials, travel to conferences for the teachers, and benefits that will help them in their professional improvement rather than providing the usual pittance of extra pay. The goal is to give teachers an adjusted load which makes provision for spending time with the student.

In the development of the public school laboratory for teacher education in the future, additional teachers provided through state funds will make it possible for the teacher to work with teacher education students or interns from a quarter to three-quarters time, depending on the circumstances. This teacher will, through his continued study, become a specialist in teacher education—one who will be more effective than any supervisor from a college could possibly be—for this will be a day-to-day interaction between supervisor and student.

Internships at the advanced and graduate level will be more common for learning specialized skills and for advanced graduate specialist degrees or diplomas. The continuous education concept will blur the distinction between pre-service and inservice education, only some of which will necessarily lead to the master's or advanced degrees.

In this type of context of teacher education, methods courses as we now know them will be outmoded. The typical methods course is based on the assumption that a teacher will be teaching a class of twenty-five to thirty-five students. In an age of technology in education and independent self-direction, this concept will not be relevant. The newer technology will make possible the study and analysis of teaching more objectively and scientifically than we have previously been able to do. The teaching of methods will be integrated with the work with students in the public schools—a cooperative responsibility among the teachers in the school, the teacher education coordinator, and the college faculty members. This will be the team that will provide for future methods "courses" that may not look like courses at all.

LABORATORY FOR COMMUNITY AND CULTURE STUDY

Another basic ingredient of teacher education of the future relevant to secondary school education will provide for an understanding of human behavior within community groups, the social structure, the culture of different countries and different socioeconomic backgrounds within this country. Such study would, of course, be related to the study of the cultural heritage but with an emphasis on the "why."

Secondary school teachers will have to be more knowledgeable about other cultures and peoples and international relationships. For high school youth, who are idealistic, will need to have their energies absorbed and their thinking stimulated as to how they can participate in building a better world for themselves. Riots, protest movements, and dropping out of society are not the answer. But moralizing about the "young people of today" or deploring the lack of "law and order" do little to remedy the situation. Unless teachers become intelligently informed about problems of a rapidly changing society and become convinced of the need and importance of working with youth to analyze the world in which they find themselves, they will be sadly ineffective. An experience I recently had in talking informally with an Upward Bound group of high school students left a deep impression on me. These young people were saying to me that the difference between the experience in the Upward Bound program and in their own high school was that somebody in this special program listened to them and was concerned in helping them solve their problems. Such problem-solving teachers are required in the high school of the future.

The laboratory for community and culture study may not even be a place, but could be many situations in which the study of human behavior, communication, and international understanding could develop.[2] Part of the study would be in seminars of an interdisciplinary nature; part would be in general education classes with the problems approach. Another facet would be in independent research activities in which a student or a group of students would dig out the facts and arrive at tentative conclusions to be further tested. The content would be selected for its value in developing skills and values considered desirable and in looking at social issues in an open-ended way.

But all of these classroom or independent library research activities would need a base of experience with a culture, with an inner city or a rural impoverished area, with an affluent suburban community, or with a foreign country. Such experiences are within the realm of possibility for a country in which young people now travel widely all over the world. If we can dream up an imaginative idea such as the Peace Corps and the Teacher Corps, we can surely develop schemes to make a laboratory of human experience operational. We are wealthy enough to do so if we are willing to make some sacrifices for the education of our youth in order to build a better world.

I have sat with Kim Wiles through many a "seminar" in ASCD. I think I knew him well enough to conclude that he would have nodded approval to some of what I have said regarding the education of the teacher for his future high school. But I also am sure that he would have challenged some of these notions in his characteristic vigorous manner. Teacher education in this country and I, personally, are the more impoverished because he cannot do so.

References

1. Vernon E. Anderson, "The All-or-None Theory of Education Applied to American Life Today," *School and Society*, 54: 426-34 (November 15, 1941).
2. See Chap. 8 of Vernon E. Anderson, *Guidelines for a New Era of Curriculum Change* (New York: The Ronald Press Company, 1969) for further discussion of this idea.

part 6

Leadership for Developing the School of the Future

chapter 18

Robert S. Gilchrist*

Leadership for Schools of the Future

EDUCATION MIRRORS SOCIAL UNREST

The intensive ferment in education of the sixties is both a reflection of and a facet of the broader social ferment in today's world. Prospects for the seventies indicate a continuation of these spasms of social change erupting with even greater intensity. In the light of the probability of additional convulsive conflicts in education, and in contemplation of the realization of the high school of the future as envisioned by Kim Wiles, we must face the critical questions which affect the future of American education:

- What is the significance to education of current waves of unrest on all fronts?

- What kind of society do Americans desire, and how can the schools be consistent with and supportive of that aim?

- What implications for an emerging educational leadership do the answers to the previous questions hold?

---

* See pp. 238–239 for the author's list of associates in the preparation of this chapter.

It is easy to recognize general unrest, but if we are to utilize the forces of change for guiding education, we must clearly identify specific sources of this unrest. Areas of tension which touch most directly upon education include: (1) The movement toward teacher power which is daily gaining momentum, (2) the patterns of shifting administrative functions with a realignment of roles, and (3) the awakening of citizens to power with strident voices demanding a share in decision making.

Additional elements in revolution include: (1) *An aroused college-age youth* demanding to be heard. Every campus across the nation has been touched in some way by a new spirit of activism in the student body. Students insist upon being included in policy making, but all too often the expression of student opinion has led to violent action and reaction. (2) *Academicians, or subject-area specialists* raising another voice for change in education with each discipline vying to promote its principal concerns. Curriculums, teaching methods, and behaviors of teachers and students are being affected as a result of new attention from subject specialists. (3) *Business and industry* rapidly accumulating power which promises to become an even greater factor with which future educational leadership must work. Big business has discovered that education is also "big business." Educational materials of all kinds are developed through the new corporations which merge a business or industry with a communications giant and a textbook company. Such mergers open up opportunities for education which could not otherwise have developed, yet they also pose a potential threat to the development of healthy participation by other groups in the selection and control of educational experiences. If education is to fulfill its responsibilities to a democratic society, it is essential that the decision-making process be broadly shared. Decisions must be rooted in a wider distribution and balance of citizen and professional groups who participate in planning educational futures.

The tremendous expansions of knowledge and technology give human beings a new sense of the possibilities for realizing the "good life" for all people. The opportunity is already before us to rise to new heights of idealism and altruism. At the same time, either our fear of the ferments of change, or our desire to use changes for our own advantage, pulls us toward selfish and materialistic ends.

In this age of rapid and basic kinds of change, the future of mankind hangs in the balance. It is yet to be decided whether we can create a world of free men or whether authoritarianism and servitude will predominate. Kim Wiles' dream for the high school of the future can and will be realized only if there are enough courageous emerging leaders among teachers, administrators, college educators, students, and citizens. With concerted teamwork toward common goals, education can become the kind which children must have if the American way of life is to be strengthened and preserved. However, no one can assume that all is going to turn out well. This is a time when a single decision may determine a direction. This is an era of daily crucial decisions. It is a time when "the chips are down," and we must roll up our sleeves and put all our energies into understanding and solving educational dilemmas. Theoretical analyses must be pragmatically tested. Education unquestionably mirrors the problems of society, and schools cannot solve such complex problems for the nation as a whole. There is no guarantee that we can be successful in developing solutions consistent with our ideals. Conditions may continue to be critical in spite of all we do, but educational leaders must make a constant effort to work with diverse groups in order to strengthen education.

SEEKING A COMMON GOAL

In order to move forward and keep perspective on the conflicts for controls in education, all groups demanding greater power must focus on the goals which they hold in common. Central to all concerns should be a conviction that schools, above all, should be environments for learning, not simply buildings where knowledge is acquired by memorization, skills developed through routine drill, habits inculcated by repetition, and attitudes formed by indoctrination. Prerequisite to a good environment for learning must be the developing of teachers and administrators who derive satisfaction not by becoming authoritarian experts, but rather by becoming facilitators and partners in learning.

Knowledge is constantly expanding, but enough is already known about learning theory, about the developmental needs of children, about the demands of living in the foreseeable future, and about the priorities society sets on values to provide a concrete basis for spelling out what constitutes a good learning environment. Basic to such a description are the following principles:

1. Pupils must be active participants in learning, in goal setting, in planning and executing a program for achieving the goals and in the evaluation of the realization of their aims. Pupils must be *involved*, not simply externally motivated. This learning environment must produce a new generation of students who will want to go on learning throughout a lifetime.
2. The curriculum must provide variety, depth, and balance of ideas and experiences for pupils who will be seeking order and se-

quence for the learning which they individually and in groups
pursue.
3. The school and classroom must be organized to provide for the
individual. Provisions must be available for independence in
learning as maturity permits. Arrangements must provide opportunities for small group instruction in order to permit peer interaction as pupils cope with problems and acquire ideas. The
entire physical and human environment of the school needs to
be organized to foster the development of pupil self-direction in
learning to the end that the individual will become eager to continue learning beyond the formal days and hours of school. John
Gardner emphasizes this belief in his book *Self-Renewal:*

> Exploration of the full range of his own potentialities is not
> something that the self-renewing man leaves to the chances
> of life. It is something he pursues systematically, or at least
> avidly, to the end of his days. He looks forward to an endless
> and unpredictable dialogue between his potentialities and the
> claims of life—not only the claims he encounters, but the
> claims he invents. And by potentialities I mean not just skills,
> but the full range of his capacities for sensing, wondering,
> learning, understanding, loving and aspiring.
>
> . . . .
>
> The ultimate goal of the educational system is to shift to the
> individual the burden of pursuing his own education.[1]

EVOLUTION OR REVOLUTION IN
EDUCATIONAL LEADERSHIP?

Who is to lead the schools of the future? We are now caught in the
grip of a struggle for power within education which may well para-
lyze future leadership or which could produce a combination of leadership from many sources stronger than any we have ever witnessed.
Even though we optimistically believe the latter will be the outcome,
the decade ahead seems destined to be the scene of a long, painful
metamorphosis in educational leadership.

Some who comment on the situation today believe the present system of school administrative organizations is obsolete. They predict
that administrators at all levels will be stripped of power or replaced by
management specialists. They predict that school boards will be phased
out in favor of city council control of schools, through overall city
budget policies, with management firms operating the schools on a
contractual basis.

A current assessment of the opinions of educational leaders as expressed by a review of the latest literature is inadequate, since the literature is already months or years behind recent developments. I chose to gather immediate reactions by reaching out horizontally across the nation, contacting people in strategic roles. Letters were mailed to a selected group of superintendents, principals, directors of curriculums, and educators holding key positions in professional organizations and institutions of higher education. They were asked to react to two questions:

1. What will be the outcome of the struggles currently waged regarding the role of the teacher in decision making, not only in respect to salaries and welfare matters, but also to the educational program?

2. What do you think administrators can and should do, in concert with teachers, to build for the best possible education in the future?

The promptness of response was a gratifying indication that the issues are viewed as critically important. The responses are powerfully written with each person presenting a unique view, although there is remarkable consistency from one respondent to the next. It is impossible to quote from or cite each letter separately, but the names and positions of all who replied are included in the reference list. These responses strengthened my own judgments, deepened my insights, and in some instances gave new direction to my thinking. The ideas presented in this chapter often reflect the contributions of those who generously responded to the previous questions.

The broad areas of general agreement among leaders include a belief that superintendents, principals, and supervisors will continue to be essential in educational leadership. There is vigorous disagreement that these roles are "done for," although change is predicted in roles for both teachers and administrators. Most respondents agree that teacher participation in decision making will increase. They also view the present ferment of teacher power as a healthy, though traumatic, development.

Concern is expressed that too many administrators expend their energies defending outmoded patterns of behavior, rather than capitalizing on current professional agitation to help move schools forward.

These responses all support the point of view that challenges for educational leadership should be attacked through application of strategy referred to by Harold and June Grant Shane as "Future-Planning."[2] The future must be planned in the present. Deliberate attention needs to be given to projecting educational designs which will create the best learning environments.

EMERGING LEADERSHIP: CONFLICT
OR COOPERATION?

The Future of Teacher Power

The recent trend toward bureaucracy in education has been an inevitable result of the growing complexity of an urbanized society. The need within school systems for organization and specialization, which are facilitated through bureaucratic structures, has also led to a mounting conflict between teachers and administrators. In a bureaucratic system, teachers frequently feel a loss of identity, a sense of relative insignificance, and consequently a feeling of deep alienation. John Goodlad has observed that the emphasis in too many school systems has shifted from an organization which exists in order to efficiently perform primary tasks, to a bureaucratic system which exists as an end in itself striving to perpetuate the status quo.[3] Frances Link calls the school a "tightly scheduled island" which has contributed to teacher alienation.[4] Teachers frequently feel themselves isolated in an impersonal system which seems to hold no concern for them as people, but is preponderantly concerned with reports, schedules, rules, and rigid controls. The eruption of teacher power as a reaction against this dehumanization of teachers is the focus of present and future controversy.

The rise of teacher militancy was one of the most significant movements in education in the 60's and will continue a wave of change in the balance of power for the 70's. Some decry a lack of professionalism in collective bargaining, but many more believe that these developments usher in a new professional day for educators. Teachers are becoming better educated, more committed to their profession, and more courageous in their personal convictions than ever before. In some cases, although still too few in number, they present a kind of leadership which does not center around salaries and welfare matters alone, but around demands for improved conditions essential to good teaching and learning. Even the salary squabbles should result in qualitative advances in professional strength. Better salaries and improved status will make teaching more attractive to the high-caliber individuals we need to recruit. This will lead directly to improved education at the classroom level, if teachers accept a professional responsibility for demanding not just what is good for teachers but rather what is ultimately best for children in the classroom.

A complaint made against teacher power is often based on the belief that too frequently teachers hold a common unspoken conviction that the schools operate for the benefit of teachers or school personnel. I share the faith, however, of the many observers who believe that the two million American teachers will increasingly not base their negotiations primarily on teacher welfare matters, but will place salary and related welfare considerations in a setting for the kinds of schools which are necessary for the best learning for children. The potential of these more than two million teachers of America to influence the education of the future is obviously important, not only because they represent by far the largest portion of those in the education profession, but because they, in the final analysis, are the professionals who will either improve the quality of the educational experiences of children or permit it to deteriorate.

In spite of the recognition that in some instances teachers are learning ways to couch their welfare demands in terms of what is best for children's learning, predominantly, teacher power, at the present is not even beginning to concern itself with children. The representatives speaking for teachers today are usually chosen for their aggressiveness and vociferousness, not for their skills as teachers or for the soundness and depth of their educational philosophies. In fact, too few teachers of professional caliber are even becoming involved in the teachers' struggles. Administrators may well view this as an ominous situation. The wise administrator should encourage his most competent teachers to become actively involved in teacher welfare movements since these teachers are the professionals who will be most qualified to think beyond immediate personal gains. More often, however, administrators reward those teachers who do not become activists in educational causes. They speak approvingly of teachers who "don't rock the boat" without realizing they are encouraging defeat of democratic principles by default.

One educator wrote that administrators (to take a leaf from Eric Fromm) have given teachers freedom *from*, but not freedom *to*. Nathaniel Ober wrote, "We have given them freedom from interference and supervision, but we have failed to give them freedom to work cooperatively with one another and to control the conditions under which they carry out their art and science."

If teachers are to rise to the challenge of their newly won power, they must learn to formulate and enforce professional discipline. They must take initiative in establishing machinery and avenues for evaluation, both of their own effectiveness as teachers and that of their peers. In the avalanche of increased bargaining rights, they must choose carefully as spokesmen those who have deepest insights regarding the educational process and the requirements of an environment for learning.

With the new power comes awesome responsibility. If teachers are to become full-fledged partners in decision making, it is hoped they will exhibit the maturity of a point of view broader than the confines of their personal classrooms. This will require continuous self-appraisal and self-development. It will require improved abilities in setting objectives, assessing personal results, and analyzing one's own teaching performance. It will require improved skill in interpersonal relations in order to work cooperatively with other leadership groups. It will require the kind of occupational commitment which assumes teaching to be a year-round, full-time profession.

The great promise in the surge of teacher voices in decision making is the belief that teachers really want to teach; they want to bring the best of their abilities into their classrooms and can no longer tolerate the violations of good learning conditions which past apathy has permitted.

Teachers, if they assume the burden of mature leadership, will soon move soberly beyond the impetuousness of the first flush of power. They will find that, if decisions are to be made and total stalemates avoided, many cooperative and, perhaps at times, compromising measures must be utilized. Without this acceptance of something less than total victory for any one group, except as it leads to better education for children, the decision-making process could become immobilized in a "dead center" struggle. School leaders, teachers, and administrators, must develop sensitivity to community concerns and long-term social goals. They must cultivate the habit of looking beyond the solutions of the moment in order to foresee conditions and consequences of today's actions on tomorrow's problems.

The Future of Administrator Power

In spite of the necessity for cooperation, teachers perceive administrators as adversaries when superintendents are forced by collective bargaining, as they increasingly are, to become exclusive representatives for the Board of Education. A parallel to the superintendent is the principal when he is viewed by teachers as part of an impersonal management team evaluating classroom operations in terms of cost and maintenance of the status quo.

Is the future of the administrator to be written in terms of the widening chasm? Or is the administrator already an obsolete figurehead for management? Far from becoming less important, the role of administrators is going to grow more essential for coordinating and harnessing conflicting sources of leadership toward educational goals.

The need now, and for the future, is for a high order of leadership which will strengthen, rather than diminish, the importance of the administrator's role in education. With greater teacher power, there will be a greater need for strong administrative leadership and coordination. Negotiations will expand the facilitating role of the administrator and will enhance, rather than limit, the possibilities of this role.

The present ferment provides a ripe opportunity to overhaul administrative practices which have long needed improving. Much needs to be done about administration to correct the tendency toward myopic concerns with budgets, busses, buildings, and bonds. There is a general acceptance among administrators that, as a group, they haven't learned how to manage both internal school problems and external public relations in terms of *educational leadership*.

A new brand of educational statesmanship is necessary to lift the administrator to a level of professional leadership which has seldom been attained but which is altogether feasible. The sharp lines existing between teachers and administrators in the old line-and-staff organization are already changing as some administrators exhibit a kind of leadership which is sensitive to the interests and needs of the schools they serve.

Diversification and specialization of administrative functions are necessary as the demands of education become more complex. Management skills will certainly be given high priority, but the administrator who is a management expert serves his schools much better when he can combine professional statesmanship with that operation.

It is useless to debate whether the administrator of the future should have an exclusive management function or an instructional-leadership function. Synchronization of these functions is of major importance whether they are performed by one man or several. James Allen makes this point clear by recognizing the expansion and complexity of the two roles which require an overall coordination. He anticipates that large school systems will have separate management and instructional staffs with heads reporting to the overall administrator. In a letter to the author he states:

> In a well-managed system, the decision makers at each level will need to get information about both the management aspects of the organization and the success with which it is achieving its instructional goals. Only by putting these two factors together can meaningful decisions be made in educational institutions that will result

in improving quality. A system that may appear to be running smoothly from a management point of view may be failing to achieve its instructional objectives. The function of administration will be to see that the resources needed to provide quality instruction are provided *and* to ensure that the resources are utilized effectively to achieve the objectives of the organization. This means that the top administrator must concern himself both with management and with basic educational objectives.

The management function cannot be isolated from the overall leadership responsibilities. These are not mutually exclusive functions; however they require an open, flexible system and a new breed of generalist in the leadership role. The new leadership must exhibit both general and specific competencies in order to constructively channel the emerging streams of power. Warren Brown expresses it this way:

> The competent school official, possessing broad knowledge about education, effective human relations skills, and managerial ability, will find his expertise in great demand as educators attempt to solve the complex problems of the future. Management and educational leadership are not dichotomous functions, since in the educational scene management is the process by which educational goals are implemented in a social system.

There is a distinct trend away from school administration of the past in which one person combined the functions of two roles: (1) the management role in which he implemented the policies of the Board of Education, and (2) the instructional-leadership role in which he helped teachers with the overall instructional problems. These roles will eventually become quite distinct except in a few school systems. For a long time and perhaps always, there will be some schools which will continue to unite these roles; however, their separation does not divide them in their ultimate goals. These two roles have separate responsibilities and their purposes are directed toward different groups, but they should be eventually integrally meshed in the smooth operations of the schools.

All who have responsibilities for educational leadership, all who participate in any way in educational decisions, must share in bringing their power to focus on what is best for children in the classroom. In the hubbub of debate about the changing roles of leadership, the basic reason for the existence of any of these roles often seems lost in the dust raised by the conflict.

The principle of working with children or adults in ways which can best develop and channel their abilities seems too easily forgotten by some administrators as they work with teachers. An administrator can be highly vulnerable to the same danger which faces teachers or citizens. The danger is that of becoming rigid, inflexible, authoritarian, and close-minded toward the approaches recommended from a different frame of reference. Administrators must demonstrate with teachers the operation of sound principles of human relationships which they expect teachers to utilize with pupils.

The Future of Citizen Participation in Power

Yet another source is demanding power through "equal time" in decision making. A better informed and often irate citizenry is putting pressure on boards, administration, and teachers to gain a position of some authority in certain areas of school policy.

School boards, as well as administrators, have in many cases, never learned to be responsive to any but the most vociferous or prestigious of community groups. Local control of schools was once a matter of geographic necessity; now it is a socio-psychological imperative. The school of the future must be controlled locally in a context harmonious with democratic goals for lifting the ceiling of educational opportunity for every individual. The dehumanization of education through institutionalized bureaucracy must be reversed with new approaches to school decentralization. The individual school with its local citizenry must have more control over the directions of education in that school. Teachers, along with the entire spectrum of professional educators, must become articulate in expressing to citizens their best judgments about educational needs. As parents and citizens at large become more and more strategically involved in decision making, educators must push themselves to communicate and become responsive in a new kind of partnership with parents.

The demands of citizens are not always polite or without expressed threat to administrators. The frustration of some citizen groups cause raw feelings to explode in many cases. This points again to the greater need for a responsive staff of educational leaders who are sensitive to the demands of the public.

Teachers alone cannot be that sensitive, nor should they need to be, since they have other primary job responsibilities. There must be some who are responsible for the total scope of the educational program from what is presently still termed "pre-school" through the post-high school program. These responsible persons will emerge as a new brand of administrator. They must be able to see that the right questions are raised; that the critical issues are kept in perspective by all groups engaged in the decision-making process.

Even if administrators were to serve ably and skillfully in their positions, they alone could not adequately assess the feelings and concerns of citizens. It is at the classroom level that the public nerve is touched. Participation of citizens in constructively shaping the program of the school strongly depends upon the attitudes and skills of the classroom teacher. Positive community participation cannot be built without the involvement of individual teachers who serve as keystones in a structure of community cooperation. Unless there is face-to-face discussion between individuals and small groups of teachers and citizens, there can be no foundation in the local school situation upon which overall decisions can be based. The larger policies will be superficial without basic community support.

ESTABLISHING PRIORITIES

Many schools are in operation without questioning their purposes and directions, simply because custom dictates. Other school systems cannot get above immediate emergencies in order to examine or define long-range goals. In many cases, citizens are pushing harder than administrators for forward-looking improvements.

When administrators, teachers, and citizens can agree upon priorities in goals for their schools, and can keep these before them as primary objectives in conferences or controversies, then it will be possible to resolve issues and apply solutions without the destructive divisiveness which occurs when each group mistrusts the motives of the other. There is no need for conflict between the administrator who is a good management person and his teachers, if both of them are performing in terms of the same goal—trying to do the best possible job of providing sound educational opportunities.

BRIDGING THE GAP BETWEEN
KNOWLEDGE AND PRACTICE

The gap between theory and practice is frequently cited as a weakness in all areas of human experience, but it is particularly acute in education. The future picture of educational leadership depends upon our ability to apply to education the knowledge we now have, to say little of applying the new data developing through behavioral science research. The profession must go through an educational "stretching machine," to borrow an analogy from Max Beberman's mathematics games. Teachers and administrators must grow into new leadership roles by deliberately "stretching" (1) to assimilate the new skills in human relations, (2) to learn the appropriate behaviors (including knowledge, skills, and attitudes) of a disciplined professional educator, and (3) to evaluate honestly, carefully, and with new precision the outcomes of the educational effort.

Growing in Human Relations Skills

If we examine closely these three areas in which we need to develop professional skills, we are brought face-to-face with this question. What have we done about the skills in human relations which have been misused for so many years?

The use of human relations skills to manipulate and control must be jettisoned. Time cannot be wasted on such masquerades. Good human relations has always been advocated in education. No one worked for human understanding and openness between administrator and staff more than Kim Wiles; but as Mel Barnes puts it, these principles have been honored more in the breach than in the observance.

Group process and mediation skills are not soft-hearted luxuries; they are essential for survival. Fortunately, developments in research in group dynamics and interpersonal relations have paralleled the need for practical training. The Institute for Applied Behavioral Science has demonstrated the value of sensitivity training for educational leaders. The techniques are not used for manipulation, but rather for improved communication, for deeper awareness of barriers to understanding, for increased sensitivity to the feelings expressed in human interaction.

These skills must be part of the training of the new teacher and the new administrator, as well as the re-educating of those already in service. Many more institutions of higher education should be designing programs for administrators which include heavy emphasis on human relations skills, as well as other newer studies in management, educational programming, systems analysis, and similar technical skills.

The classroom must be brought into focus as a microcosm in which broader human relations principles can be seen in live action. The way in which teachers relate to children in a classroom must be consistent with the way in which they expect to be treated by one another or by the administration. The teacher who rules a classroom as a dogmatic

The High School of the Future

authoritarian, organizing and executing without including children in decision making, cannot expect his relationships with others on the staff to be any more democratic. The principles of respect for individual opinion and belief in human capacities for wise self-direction must be extended, first of all, to children in the classroom.

Growing Professionally in Knowledge, Skills, and Attitudes

Professional growth encompasses a wide range of abilities which need attention if educators are to become leaders in a profession. Heavy emphasis in the future will be upon research methodology, ability to apply technology to educational planning, skills in analyzing in depth the teaching-learning process, as well as numerous other specialized abilities.

Without desiring to reopen old semantic arguments about whether or not teaching can be labeled a profession, or whether unionism is the antithesis of professionalism, it is simply evident that leaders of schools in the future must have many more specialized professional skills than have been required in the past. A sharpened understanding of the specialized roles of the members of the new leadership team will be necessary. If educators are to function effectively in their new roles, the expectations of others with whom they work must be changed. For example, an administrator can hardly be successful functioning in a democratic framework if teachers view him as still governed in his behavior by authoritarian principles. Teachers' roles with children must change sharply as teachers learn to behave as guides, evaluators, and prescribers in the learning environment. The teaching function of the future will be so complex that it is unwise to speak of a single teaching role when many different and equally important roles are emerging.

One of these new roles is that of the educator as a researcher. Professional development and teacher education will soon give even more rigorous attention to research and its possible applications in education. While research and development will be the special full-time interest of certain members of the profession, all categories of leadership will be required to keep abreast of these developments. The professional educator will of necessity be involved in some form of applied research and will need to be knowledgeable about planning, designing, and evaluating.

Another mark of professional leadership will be the year-round employment of all teachers. We can no longer tolerate the waste of talent and resources which comes from a lack of utilization of professional energy devoted full time to the business of improving education. Those who would cling to teaching as a part-time responsibility will be misfits in the system and will be outside the professional ranks.

Growing Toward Precision in Evaluation

Evaluation of processes and goals is integrally related to the previous areas of needed growth. Educators must build in the process of continuous evaluation at all levels. Teachers individually, faculties of a school unit, school systems as a whole, and colleges of education must take seriously the question of how well the schools are achieving their goals. Ralph Tyler and others for many years have insisted upon the need for clear objectives and clear programs for attaining those objectives. Schools have neglected to study the outcomes of the various elements of their programs or their total effectiveness.

The current movement toward a national assessment is an outgrowth of the frustration of those who believe schools must become goal-oriented and specific about what they are doing. Regardless of the outcome of national assessment, educators must evaluate incisively in the local school. Educational leaders are needed who can assist teachers in self-evaluation through more objective methods, through the use of technology and varied techniques such as video, for analyzing their instructional behavior and the interaction in their classrooms.

Daniel L. Stufflebeam at The Ohio State University is illustrative of a group of evaluators bringing new and valuable contributions to those who are serious about wanting to evaluate. Stufflebeam says evaluations must fit the kinds of educational decisions to be made at each point. The decisions are classified as (1) planning, (2) programming, (3) implementing, and (4) recycling. Consequently, there are four kinds of evaluation, one for each decision step: (1) context evaluation, (2) input evaluation, (3) process evaluation, and (4) product evaluation. The adequacy of the evaluation must also be judged in terms of validity, timeliness, and creditability.[5]

The major problem for schools is in becoming clear on goals and in spelling out in objectively measurable terms the precise steps for evaluating their successes and failures. In addition to designing a plan for careful evaluation, the schools all too frequently do not provide the personnel or the channels through which to execute ongoing evaluative processes. Schools of the future will have a specialized research, development, and evaluation staff with a sizeable portion of the budget to support the collecting of concrete answers for critical questions about education.

CULTIVATING THE RESPONSIVE
ENVIRONMENT

The major task facing the leaders who will guide schools of the future is the creation and nourishment of a responsive environment in which there is honest interaction and dialogue between professional groups and citizens in all possible combinations. This environment must provide for true teamwork which will produce the best types of cooperatively planned educational programs. Teachers can no longer be individual entrepreneurs insulated by their classrooms against external interference. Neither can administrators command an awesome respect through distance on a hierarchical line. It is to be hoped that citizens, too, will be willing to share, rather than control, in decision making.

The new role for teachers as educational leaders is dramatic. But equally significant are the opportunities for principals, supervisors, and superintendents. As power between these groups equalizes, cooperative team efforts must materialize.

Of course there will be conflict. The kinds of people to whom teaching is attractive should be bold innovators, independent thinkers, courageous leaders who are almost certain to keep the "pot boiling." The administrator who is a human resource engineer can provide a climate responsive to diversity of opinion and uniqueness of individual teachers.

The professional climate should be designed to support unconventionality in teachers. W. W. Charters of Oregon University expresses this need clearly in his response to the author:

> It is my distinct feeling that forces are abroad in today's schools to drive out of teaching (and to prevent entry into teaching) all but the most compliant, safe and conventional persons. To foster unconventionality, of course, is to create tensions, conflict, and controversy. By definition, a bureaucratic system cannot operate smoothly and efficiently when filled with people who challenge even the smallest routine. Yet I am ready to risk a good bit of this for the sake of creating learning environments that are non-routine in themselves.

The point of emphasis is on what happens in the classroom between the teachers and students who are learning there. We cannot regiment and rigidly control teachers and students in a democratic society. We nourish independence and responsibility; we cherish individuality again in a context of responsiveness to others. The crux of all the ferment in educational leadership comes down to the quality of relationships and experiences between individuals within the learning environment.

Challenges and threats to leadership for the future are many, but the opportunities for realizing the dream of the future school are greater than ever before. We must decide in advance which way we shall go and work toward that end. Two alternatives emerge in bold outline: We can go in the direction of alienation through protection of old administrative structures, through further dehumanization of teachers and students by unwieldy bureaucratic practices and impersonal relationships; or we can go in the direction which requires recognition and respect for a new kind of teacher who must demonstrate superior professional skills, and which requires a new framework for leadership emphasizing specialization of functions, decentralization of authority, high competence in working with diverse groups in order to move education forward through shared responsibility for planning goals, designing procedures and implementing evaluation. To go in the latter direction requires an invigorating and responsive professional environment in which educators are committed to life-long teaching in an atmosphere which will produce students who are committed to life-long learning. This cannot happen automatically with the passing of time. Today's leaders in education must become much more energetic in working for the development of commitment to education.

The principle upon which decisions of educational leaders or citizens involved in the selection of educational priorities should be based was expressed by Carl Rogers in this climactic statement: "The only man who is educated is the man who has learned how to learn; the man who has learned how to adapt and change; the man who has realized that no knowledge is secure, that only the process of seeking knowledge gives a basis for security."[6]

The final product we in education are seeking is the kind of person just described. The ultimate goal for leadership in education, regardless of whether it comes from citizens, teachers, or administrators, is the provision of a learning environment where a child can grow toward becoming an educated citizen. All who influence educational decisions must keep the final goal before them as they work through the tangle of immediate problems and intermediate goals. The educational leader today must set the stage for tomorrow's schools by becoming more sensitively aware of the dynamics of the present conflicts, and by becoming more vigorous in his determination to not weaken in pursuit of the quality of education needed in our nation's schools.

References

1. John Gardner, *Self-Renewal: The Individual and the Innovative Society* (New York: Harper & Row, Publishers, 1963), pp. 3-4.
2. Harold G. Shane and June Grant Shane, "Future-Planning and the Curriculum," *Phi Delta Kappan*, 49(7):372-7 (March, 1968).
3. *Los Angeles Times*, July 23, 1968, Part II, p. 6.
4. Frances Link, "Social Planning and Social Change," *Educational Leadership* (February, 1968).
5. " 'CIPP'—Stufflebeam's Evaluation Model," *PACE Report* (November, 1957), pp. 10-13. Duplicated by Eastern Illinois Development and Service Unit, 410 E. Polk, Charleston, Illinois.
6. Carl Rogers, "Quotation," *SRIS Quarterly*, (Spring, 1968), p. 1.

List of Contributors

Dr. James E. Allen, Commissioner of Education, State of New York, Albany, New York; Edwin R. Bailey, Chairman, Division of Educational Administration, University of Missouri at Kansas City, 5100 Rockhill Road, Kansas City, Missouri; Dr. Melvin Barnes, Superintendent of Schools, Portland, Oregon; Dr. Leslee J. Bishop, Former Executive Secretary, Association for Supervision and Curriculum Development, 1201 Sixteenth Street, N.W., Washington, D.C.; Dr. Alden Blankenship, Assistant Director, Educational Research Council of America, Rockefeller Building, Cleveland, Ohio; Dr. Warren M. Brown, Superintendent of Schools, 655 January Avenue, Ferguson, Missouri; Dr. Roald Campbell, Dean, Graduate School of Education, University of Chicago, Chicago, Illinois; Dr. W. W. Charters, Professor of Education, University of Oregon, Eugene, Oregon; Dr. Stanley Elam, Editor, *Phi Delta Kappan*, 8th and Union, Bloomington, Indiana; Dr. Lawrence D. Fish, Executive Director, Northwest Regional Educational Laboratory, 400 Lindsay Building, 710 SW Second Avenue, Portland, Oregon; Dr. John Hemphill, Director, Far West Laboratory for Educational Research and Development, 1 Garden Circle, Hotel Claremont, Berkeley, California; Dr. Robert E. Jenkins, Superintendent, Unified School District, San Francisco, California; Mrs. Helen Johnson, Area Director, Montgomery County Schools, 850 North Washington Street, Rockville, Maryland; Mrs. Frances R. Link, Cheltenham Township Schools, Elkins Park, Pennsylvania; Dr. Lloyd S. Michael, Professor of Education, Northwestern University, Evanston, Illinois; Dr. John Michaelis, Professor of Education, University of California, Berkeley, California; Dr. Nathaniel Ober, Assistant Superintendent in Charge of Secondary Education, Minneapolis Public Schools, Minneapolis, Minnesota; Dr. Arnold W. Salisbury, Associate Professor of Education, Western Illinois University, Macomb, Illinois; Mrs. Glenys Unruh, Assistant to the Superintendent for Curriculum and Instruction, 725 Kingsland Avenue, University

City, Missouri; Dr. Herbert W. Schooling, Dean of Faculties, University of Missouri, Columbia, Missouri; Dr. Irwin Wapner, Director, Pupil Personnel Services, Lompoc Unified School District, Lompoc, California; Dr. Glen F. Wegner, Superintendent of Schools, Lompoc, California; Dr. Fred T. Wilhelms, Executive Secretary, Association for Supervision and Curriculum Development, 1201 Sixteenth Street, N.W., Washington, D.C.

Mrs. Edna Mitchell, Associate Professor of Education, William Jewell College, and Research Associate, University of Missouri at Kansas City, contributed valuable editorial services in preparation of this chapter.

chapter 19

John T. Lovell

Ideas, Supervision, and Kim Wiles

To speculate about the schools of tomorrow is at the same time exciting, challenging, and hazardous. Therefore, it is not surprising that Kim Wiles devoted the last chapter of his curriculum book to such an endeavor. Kim's life was wrought out of a curiosity and zeal for new experience. He was interested in new ideas, concepts, and theoretical formulations and the implications of these ideas for building a new education and a new society. The purpose of this essay is to identify and discuss a number of ideas which I associate with Wiles and which have had greatest meaning for me as a professional educator.

IDEAS FOR PROCEEDING FROM THE KNOWN TO THE UNKNOWN

Kim Wiles accepted change as a fundamental characteristic of the universe. The question was not one of whether or not to change, but rather concerned the possibility for man to control the direction and quality of the change in such a way as to increase the probability that his own purposes would be served. In other words, Is man merely a victim of some inevitable cycle of change? Or can he to some extent reduce "clogged up parts," develop new parts, change his own behavior and the behavior of others, and thereby control to some extent his own destiny? Wiles' answer to the latter question was a resounding "yes." He felt that man can change both himself and his environment and thereby improve his own state of existence. Based on this assumption, he suggested a number of propositions to improve the chance that innovations would indeed be fruitful:

1. Change should be based on sound evaluation.

2. Change should be based on theoretical formulations and research data.

3. Change should be based on inferences made from consulting theoretical formulations and research data from related disciplines.

Sound Evaluation

Wiles indicated his concern for change based on evaluation as follows:

> The hope for the improvement of the school program lies in the revision of existing practices and procedures in the light of sound evaluation.[1]

The critical focus was that man could never proceed from nothingness. There is always a history and a present "state" that can help to give meaning to the constant search for an improved state of affairs. In order to improve the chance of achieving a new and preferred situation, it is necessary not only to have a clear conceptualization of goals, but also a clear definition of the strengths and weaknesses of current conditions. This makes it possible to build on strengths and develop innovations in areas of weakness. The description of present conditions serves as a "bench mark" for making judgments about movement toward a preferred condition.

Wiles developed a comprehensive statement of the process of evaluation:

> Evaluation is the process of making judgments that are to be used as a basis for planning. It consists of establishing goals, collecting evidence concerning growth or lack of growth toward goals, making judgment about the evidence, and revising procedures and goals in light of the judgments. It is a procedure for improving the product, the process, and even the goals themselves.[2]

Included in this complex statement is not only the process of collecting evidence about growth but also the process of goal development and goal evaluation. A goal is a man-made idea of a preferred state of existence. It can never exist in reality; at that point it is no longer a goal. Thus, in evaluation, man must somehow develop an operational definition of his goals that is clear enough to serve as a frame of reference for making judgments about growth or lack of growth toward those goals. This is difficult in any organization, but it is especially difficult in educational organizations because of the nature of the expected output. There is little doubt that in his discussion of the process of evaluation, Wiles identified one of the major problems of the institution of education.

One way of viewing the institution of education in our society is as a social system. The educational organization can be thought of as a sub-system of the society. From this perspective, the society specifies the expected output of the educational organization. These specifications can be visualized as inputs along with human and material resources. After the organization interprets these expectations, develops operationalized goals, and implements a system of operations, the hoped-for outcomes will be realized. These outcomes are the output of the social system which is fed back into the society. Figure 1 (p. 243) may help to clarify this way of viewing the educational organization. The various dimensions of the social system are indicated and a number of problem areas in the evaluation process with which the educational institution must come to grips can be identified. First, an adequate way for the society to define and communicate its expectations to the educational institution has not been developed. Second, the educational institution has had difficulty in operationalizing educational objectives and, therefore, there is no adequate method to determine the effectiveness of operations for achieving these objectives. Third, an adequate body of educational theory from which educational operations can be derived does not now exist. Fourth, it is very difficult for the society to judge the output of the educational organization since the "pay-off" is behavioral change which is very difficult to measure. Also, since the society does not provide an independent agency to evaluate the output of the educational operation, it is forced to rely on what the educational organization "says" or on casual observation. Both of these methods are woefully inadequate. It would appear that if the schools of tomorrow are going to emerge as a significantly improved institution, the society and the educational institution must take immediate steps to develop an improved approach to evaluation.

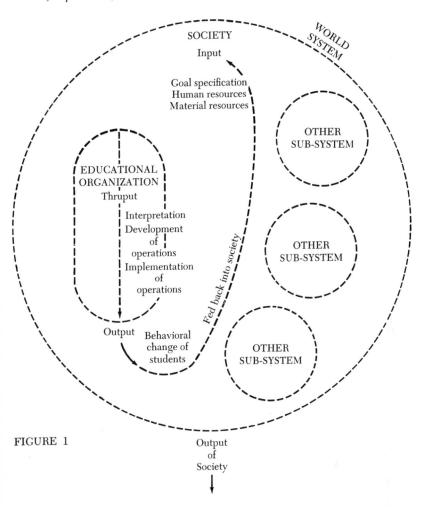

FIGURE 1

Change Based on Theoretical Formulations and
Research Findings from Education

It is significant that Wiles prefaced his chapter, "The High School of the Future," with the following statement:

Today's dream is tomorrow's reality. To increase current vision and build future reality each of us must use existing data, frontier practices, and projected social trends to attempt to invent the secondary school of tomorrow.[3]

It is apparent throughout the writings of Wiles that he had a deep commitment to scientific research as a basic approach to describing, explaining, and controlling reality. His book, *Supervision for Better Schools,* is based on scientific research. In this book, he introduced a "new" concept of, and a "new" approach to, instructional supervision. The research he utilized is explicitly defined and presented under the heading, "*Selected Significant Research.*" In graduate classes in supervision and curriculum, Wiles constantly made the effort to relate propositions and projected practices to research or the lack of research.

In developing his conceptualization of the high school of tomorrow, Wiles began by deploring the lack of a scientific body of theory and research data in education which could be used as a frame of reference for projecting ideas for the schools of tomorrow:

> Many of the present answers to questions about the type of secondary curriculum needed must be based on inferences made by consulting research data from related disciplines. This approach is not satisfactory. Basic research studies designed to provide evidence concerning the needs of youth and the most effective educational procedures should be undertaken.[4]

He then identified some of the areas which need to be investigated immediately. It is very interesting that he did not stop and wait at this point. Even though aware of the limitations of educational research, he went on to develop an idea of the high school of tomorrow based on research from related disciplines, a study of social trends and rising technology, knowledge of human needs, and his own value system. He invited critical study and evaluation, and he hoped for more adequate research from which new ideas for the schools of tomorrow could emerge.

Change Based on Theoretical Formulations and Research Findings from Related Disciplines

Wiles indicated his commitment to utilize research findings from related disciplines to improve educational practice in the following statement:

> This entire book has been an attempt to state the implications of present research in the fields of learning, group dynamics, psychiatry, group therapy, social psychology, human relations, and communications for the way in which supervisors should seek to fulfill their function.[5]

The great contribution that Wiles made to the study and practice of instructional supervision and educational leadership was at least partly a function of his utilization of research findings from related disciplines. The principles and practices of instructional supervision which he described and which had such a profound effect on American education were gleaned directly from research developments in other fields such as the Lewin, Lippitt, White, Hemphill, and Jennings studies in leadership and the human relations studies of Roethlisberger, Dickinson, and the National Training Laboratory Group. A new basis for explaining human motivation and group production was gradually emerging, and Wiles caught the sense of this theoretical development and had the imagination and skill to apply it to the study of educational supervision.

Wiles' valuing of research from related fields was expressed at the behavioral level in many other areas of his activity. For example, while he was president of the Association for Supervision and Curriculum Development he was instrumental in the activation of commissions to study supervision theory, curriculum theory, and instructional theory. The following statement which is quoted from a letter sent to members of the Commission on Supervision Theory explains the charge:

> The Association for Supervision and Curriculum Development has established a new Commission to be known as the Commission on Supervision Theory. The Association has been interested in the development of a theory of supervision based on research relating to the various aspects of the process of supervision. The charge to the Commission is:
>
> To take leadership in the formulation of a theory of supervision based on an analysis of the research in leadership, communication, community power structure, decision making, the process of change and other relevant areas. It is hoped that the Commission will accept the responsibility for planning and conducting seminars or institutes or other appropriate activities centered around an exploration of segments of research statements and interpretations that are important in evolving a theory of supervision.

The charge to the members of the commissions on instructional theory and curriculum theory was similar. The expectation was that the commissions would develop a "system" of concepts that could serve as a conceptual framework for viewing and studying the phenomenon of instructional supervisory behavior in educational institutions. There was an assumption that theoretical formulations had been developed in other fields of inquiry that would lead to the development of such formulations as would become a base for the scientific study of instructional and supervisory behavior.

IDEAS ABOUT INSTRUCTIONAL SUPERVISION

Kim Wiles' ideas about instructional supervision were primarily a function of his assumptions about the factors which help explain human behavior in educational organizations, his assumptions about the functions of instructional supervisory behavior in educational organizations, and his reliance on the "scientific method" as the basic factor in man's way of describing, explaining, and controlling reality.

Assumptions About Human Behavior

March and Simon, in 1961, grouped propositions about organizational behavior in the following three categories:

1. Propositions assuming that organization members, and particularly employees, are primarily *passive instruments,* capable of performing work and accepting directions, but not initiating action or exerting influence in any significant way.

2. Propositions assuming that members bring to their organizations *attitudes, values,* and *goals*; that they have to be motivated or induced to participate in the system of organization behavior; that there is incomplete parallelism between their personal goals and organization goals; and that actual or potential goal conflicts make power phenomena, attitudes, and morale centrally important in the explanation of organizational behavior.

3. Propositions assuming that organization members are *decision makers* and *problem solvers,* and that perception and thought processes are central to the explanation of behavior in organizations.[6]

The assumption of the organizational member as a "passive instrument" to be used and molded by administration to achieve the goals of the organization was a prominent characteristic of early literature on supervision. In recent decades, the literature and practice of supervision has been based more on the idea of man as a goal-seeking animal with his own need dispositions. This means that there is likely to be incongruence between the needs of the organization and the needs of the organizational member and, therefore, the member must be "motivated" or "induced" to behave in a way consistent with the expectations of the supervisor.

It is exciting that a book on educational supervision based on the assumption of organizational members as policy developers, decision makers, and problem solvers was first published in 1950. Wiles made the assumption that teachers have the competence, the skills, the motivation, and the commitment to share in the decision-making process. The following quotations illustrate this point:

> The concept of "power over" has been a part of human culture for many years. It is only as we begin to discover that sharing decisions is a more effective way to release the power of a group that we see a different function for the leader. Conceiving of the leader's role as that of decision-maker, is only possible in situations where teachers are willing to surrender their professional judgment.[7]

> The administration shares the decisions within its authority. The simple process of sharing decisions is the most powerful tool a leader has. It is the key to the securing of leadership, the assumption of responsibility, the acceptance of assignment, and the development of high morale.[8]

The proposition of personal integrity is related to the assumption of organizational members as problem solvers. Wiles maintained that permissiveness is basic to self-respect and that each individual must be free to be authentic in his behavior in group goal development and problem solving. He advanced the idea if teachers are free to speak out, this increases the range of possible solutions as well as the commitment to the implementation of the decision. He valued the individual and his ideas. The way people feel was important to him. Their behavior is not so much a function of the way things "are" but rather the way they feel things are. He recognized that each group member has a need to belong and a need for friendship. The supervisor seeks to provide a climate in which group members can fulfill their personal needs as well as contribute to the achievement of organizational goals.[9]

The power of the book is not only in its definition and synthesis of a group of propositions about supervision that reflect an exceptional understanding of the behavior of man in organizations. Even more important is the assumption of the idea of "supervision" as the "behavior" of the official leader and, therefore, a phenomenon which is subject to the application of scientific knowledge. This led to the conceptualization of supervision as skill in leadership, skill in human relations, skill in group process, skill in personnel administration, and skill in evaluation. The applications of the propositions were described in major areas of supervisory activity and thus, the book became a major tool for practitioners, as well as for students in college classes.

The Function of Instructional Supervisory Behavior

Wiles defined instructional supervision as behavior by the "official" leader that has the purpose of improving the learning situation for children. Because of his assumptions about employees (teachers) in the educational organization, he conceptualized the release of the creative power of group members as the basic function of the supervisor. The focus was not so much "to tell," "do to," or "get the teacher to," but rather to provide a climate in which the full potential of the teacher could be released:

> All teachers have greater potential than they use. Many factors— lack of vision, past experience, community pressure, lack of adjustment in human relations, poor personnel administration, inability to evaluate their work—prevent teachers from utilizing all their skills and abilities. The supervisor's function in the school is to help teachers release their full potential.[10]

It is an important fact that Wiles did not question the authority of the supervisory role. His concern was with the utilization of authority bestowed on the official leader in such a way as to assure the release of the energy of the group in creative problem solving.

Reliance on the Scientific Method

The definition of instructional supervision as behavior made it possible to identify the behavior and subject certain assumptions to the light of scientific knowledge. Wiles applied scientific findings in such a way as to challenge old assumptions and develop new ones more consistent with modern knowledge. He questioned such long-term assumptions as the following:

1. Administration is decision making.
2. Feelings are not important.
3. Appointment to an official position makes a leader.
4. The flow of communication follows official channels.
5. Teachers can be forced to grow.

However, it is even more important that Wiles provided and utilized a significant base of scientific evidence not only to devastate supervisory principles and practices of long standing, but also to logically derive a new system of principles and practices. When he revised his supervision book in 1955, he made the following statement in the preface which sums up the value he placed on scientific evidence:

> The past five years have not led me to revise the basic principles advanced in the first edition. In fact, the research in leadership and group work has given even greater support to the supervision procedures proposed. . . . But the evidence is still not conclusive, and the following statement from the preface of the first edition remains an accurate expression of my feelings:
>
>> You may use this book to supplement or contradict your own experience. If it is at variance with your conclusions, I hope it will lead you to re-examine your own analysis. Groups will be able to use it as an hypothesis to test against their experience and *through their work together*. . . . I hope these ideas will not be accepted unquestioningly by anyone. They are truth as we know it. They will be revised as we gain more experience and research data in the area of democratic living.[11]

SUPERVISION IN THE SCHOOLS OF TOMORROW

The nature of instructional supervision in the schools of tomorrow will be at least partly a function of a growing body of theoretical formulations and empirical findings not only from related disciplines, but from the field of education itself. Wiles made a substantial contribution to this expanding body of literature, and the work is being carried on by a growing number of scholars both as individuals and through special structures such as national commissions and committees. Therefore, I would predict much more specific definitions of instructional supervisory behavior and more clearly developed explanations of the phenomenon from which hypotheses can be derived and tested. This will provide the basis for large-scale research programs from which new operations and procedures can be defined and implemented.

It is recognized that leadership behavior is not necessarily a function of formal position, but rather is a function of many factors. Competence in the area of group concern and level of esteem by fellow group members have already been identified as significant factors. Therefore, it is reasonable to assume that organizations will broaden the distribution of leadership behavior on an ad hoc basis in order to capitalize on the special competence and esteem of a much larger number of staff members. Since leadership, decision making, and policy formulation will not be thought of as the prerogative of administration, organization members will be allocated more time for participating in these activities.

There will be a rising emphasis on "colleaguial supervision" in which colleagues with special competence, interest, and staff acceptance will be provided the necessary allocation of time and authority to carry out special projects and programs. The need for constituted authority will be just as great, or greater than ever, but the distribution of this authority will be on the basis of need and special competence. Since the focus will be on supervision by colleagues, there will be a gradual disappearance of special status and privilege based on position in the hierarchy. Special status has long been recognized as a barrier to creative and cooperative group problem solving.

New technological developments and rising specialization will create the basis for innovations in the schools of tomorrow. Many worthwhile changes have already been predicted and described by Kim Wiles and other authorities. These changes create great challenges and problems for educational supervision. While specialization provides the possibility of more efficient and effective behavior, it also increases the possibility of bifurcation of interest in organization. This indicates a greater need for "coordinating behavior" that will have the function of keeping organizational parts working together toward common goals. It is through supervision that the total organization will be able to maintain communication and cooperation among its parts.

The development of technology assures that more and more organization members will be working with things rather than people and, therefore, it will become more and more difficult to meet personal needs for belonging and affection. The process of keeping the educational organization "humanized" is and will continue to be a great challenge to educational supervision.

References

1. Kimball Wiles, *Supervision for Better Schools* (Englewood Cliffs, N.J.: Prentice-Hall, Inc., 1955), p. 293.
2. *Ibid.*, p. 292.
3. *Ibid.*, p. 298.
4. *Ibid.*, pp. 299-300.
5. *Ibid.*, p. 333.

6. James G. March and Herbert A. Simon. *Organizations* (New York: John
   Wiley & Sons, Inc., 1961), p. 6.
7. Wiles, *Supervision for Better Schools*, p. 335.
8. *Ibid.*, p. 339.
9. *Ibid.*, pp. 337-342.
10. *Ibid.*
11. *Ibid.*, p. x.

Index

Index